D0841156

AGILE PROJECT MANAGEMENT

3 BOOKS IN 1 - THE ULTIMATE BEGINNER'S, INTERMEDIATE & ADVANCED GUIDE TO LEARN AGILE PROJECT MANAGEMENT STEP BY STEP

JAMES TURNER

CONTENTS

AGILE PROJECT MANAGEMENT

AGILE PROJECT MANAGEMENT

AGILE PROJECT MANAGEMENT

AGILE PROJECT MANAGEMENT

THE ULTIMATE BEGINNER'S GUIDE TO LEARN AGILE PROJECT MANAGEMENT STEP BY STEP

What is Agile Project Management?

In the current job environment, the undertaking of overall work as projects is rampant. A project is simply a planned piece of work that contains a series of tasks that have a defined start and completion date. Every project has a specific deliverable, and it is paramount for project managers to conform to the stipulated guidelines for success to be achieved. There are some project management strategies that are undertaken to facilitate the successful completion of projects. Among the best strategies is the use of agile project management. Agile project management (AGP) is a process whereby projects are managed and implemented in small chunks. Ideally, the management strategy requires the iterative and incremental delivery of variables throughout the life cycle of the project. With each delivery of a variable, the requirements are re-evaluated and the work refined until it meets all the specifications of the client. For this reason, agile project management is immensely desirable and highly sought by high-value clients. The type of projects that can adopt the agile project management methodology is not restricted, and they range from civil, construction, and software, to typically any piece of work that can be divided projects. This guide will delve into the systematic analysis of the core aspects of agile project management, illustrating all that needs to be known about the methodology.

1

HISTORY, BENEFITS, AND TENETS
OF AGILE PROJECT MANAGEMENT

gile project management has not always been in existence. The foundation of the methodology was laid in 1986, in an article that was published in the Harvard Business Review. The article authors had noted that there was a widespread deviation from the traditional project management methodologies, and they were determined to find the reason why the people were shifting to a modern project management methodology. In the new technology, a hands-off approach was increasingly being implemented in favor of better product evaluation and improvement strategy. According to the analysis, the proponents of the new methodology insisted that the traditional waterfall method was not well-suited for the rapid pace through which technological advancements was occurring. In many instances, projects were canceled before delivery since software that was in the curse of being developed became obsolete before the actual product was fulfilled. Therefore, there needed to be a system where the development would be improved, to prevent the recurrence of such disadvantages.

The first crisis which the developers hoped to eliminate was the application development crisis, where the products could not be used after completion, mainly due to their nature of being outdated. Further, there was a delivery lag experienced, where the time to complete the project was too long. With such a realization, the industry discovered that it needed to make adjustments so that it could move fast enough and meet the customer demands as efficiently as possible.

The second crisis was the disadvantages that accrued as a result of revealing the products to the customers when they had already been completed, and not earlier. This circumstance made it immensely hard to solve any issues that may have been discovered in the course of developing the products since it would mean that the team would have to start from scratch to rectify such deforms. The developers had to look for an alternative to the problem, and think of a way through which they could be able to incorporate changes before the product was completed. What the developers were most inclined toward improving was flexibility, to facilitate changes and progress reviews.

After a series of wasted money and time in the developing of products which were ultimately rejected, the leaders decided that it was time to develop a new approach that would help solve all the problems. In 2001, 13 individuals were gathered in Utah, most of who were looking forward to the development of new and improved systems. They decided that the best system was one which would ensure that the team had enough flexibility of operations that would allow them to make changes early enough. The strategy would help avert troubles realized after the completion of a project. With such a strategy in mind, they came up with the agile manifesto.

The agile manifesto is a declaration of the principles and

values that would be recognized in agile methodology. The main aim of this principle was to provide a clear structure which interested parties could follow. The manifesto was made up of four key foundational values and 12 principles. Five years after the making of the manifesto, a declaration of interdependence was written to enable the original manifesto to be extended beyond software development. Value-added development, iterative work, team accountability, shared responsibility, and the encouragement of non-software teams were the important addendums. The tenets were not meant to serve as hard-set rules, but rather as a guide

The tenents that were incorporated in the declaration for interdependence included:

1. Increased return on investments through the making of continuous value flow as the main focus.
2. The delivery of reliable results by engaging customers in the project, and shared ownership of the project.
3. The unleashing of creativity and innovation by recognizing individuals as the major facilitators of the ultimate value source. The creating of an enabling environment where the individuals can make a difference is a major priority.
4. The boosting of performance through the sharing of responsibilities, as well as group accountability, to enhance team effectiveness.
5. The improvement of reliability and effectiveness through specific practices, strategies, and processes which are situational.

The four key values that define the agile methodology are:

1. Individual and team interactions over tools and processes.
2. Software that is working effectively, comprehensive documentation of activities;
3. Collaborating with customers over contract negotiation; and
4. Responding to changes as they arise over following a predetermined plan.

Benefits of Agile Project Management

For any company or organization to grow and develop, change is fundamental. Agile project management is amongst the changes that continue to impact the management arena and has continued to prove its efficiency. Before its inception, there were a series of project management methodologies in use. A common traditional methodology is the waterfall approach, amongst other methods. Even though such approaches have continued to be beneficial throughout their time, agile project management is much better.

The major difference between agile and traditional project management methodologies is that the latter establishes a detailed plan which is systematically followed from the onset to the completion of the project. This strategy differs from the agile project management methodology, where operations begin based on a rough draft and are delivered in short bursts repeatedly, to ensure that the client is satisfied with the end product. The many iterative submissions are the core of agile project management since they ensure that a relationship is formed between the two parties in the course of carrying out the work.

Worth noting is that agile project management is based on certain principles which the traditional methods do not conform to. First, AGP honors and prefers customer collaboration over contract negotiations. The whole essence of customer collaboration is to work step-by-step with such a client and ensure that they get exactly and beyond what they require of a project. The strategy is immensely different from contract working, where in most cases the clients are presented with the end product. While a contract is beneficial, it restricts the workers as they are only required to give exactly what the clients want, with no room for compromise. However, when one works with the clients, there is room for negotiation, and the project managers can evaluate alternatives with the clients. Through such an interaction, the clients end up getting better output, consequently increasing their satisfaction.

Further, agile project management facilitates personal interaction with clients over using processes and tools. The traditional project management methodologies operate in such a way that the clients and the workers do not have a personal relationship. They are only connected through particular projects, using a predetermined checklist to evaluate the performance. With agile project management, a personal relationship is paramount, and the client is updated of the happenings regularly.

More importantly, agile project management advocates for the response to change, as opposed to following a specified structure. As a project is ongoing, unexpected results may occur. Traditional project management methodologies warrant sticking to the plan despite the results. With AGP, the results of a particular step determine the associating response, which ensures that all challenges are handled promptly and well in advance.

Agile project management is also very beneficial to the workers involved since it empowers them by helping build accountability. The fact that all persons involved in the project are interconnected to one another means that there is a lot of idea sharing, which enables the workers to learn and grow in the given field. Working in a team ensures that the workers always have to give reasons behind why they think certain processes and ideas are the best, consequently promoting continuous development and improvement of skills.

Core Principles of Agile Project Management

The favorable outcome of agile project management across its diverse fields of operations is subject to its principles, which are geared toward success. The agile philosophy is normally inclined toward early empowerment of people and their interaction, ensuring value in the end product. The agile mode of operation has a very high drive to deliver maximum value, regardless of the risks in a particular project. In essence, for one to fully understand what the agile project management methodology entails, they must be privy of the 12 key principles that define the concept.

1. **Customer Satisfaction through Constant and Fast Delivery**

Agile project management aims at ensuring iterative development that proceeds incrementally. Typically, projects are given in the form of a contract that has a specified piece of work. Contracts stipulate the scope of the work, as well as the expected outcome at the end of the project. The agile methodology requires the given project to be divided into small chunks of work and handled individually. The chunks are then given to the professionals, who engage the clients to get a clear idea of what exactly is needed. Depending on the scope of the work, the iterative pieces of work take an undefined time to complete, ranging from a few days to many months. The project managers then take time to evaluate the functionality of each completed segment, evaluating the resultant performance, as well as any risks and challenges that present themselves. Once evaluated, any misgivings are reported to the client before the accompanying segment begins, giving both groups a chance to make conscious decisions about the best way to proceed. Through this working process, the result is better valued and with minimal mistakes. A graphical representation of the iterative development of each deliverable is as shown in Figure 1.

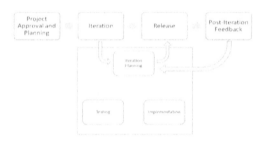

Figure 1: Illustration of the iterative process for each deliverable.

Source (Dmitry, 2019)

As illustrated, the first step is planning and following the approval process for the project. This step normally involves defining the scope of the project, aspects such as budgeting, as well as setting the timeline for the entire work. Once the requirements are all clearly defined, the first segment can proceed. Typically, each division has a given timeline, which the project managers must adhere to. Each division also has its guidelines, which guarantee the successful implementation of the said project. Since agile project management warrants the close interaction with the client, the workers must ensure that they seek clarification from the client where necessary to ensure that they get the job description right.

Once this step is completed, the client is involved, and they go through the finished division with the contractor. This is the release step, where the completed segment is analyzed. Depending on the project, the stakeholders have their parameters through which they test the functionality so far. Diverse projects are tested differently. For instance, if the contract involves software development, the client can test the coding so far. If it is in the civil and construction industry, the clients can analyze aspects, such as how well the foundation and such preliminary activities have been completed. Once analyzed, the clients will either be satisfied or dissatisfied.

When satisfaction is achieved, the contractors can then proceed to the next phase. In the case of dissatisfaction, the contractors must work with the clients and identify the areas of conflict. After that, re-planning for the work is done, and the contractors move ahead with implementation as guided by the client's wants. When done, they test the work using the given parameters. Satisfied that they have indeed taken the entire client's comments into consideration, the work is resubmitted to the client, who determines whether the expectations have been met.

All steps in a given project go through these phases, consequently ensuring that the clients are satisfied with each phase. The benefit of such a strategy is that there is minimal risk of the entire project being rejected since the client approves phase by phase. Further, working with clients ensures that they get exactly what they want.

2. Embracing Changing Environments to Provide Competitive Advantage to Customer

The world is shifting rapidly, mainly due to technological advancements. Most projects are meant to boost the functionality of a given business/enterprise. Aspects such as software development and even construction works are done to facilitate the company's operations so that they can become profitable. With each project that a company undertakes, there is normally the hope that with the completion of such a project, competitive advantage will occur.

Competitive advantage is defined as the leverage that a company has over other similar/competing firms and enterprises. For a company to have a competitive advantage over others, there need to be aspects such as higher-quality products, as well as overall methods of conducting business. The technological and business advancements in the current times have resulted in the discovery of better business practices as time goes by. Worth noting is that all the developments and advancements that we have to date are instigated by a change. Therefore, adherence to change is among the best ways through which the success of an implementation can be assured.

As stated in the first principle, the major objective is ensuring that the customer is satisfied by the end product. Therefore, there is always the need to ensure that value is added to every completed project. To meet the value definition, there is always the need to embrace changes as they occur in the course of the project, even if it means having to adjust mid-stream as better modes of performance are realized. Worth noting is that change is unavoidable and it is not final either. That means that, however good the current innovations may be in fulfilling a particular problem today, there is always a chance that better methods would be devised at a later date. Being privy to such advancements is critical, as it is the only way through which performance can be improved. Also worth noting is that, for the changes to be beneficial to a project, the project managers must be willing to adapt and shift to such modern innovations.

Dwight Eisenhower, the 34th President of the United States, is amongst the major advocators of change. Eisenhower always insisted that in as much as planning was everything, the plan was nothing. In the course of his leadership, Eisenhower's role in the success of the army was well known. His advocacy of change always saw him aim to get the best weapons and tools for war, even though most of the fighters in the army were used to traditional weapons of war. Eisenhower always knew that change was imminent and that having the latest weapons would ensure that his army had an advantage over the opposition, consequently resulting in success.

This principle is highly advocated in agile project management. Eisenhower's saying is not meant to invalidate planning, but rather insists that change is inevitable. Further, there is always the need to ensure that the plans and the processes leave space for change with minimal impact on the outcomes. The fact that some projects may take years to complete means that there is always a high probability that some new methods of operations are devised as it is ongoing. As much as there is always a plan meant to guide how the project is expected to proceed, it is important for new changes to be embraced.

In agile project management, there are certain things that must be observed to ensure that there is room for possible changes in the course of an operation.

i. First, there must be the understanding that in every company, regardless of how successful it is, there are processes that the staff is accustomed to. By nature, change is uncomfortable, and the project managers must be on the forefront to instigate it. Most of the staff would rather proceed with operations as they are used to, due to the uncertainty of the changes and comfort. When the project managers take it upon themselves to educate the staff about the importance of constantly shifting to better modes of operations, it increases their level of reception to current and even future changes. For some of the major operations, there are conferences and lessons that can be undertaken to teach willing persons about the latest innovative practices and ways of accomplishing some works. Therefore, the company must be open to taking their staff through such training, so that their levels of expertise can be developed.

ii. There is always the perception that change is instigated when the previous modes of operations do not proceed as planned. This is a myth that must be disbanded. Change is not only applicable where the current methods of operations are problematic or prove to be inefficient. On the contrary, the operational methods require a constant upgrade, regardless of how well they are working, conforming to the changing innovative strategies. With the correct mentality, the involved persons would always be eager to look for better ways of carrying out an activity, even if the existing one works perfectly. Ultimately, the value and quality of output improve.

iii. It is a fact that most managers put in excessive control of projects to determine the outcome of the activities. In agile project management, even though the managers are mandated to look over the projects, they must be responsive to ideas given by the team members. Different people in a team have different capabilities and ideologies, and taking into account all of them ensures that the best methodologies are selected.

3. Delivering Product/Service Fast and Promptly

Agile project management ensures that the products and

services are delivered promptly; faster than in traditional methods. The fact that the milestones are delivered incrementally means that the benefits of the completed sections can potentially be realized, before full completion of the products/services. Further, the system promises a faster return on investment since customer reaction can be gauged well in advance, and adjustments made depending on the response. The major benefit of such a strategy is that, when the product/service is finally complete, it is in line with the needs of the consumers, promoting competitive advantage. Statistics show that the agile methodology has a 37% faster time-to-market than average, and 16% higher efficiency than the average.

Worth noting is that, even though the agile methodology is inclined to fast delivery of products and services, there is always caution not to do so at the expense of quality and value. The latter constitutes the major requirements and factors that must be safeguarded at all time. Fast is never recommended if it pertains compromise to the quality of the output, and the agile methodology strives to safeguard the quality of the product at all times. Further, sustainability is highly advocated for, since it is the only way through which such good performance can be replicated.

Another way through which quality and value are safeguarded in the course of carrying out a project is prioritization. Different projects have different segments, which can either be carried out concurrently or individually. Further, some staff members can be able to carry out some functions better than others. This realization is imperative since it ensures that all functions are handled by persons who are best suited, resulting in better results.

Also, a company should acknowledge the capacity of work which they can be able to handle at a particular time, to prevent instances of failed delivery. Project managers using the agile methodology know the importance of delivering quality output to the clients. When they take on multiple jobs at once, the team becomes pressurized, ultimately resulting in not giving the deserved attention to either of the projects. The interference hinders speed, which does not conform to the agile methodology.

4. Fostering Collaboration between the Stakeholders and the Developers

The term collaboration refers to working together of people with similar interests. Agile project management highly encourages collaboration between the team members, as well as between the stakeholders and the developers/contractors. It is important to define and identify the stakeholders in any project, to be able to evaluate how their needs can be safeguarded effectively. The major stakeholder is the client who pays for the project. That notwithstanding, the developers must analyze the needs and requirements of stakeholders, such as the end consumers and potential clients, since the success of the product depends on how well the consumers react to it. Therefore, the agile approach is greatly inclined toward the undertaking and exploring of technical expertise necessary to develop and test new product lines.

Customer collaboration can be facilitated in various ways. First, the client, as well as the developers, must identify the end users of the products. There is also a need to identify the social class which the service/product targets. Such parameters make it easier to develop the products and also carry out preliminary tests before the final product is developed.

Notably, a collaborative relationship can only be possible when all stakeholders are privy of what is needed to be successful. All parties must be respectful and mindful of what the fellow collaborators need to succeed, regardless of whether they agree with it. In the course of carrying out all the works, it is always important to keep in mind that all the stakeholders share the common objective of facilitating the success of the project. With such a notion, it becomes easier for all parties to work together harmoniously.

Most developers are inclined to the notion that it is easier for people to be able to identify what they like and dislike in a product when an option is presented to them. Therefore, the initial instructions given by a client are insufficient to ideally cover everything that they have. However, when the agile methodology is adopted, the iterative mode of delivery ensures that the clients are presented with options from the beginning. Therefore, they can be able to point out from the beginning what they want and what they do not want, ultimately enabling the contractors/developers to devise an item that fulfills their needs in entirety.

Among the key processes and activities that all stakeholders ideally should be involved in include:

i. Reviewing the design documents. As previously discussed, the agile methodology involves a constant change to the designs and modes of operations in response to changes in technology and operational methods. In most cases, the clients may agree or disagree with such changes, and it is vital to involve them so that they can make informed decisions about such developments.

ii. The stakeholders must also be involved in prototype development. Prototypes are replicas of the expected end product, and they are mostly developed for electrical products and machinery before mass production starts. The prototypes are designed to replicate how the end products would operate, and so proper scrutiny is vital. Based on the operations of the prototype, the clients can be able to point out what they like and the areas where improvement is needed. Further, potential users of such products should be involved so that they can give vital feedback about the effectiveness of such a product. With such developments, the end product is deemed perfect.

In cases where the project involves construction and civil works, three-dimensional prototypes can be developed from the architectural arena, and the clients are presented with the expected end product. Depending on the needs that such works are expected to accomplish, they can either approve or modify such designs.

iii. Defining the Transition Requirements. Many requirements are required every time a change is meant to be incorporated. The stakeholders should be available to help define such changes, to ensure that all people are on board with the expected results.

iv. Providing instructions where the requirements are unclear. When a contract/job is given, it is a fact that some of the requirements may not be given satisfactorily. Therefore, the stakeholders should take time and participate in the actualization of the projects at hand, to ensure that indeed what is done is what is expected. The agile methodology prides itself in the fast and prompt delivery of a product, and it would be a major loss of time and resources to finalize a product with the wrong specifications. When a stakeholder is involved, they can identify places where instructions may have been misconstrued early on, so that it can be rectified and facilitate the production of a product/service that was required.

5. Building the Project Around Motivated Individuals

Motivation is among the greatest aspects that must be safeguarded in agile project management. As businesses and organizations work on leading an agile environment and workforce, it is important to realize that agility can only be attained when all persons are on the same page. Further, all the team members must be motivated to work by the laid-down guidelines, so that success can be achieved. The major hindrance in this principle is that it is highly unlikely that employers can be able to identify motivated individuals at face value during the hiring process, as there is no parameter through which motivation can be tested. The real illustration of the motivation levels arises when they are put to the task, at which point it is difficult to change the workforce. To prevent this situation, there is always the need to build a motivated workforce, even before a task is given out. The more motivated the team is, the better the overall output.

There are some ways through which motivation can be enhanced around the team members:

1. Doing Away With Micromanaging People

The project managers must know that motivation is ideally the art of getting people to act and work based on their own accord, without forcing them to carry out any activity. The best way through which such motivation can be fostered is through the breaking of the addiction process, through doing away with micromanaging people. The project managers must always realize that they are better suited for choosing the team members well, then trusting them to do the right thing without any form of coercion. Contrary to what many people believe, being hard on employees and junior members of the team seldom gets them motivated, but rather creates distrust and a wide distance with the management.

Agile project management encourages the cutting down of heavy management and giving the team members the chance to operate as they feel best. People involved must always be allowed to take risks. Ultimately, they learn better. Further, it is a fact that it is preferable to have people on the team who solve their problems and learn from any mistakes, then having to give all instructions to team members and prohibiting them from making any decisions out of the instructions given. If people are enabled to succeed within their scope of capabilities, they will naturally be motivated to grow for the sake of their betterment. Consequently, this results in the success of company operations.

2. Allowing People to Choose What to Work On

In any project, different team members have different capabilities. As much as the project managers may want to assign duties, it would be much better to allow the team members to assign themselves what they feel would best suit them. In agile project management, the people are more motivated, since they choose what to work on by themselves and are, therefore, determined to do such activities in the best way possible. Putting trust in people gives them the motivation to deliver more than was expected, and they are more likely to take more responsibility since they strive to meet the goals they set by themselves. Further, the fact that they are responsible for dealing with all the challenges ensures that they learn better, enabling them to handle the accompanying tasks with more ease.

3. Giving Up Control

The project managers must always realize that as much as they are responsible for everything that goes on within the project, they have to be careful and avoid over-controlling the team members. The managers ideally pick a team whenever a task arises, and depending on how they handle the team from the start, the level of motivation varies.

Giving up control does not amount to laxity, and the

managers should set clear rules about how they would like the task to be carried out. Due to the strictness of the agility methodology, there is always the chance that some team members cannot be able to cope with the pressure, and the manager should not stop them from leaving. Consequently, unmotivated members have no choice than to up their game, since most of the decision-making is left to them.

4. Provisions of an Enabling Environment

Giving the team an environment where they feel appreciated and valuable is also vital in improving motivation. An environment encompasses the physical space where the team operates. The environment can also be non-physical, relating to the emotional, intellectual, and spiritual feeling that the team gets while working in a place. A good environment creates a sense of fulfillment to the team members, ultimately facilitating the successful implementation of the work required.

The physical environment is the first thing that the team resonates with. Where the environment is well-kempt, with proper lighting and proper infrastructure, it creates a sense of professionalism. Walking into such an environment, the staff automatically and subconsciously gets into the working mode. In the case the environment is rowdy with insufficient or no proper infrastructure and equipment, there is bound to be increased feelings of unease. The latter affects performance significantly, rarely resulting in success.

The non-physical environments mainly encompass how the top-management relates with the staff. The staff is more likely to be motivated and content in an environment where they are appraised, positively criticized, and are encouraged to be the best versions of themselves. The assurance that one can grow in a particular environment is a major motivator to work hard, resulting in positive results ultimately.

5. Fair and Reasonable Remuneration

It is a fact that people do not go to work just to develop their skills. The major motivator is the salary that they receive. It is also evident that the fairer the remuneration, the more motivated the workers are bound to be. The project managers must always keep this in mind, even when bidding for contracts and tenders. Even though they are more likely to get contracts when they quote lower amounts, it must never be at the expense of the employees.

Ideally, a company should adopt policies where they reward good performance. Most companies have annual parties where they reward the employee of the year, motivating others to work hard too and become recognized as well. Further, whenever a completed project becomes an undoubted success, the giving of bonuses where they are due is important. Such forms of appreciation go a long way in motivating the employees to perform significantly better in their work.

6. Adopting Face-to-Face Communication, as it is the Most Efficient Method of Conveying Information

Communication has the sole purpose of conveying information between people for different purposes. In the course of carrying out a project, the information can either be about the project process, including the risks, approach, and plans. For any project to be successful, communication management must be deeply scrutinized and improved. Project managers must be on the forefront and guide their team about the acceptable mode of communication, to ensure efficiency and cooperation. Undoubtedly, the most efficient way through which information can be conveyed within a development team is through the adoption of face-to-face communication.

Many people may argue that the technological advancements that have taken place in the communication arena are the best. While these technological measures may be beneficial in instances where there is no option, it is apparent that there are a lot of disadvantages that ensue. Among the key disadvantages are:

1. Distractions. It is a fact that using modes of communication, such as teleconferencing, comes with a lot of distractions. First, some people can work on some other work, such as emailing during the calls, resulting in a lack of attention. The fact that the participants are invisible to the leaders during the calls may make them somewhat inattentive, a situation which is not realized in face-to-face communication.

2. More importantly, communications through technological mediums block non-verbal cues, which are very important. Since people cannot detect facial expressions and cues, such as body movements, it renders communication incomplete.

3. The duration of the web and teleconference meetings is much higher than in face-to-face communication. Ultimately, it takes more time and resources to cover certain topics than it would have where face-to-face communication was upheld. That notwithstanding, it might be important to note that in instances where geographical differences are apparent, there may be no option other than using the technological modes of communication.

Agile project management strives to ensure that face-to-face communication is prioritized over all other forms of communication. This communication is not only encour-aged between the stakeholders and the contractors/developers, but also within the team members. There are advantages to a company/organization where face-to-face communication is adopted. Maximizing personal communication enables the following;

1. Elimination of waste. Face-to-face communication facilitates the elimination of time and resource wastage. Going straight to the source means that any questions can be handled promptly and directly, saving on time. Using the other means of communications means that one must take time off to schedule for calls or sending emails, then waste time waiting for the response. The conversation that ensues either through emailing or other messaging platforms may take many days, which is a loss of time and affects the continuity of the project.

2. Enables osmotic and non-verbal communication. Non-verbal cues are considered pivotal in any communication. It is only face-to face-communication that allows the full enjoyment of non-verbal cues, and a lot can be assumed from the body language of recipients. Eye-contact, voice deflection, and intonation undoubtedly offer more detailed communication than phone calls and emails can ever provide.

3. Further, through face-to-face communication, the project managers can show the stakeholders/team members what exactly they mean when they describe certain issues. For instance, in the case of construction work, it is easier to work directly with the involved team members and show them where construction has gone wrong, instead of attempting to tell them through calls. Where prototypes are being developed, it is also easier to show the relevant parties the functionalities and the areas of dispute

face-to-face, rather than explaining through technological media.

4. Finally, face-to-face conversations enable the project managers to get the leverage for ensuring that they get a commitment out of everyone involved. There is always a big difference between asking people through the mail or phone calls if they agree to some terms of conduct, and looking at them straight in the face to get such responses. Having a face-to-face talk makes the people develop a feeling of accountability, which increases their chances of fulfilling what they promise.

7. The Final Working Product is the Sole and Pivotal Measure of Success

Progress and success of a project in agile project management are analyzed through various parameters. The fundamental measure of the progress is through the evaluation of the finished product/service. A product is considered to be complete when it is successfully delivered and tested. Therefore, the end product must be readily available to be transferred to the client in its entirety for the project to be considered complete.

Worth noting is that the fact that the clients are involved in all the development steps of the product ensures that the end product had little-to-no issues. Therefore, in most cases, the end product is the final product that does not require any adjustment.

8. The Agile Processes Aim at Promoting Sustainable Development. All the Stakeholders Must Maintain an Indefinite Constant Pace

Sustainable development refers to the constant development of a product, until its completion. The fact that it is regarded as sustainable means that the activities should be fulfilled without any loss of concentration within the team. As such, the activities need to be carefully planned to ensure that all there is no unnecessary pressure on the team, which may result in increased mistakes in the execution process.

Sometimes, project managers may be so inclined to delivering a product fast, that they do so at the expense of the well-being of the team. The agile methodology advocates for the needs of the team members to be put first so that concentration and motivation can be enhanced. Worth noting is that consistent delivery of the milestones is pivotal, which results in the whole project being divided into manageable iterates.

It is important to note that some scholars assert that the use of the Gantt chart is highly beneficial in the control of iterations in agile methodology. However, some scholars are of the school of thought that the use of such charts should be restricted to traditional project management practices. Most diverse business processes have revealed that the use of the Gantt charts is very beneficial, even in the agile environment, thus advocate for its use. When the use of the Gantt charts is incorporated correctly, it helps in the clear illustration of the timeline of each milestone, thus keeping the team members on their toes. Sharing the chart with the stakeholders enables them to have a clear understanding of the order of activities, facilitating their prediction of when they can expect the various milestones to be complete. A simplified Gantt chart is as illustrated in Figure 2

Time / Activity	Weeks 1-4	Weeks 5-7	Weeks 8-12	Week 13
Activity 1				
Activity 2				
Activity 3				

Figure 2: Illustration of how a Gantt chart is used.

As illustrated, all the activities are listed clearly on the chart, along with their expected duration. In the above illustration, the first activity is expected to take four weeks. With such a realization, the team members are motivated to plan their activities well to ensure that they beat the set deadline. Consequently, the stakeholders have a clear picture of when they can expect the product, in addition to the completion of some of the vital milestones.

Ideally, the Gantt charts showcase the expected timelines for the product-related activities, as well as the process-related activities. The product-related activities are normally performed before the launch of a product/service, and they include acts such as the testing of the prototypes, testing civil and construction works in engineering or testing the efficiency of systems in software development. The support staff must also train in the activities expected of them during the launch of the product, as well as the marketing strategies that are expected to be adopted. The process-related activities include aspects such as documentation and formal verification of some of the processes.

The Gantt chart is beneficial in the agile management process, majorly since it helps pinpoint at a glance the activities that must be conducted at a given time.

9. A Continuous Focus on Technical Excellence and a Proper Design Enhances Agility

An agile environment never occurs by accident. This principle reiterates the importance of paying attention to every detail in the development process, to ensure that the end product is of the highest quality possible. Therefore, in as much as there is the need to have a fast turn-around, it must never be at the expense of the quality of the final product.

The enhancement of agility is the end goal of this principle, and it can only be achieved where technical excellence and proper designs are put first.

Learning about the components of good design and the factors that amount to technical excellence is important for the principle to be fulfilled. For a product to be deemed as having a good design, they have the following characteristics:

1. Good designs are error-free since the key components and instructions are right from the onset. For this goal to be achieved, the team must listen carefully to the clients' needs and wants, and work with them in the designing of such a product. It is evident that in the development process, there may be a lot of unpredictable occurrences, which can disrupt the quality of the end product. Working with all stakeholders helps prevent distortions since everyone is on the same page regarding what the end products should look like.

2. Good designs are also repeatable, whether in part or in full. This saves time for similar projects in the future since the team uses methods and processes that have already been established to work effectively. For instance, a checklist about the order of steps proven to work in the past is a major guarantee that the results will be similar to the previous successes.

3. Good designs are also shareable since there is confidence in the communication of the strategies used. When qualified people take part in the development of a product or a service, they are sure of what they have done. Therefore, any question about the operations and the capability of the end

product is easily communicated with others, since it derives out of proven facts.

Technical excellence, on the other hand, involves paying attention to detail and doing what is expected, as well as the refraining from over-doing things. Some of the characteristics that define technical excellence are:

1. Proper performance from the onset. Technical excellence amounts to doing things the right way from the start. Therefore, where it is employed, there is the avoidance of making mistakes. The fact that good performance facilitates quality and speed ensures that time and resources are well spent. An excellent team displays a surety of all activities that they engage in, and do not have to learn from their mistakes. The key goal always is the avoidance of mistakes.
2. Confidence is also a major characteristic of technical excellence. When a team is well-qualified, they can undertake any task without the fear of making mistakes. When such confidence is displayed by the top management, the junior members attain a level of trust in the occurrences, serving as great motivation
3. The ability to re-do and teach. When a team attains technical excellence, they can be able to teach others effectively, and attain the same success in a similar future project.
4. Good designs and technical excellence are undoubtedly enablers of an agile environment. Therefore, the choices made in terms of the team and the methods of operation play a great role in the determination of the success of the projects. The agile methodology requires all choices to be in line with the core principles of excellence and

quality, to facilitate quality service and product delivery.

10. Simplicity is of Essence

The agile methodology is highly inclined toward the notion that less is more. Therefore, it is never about the amount of work that is done, but rather the quality of the reasonable work done. For the principle to be achieved, it is always vital for the project managers to carefully consider every aspect of the project, which is not a small undertaking. Worth noting is that, in projects such as the development of a product, there is always that some of the functions that the team may concentrate on are unnecessary. Discernment is, therefore, very necessary to evaluate what is worth doing and doing away with clutter activities. There are numerous strategies that can be put in place to ensure that the principle becomes a success.

1. The project managers should have a sit down with the clients and go over the expected functionalities of the desired product. Although the clients cannot create the products/services on their own, they usually have a clear picture of what they want. Since the project managers are the professionals, they can go through the checklist one-by-one, and identify specifications that are not necessary. Such specifications can either be merged with other functions or removed in entirety, reducing clutter.
2. The documentation should be simplified as much as possible to give clear instructions. There is no need for documenting a lot of material just for the sake of it. Even though some projects may be highly valued, adding unnecessary instructions and documentation does not amount to seriousness. On the contrary, a

lot of vague materials only serve as confusion, which affects the quality of the end product.

3. Simplicity also applies to the team, as it is necessary for them to be honest with themselves about their capabilities. First, the team members should only handle what they can as at a particular time and avoid undertaking multiple roles. The danger of taking too much is that pressure may arise and disorient their operations. Cluttering of the mind is a real phenomenon that prevents the team members from performing as well as they should.

The Best Architectures and Designs are Mostly Developed by Self-Organizing Teams

Product ideas and challenges are unique to each project. There are many ways through which project managers can respond to the varying advancements. First, the managerial team can decide to be the sole decision-makers and guide the direction of all the projects' occurrences. The agile methodology is against such restriction, and it encourages all the team members to be actively involved in the identification of problems, as well as the resultant solutions. With such a team spirit, there is always a very high chance of growth, since the members learn from each other and learn from mistakes.

Further, the principle reiterates the importance of growing and learning along the way, and not trying to get everything right from the start. It is a fact that in the development of a product, there is always the chance of incurring unexpected challenges, which must be handled as they come. Attempting to identify all possible mistakes at the beginning of a project is not possible, and it may influence how the team reacts to challenges. If the team starts a product with the assurance that no mistake will occur, it is bound to be very demoralizing when a challenge does arise.

Self-organization is also a major component for this principle, and it involves the giving of the team members the chance to choose what they are comfortable working on and timelines. Being a project manager does not amount to forcing teams to do what they are not comfortable in since it will only fail. When the team chooses its activities and timelines, they are more obliged to conform to it. Ultimately, success is attained.

Efficiency and Fine-Tuning Behaviors are Achieved through the Use of Regular Intervals

This principle asserts most of what was discussed in the other principles, particularly about developments in the iterative process. As has been described, the agile methodology requires the project to be handled in such a way which guarantees quality, through constant improvement. With every step that occurs, results are analyzed, as well as the accompanying functionalities and deformities. If the process is considered to be a success, the team is free to move to the next phase. Where mistakes are realized, the team takes time to learn from it, ultimately identifying the best modes of operation.

Chapter Summary

- Agile project management bases its operations on 12 distinct principles.
- Through the adoption of the principles, success is guaranteed.
- The 12 principles are:

1. Customer Satisfaction through Constant and Fast Delivery
2. Embracing Changing Environment to Provide Competitive Advantage to Customer

3. Delivering Product/Service Fast and Promptly
4. Fostering Collaboration between the Stakeholders and the Developers
5. Building the Project Around Motivated Individuals
6. Adopting Face-to-Face Communication, as it is the Most Efficient Method of Conveying Information
7. The Final Working Product is the Sole and Pivotal Measure of Success
8. The Agile Processes Aim at Promoting Sustainable Development. All the Stakeholders Must Maintain an Indefinite Constant Pace
9. A Continuous Focus on Technical Excellence and a Proper Design Enhances Agility
10. Simplicity is of Essence
11. The Best Architectures and Designs are Mostly Developed by Self-Organizing Teams
12. Efficiency and Fine-Tuning Behaviors are Achieved through the Use of Regular Intervals

2

TRANSITIONING FROM TRADITIONAL TO AGILE PROJECT MANAGEMENT

Agile project management has been tested around various sectors and undoubtedly proven to be the most effective methodology in the running of projects. One of the major setbacks of handling typical projects is that they are prone to inefficiencies, such as delays, ultimately being a major hindrance to the effective functioning of a company/organization. The use of the agile methodology is a great asset to any company, and greatly increases the chances of success. There is a need to distinguish between adaptive vs. predictive methodologies, as well as agile vs. waterfall methods to gain a deeper understanding of the differences.

Adaptive vs. Predictive Methodology

The adaptive philosophy is based on the idea that the developmental methods normally exist on a continuum, from the adaptive methodologies to the predictive ones. The agile methodologies lie on the adaptive side of the continuum, while the more traditional methodologies lie on the predictive side. Amongst the key developmental methods used is the "rolling stone" approach, which is beneficial in the planning of schedules and identifying the milestones. Despite these functions, the approach is flexible in the path which can be used to reach them and also allows for instances of change. The adaptive methods have a major focus on the quick adaptation of the changing realities. Therefore, when the specific needs of a project change, so do they in the adaptive team. Well-known is that an agile project is subject to human changes. The unpredictable nature means that the team may have difficulty explaining what may happen in the future since they know changes are imminent. The longer the project is, the more difficult it is to make any predictions, since one may not know the changes that may be necessitated. The fact that the agile team cannot be able to report about tasks that they will do in the future means that the activities are open and the team members are free to do what they feel is best for the project, even if it was not in the initial plan

The predictive methods greatly contrast with the adaptive methods. The predictive approach focuses on analyzing and planning future events in detail as a means of catering for known risks. In extreme circumstances, the predictive team may analyze the events so deeply that they can be able to report exactly what they're hoping would occur in the future, as well as the features that are planned for in the entire project cycle. Predictive methodologies have a major reliance on the effective analysis in the early phase of the project. The major disadvantage of using such a system is that in case anything goes wrong at the beginning of the project, the team may have great difficulty changing direction. Predictive teams normally use a change control board to ensure that it is only the most valuable changes which are considered. With the rigidity, it is evident that making simple changes is a very complex idea which requires maximum input from the stakeholders

Agile vs. Waterfall Methodology

The waterfall methodology is also known as a traditional method/approach to project management. The waterfall methodology is ideally a linear approach to software development and has a predetermined sequence of events. There is a series of steps that accrue in waterfall management. The first process is the gathering of the required documents, which normally consist of the instructions from the clients as well as all the paperwork about the cost, timeline, and budget. Once all the paperwork is in place, the designing of the project takes place in line with the needs of the clients. In a software development scenario, aspects such as coding and unit testing of the finished phases are done systematically to allow the fixing of any issue and the ultimate delivery of the finished product. The waterfall methodology is not restricted to software development, in as much as the idea originated from there initially. True waterfall development projects consist of distinct stages in the development process where each page must be completed before the other one can begin. There is also a typical stage gap between each of the phases since paperwork and approval are done in between to ensure that the project is proceeding as planned. The biggest benefit of the waterfall approach is that the developers and their clients agree on what will be delivered at the end of the project. This straightforward nature means that the clients get exactly what they want, regardless of whether it is the best choice or not. The major shortcoming is the fact that most of the products may become obsolete as making changes is not recommended.

The agile methodology, on the other hand, is an iterative and team-based approach, which is the most popular amongst all the project management methodologies. Major emphasis is placed on the rapid delivery of a project with complete functional components. Also, a lot of flexibility is enjoyed in the methodology, and the team members can make any changes which they feel would be best for the increased value of the project. The fact that project managers are not regarded as the boss means they work hand-in-hand with the team members and learn from each other. Consequently, building trust and great relationships occur, which is an advantage in the handling of future projects. The product is evaluated phase-by-phase, and brainstorming is done among the team members and with all the stakeholders to ensure that indeed what has been done is what they wanted. Further, the determination of whether any adjustments should be made occurs, and it is monumental for quality products.

Currently, traditional methods of project management, such as the use of the waterfall methodology, are very inhibiting and continue proving to be inefficient and cumbersome. Agile projects are considered to be three times more successful than their non-agile counterparts. It is, therefore, not a wonder why most organizations are considering a shift to the methodology. Figure 3 illustrates the results of a study that was conducted by the Standish group in 2012, comparing the success of projects conducted using the waterfall method against the agile methodology.

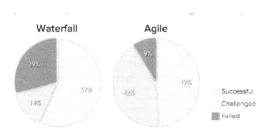

Source: The CHAOS Manifesto, The Standish Group, 2012.

Figure 3: comparison of success statistics of the waterfall against the agile methodology

Source : (Alexander, 2019)

As per the results, it is evident that the agile methodology is much more successful than the traditional project management method. The results are from a survey that was undertaken between 2002 and 2012, a complete ten years. As is evident, an overwhelming 42% of the projects managed through the agile methodology were successful compared to a measly 14% done using the waterfall methodology. The failure rate in the agile methodology is also significantly lower, which explains why it is so highly rated.

Many companies and organizations have resolved to shift to the agile methodology to experience such benefits. A recent interview by VersionOne, a software giant, illustrates this shift. Out of 4,048 software developers involved in the 2013 research, 84% said that their companies had already shifted to agile project management. The percentage was a significant rise from 80% in the previous year, conducted from the same respondents. With the shift to the agile methodology, the respondents asserted that they had already started experiencing significant improvements, which boosted the success of their projects. It is these success statistics and realizations that are prompting more organizations and project managers to go agile.

Even though the transition to agile project management is highly recommended, there is a need to note that it should be done in a specific manner. Shifting without a clear plan and strategy is bound to result in failure and confusion, and may result in the worsening of the situation. That notwithstanding, it is worth noting that shifting to agile is simpler than it seems, as long as one has the full knowledge of what the practice pertains.

Factors to Consider Before Going Agile

While there is no defined formula of shifting to agile project management, some of the factors that should be considered before the transition process are:

i. Organizational Goals and Objectives

Every organization has its distinct goals and objectives. Once all of them are identified, it is important for the team to evaluate how shifting to the new mode of operations will help meet those goals. It is a fact that not all business methodologies require the use of agile project management, and the management must be on the forefront to evaluate which ones do. Where the goals include aspects, such as faster delivery of milestones and increased efficiency, agile project management is undoubtedly the best.

ii. Company Culture and Hierarchy

Not every company can be able to benefit from agile project management and so, there is a need to map the company hierarchy, as well as determine the culture of the organization. Company hierarchy refers to the organization of the individuals in a work environment. The arrangement can either be based on the power, status, or job function.

Where hierarchy is observed, it means that all the work done therein is clearly defined, and there is little room for advancements and changes. Hierarchy is also known as the chain of command, and it stipulates the direction of the authority, and who people are supposed to listen to. Normally, the top management is in charge of making nearly all decisions in the company, and the subordinates must follow all the instructions laid.

The level of adherence to hierarchy is different from corporation to corporation. Some companies may be strict and unwilling to compromise when it comes to the sharing of power. Some may be flexible and willing to give up some level of control. In the former, the agile methodology would not work, and such a company is better-suited sticking to its traditional methods. In the latter, the company can adopt agile methodologies and prosper.

Culture is also very important. In a company, the term culture may refer to the practices that the people are used to, in terms of the beliefs, values, and ways of interaction. Some companies have a very strict culture which is very hard to change. For instance, some companies may divide tasks by the capabilities of the staff, and require them to stick to such work, even though they may be qualified in other areas. Once the staff is used to such arrangements, they eventually accept it as a norm, which is hard to change. A culture which encourages people to go out of their comfort zones is also present in some companies, and these are the ones which would be better suited to shift to agile project management. The organization must scrutinize its culture before attempting to make any shift so that they can know where to start without disrupting the overall company functions.

iii. Impact on Customers

Customers are the major stakeholders of any company since without them no company can survive. Any change that occurs within a company is bound to affect the customers, and the management must evaluate the positive and negative implications. If a shift to agile project management would result in the loss of customers, then the move is not worth it, and the company must do away with it. On the other hand, where such a shift promises positive inferences to the customers, then it is worth undertaking.

There are three major questions that can help any company determine what the impact on customers would be.

1. In what way will the shift to agile project management improve customer experience? Any shift that must be done in a company is considered to be effective and necessary when the overall implication is better customer experience. Some customers and clients prefer working with contractors and developers who follow a stringent set of rules. For instance, in the construction industry, some clients may prefer to work with clients who follow the plans to the letter, without question or compromise. However, some clients require the developers/contractors to react based on their knowledge and determine the best approach through which they can accomplish various tasks. Therefore, they do not require contractors to work with exactly what they are given, since some of the requirements may not be ideal/best.

In order to determine what most of the customers want, the companies can analyze and re-evaluate previous feedback from clients whose works have already been completed. Where most of the clients express satisfaction with the team for following the rules to the letter, then the traditional method is the best. However, where the clients have had to change some of the rules after the completion of the project due to satisfaction; and where the team feels that they noted the impending problem before the completion of the project, then agile methodology would be perfect.

2. Will the shift to agile project management result in better value and quality output? Sometimes, a team may feel like they can be able to offer better quality output when they are allowed to make vital decisions about some of the processes. In this case, the agile methodology is perfect, since it would give such persons the flexibility to get involved in decision

making. On the other hand, where the staff would rather follow predetermined regulations, the traditional methods are better suited to be used.

3. How will the shift affect the collaboration between the rest of the team and other stakeholders? Agile project management is said to be beneficial in that it improves the relationship between the top management and the team members to a very large extent. That notwithstanding, it a fact that the management must be willing to let go of some of the control, for the method to work. In some organizations, the team members may appreciate the chance to be given some level of freedom, and it would undoubtedly improve the relationship with the management and other stakeholders. In some cases, the team may take advantage of such freedom and misuse it. For instance, in case of casual work where a team is paid on an hourly basis, giving them the freedom to choose what to do would result to their selection of the easiest jobs, and doing it slowly. Ultimately, the company loses out. However, where the work involves the accomplishments of milestones, the team can be able to organize itself and ensure that they finish given tasks and on time. Therefore, the agile methodology would be appropriate.

iv. Resources Available in the Company

In any business, there are three key resources that are monumental: physical, human, and intellectual. Physical resources refer to all the monetary assets that are at the disposal of the company that can be used to ensure its success. Money is amongst the physical resources that greatly determine the capability of a company to adopt other forms of operations. Where a company has enough money to purchase equipment required in agile management, they can go ahead and shift to it.

The consideration of human resources is also very important

since it consists of people who are involved in the under-taking of the company operations. Therefore, the company must evaluate the skills and talents that all the members have so that they can be able to gauge whether the transition will work. Where the skills and available talent are proven to exist, the transition can be undertaken, since it would undoubtedly be successful. On the other hand, if the work-force does not have the required skills and expertise, the company must rethink transitioning immediately, and is better placed availing such skills through training the staff first. Intellectual expertise is part of the human resources' skills and must be proven to exist before the transition.

v. Risks and Potential Shortcomings

Each project process has its own advantages and disadvan-tages, and agile project management is no different. There are some risks that would undoubtedly be imminent after the transition unique to the different companies. The company must, therefore, consider all the risks and deter-mine whether they would be comfortable exposing them-selves to such risks. The effects of the risks must also be evaluated, to give the management a clear picture of what they are getting themselves into. In the cases where the risks are minor and not very harmful to the company, the management can go ahead and start the transitioning process. On the other hand, if the risks are too serious and would result in major losses and negative effects, then the company can reconsider.

vi. Opinions of the Other Stakeholders.

Involving key stakeholders in the decision-making process is very important. Each person has a diverse level of under-standing when it comes to issues, and the transitioning process is no exception. The opinions of the other stake-holders may be monumental in the bringing-to-light aspects that the management may not have considered. Further, where some risks are identified, the stakeholders may identify possible remedies, which the other persons may not have considered. Through such sharing of ideas, the best strategy can be discussed and ultimately executed.

vii. Feedback about the Transition Plan.

Where a go-ahead has already been given to shift to the agile methodology, there is always the need for putting together a comprehensive project management plan to clearly illustrate the functional areas before proceeding. Once all the stakeholders agree to the plan, it being a positive sign that it would work, the management can go ahead and implement it. Where there are doubts about some of the processes, the management can go through it with the disgruntled stakeholders and come up with the best strategy of addressing such issues and problems.

viii. Availability of a Change Management Expert

Switching to a new methodology does not only affect the management but all the stakeholders in a particular company. When the change is implemented, there is a need for the management to know that it may be forced to cut out some staff or add others. Involving an expert in the transition process ensures that the management knows all vital information about the shift. In so doing, the stakeholders can decide whether they are willing to conform to some of the changes or not.

ix. Experiences of Other Companies

No company operates by itself, and all have competitors. Amongst the best ways through which the company can be able to predict the functionality of the change is by evaluating how well/badly off companies that have shifted to agile are. Currently, getting such information is not difficult, as the internet is full of case studies. The companies can also carry out their individual due diligence, and get information from credible and willing firms. Where the shift has a positive track record, it is an assurance that the company would also benefit from the transition. However, where similar and competing firms have failed as a result of the shift, the company should reconsider.

x. Results of a Pilot Project

A pilot project is a preliminary short-scale experiment that a company conducts so that they can see the end result. This is amongst the best ways of gauging the expected functionality of the shift, since the team operates as they would if it were a real project. If the pilot project is a success, it serves as a sign that the methodology would work. Where the converse is experienced, the managers should reconsider, since it means that real projects would fail as well.

xi. The Extent to Which Everyone is on Board

A company is a conglomerate of diverse people and talents. Shifting from one method of operation to another requires cooperation from all persons for it to be successful. Worth noting is that any major decision must have its proponents and opponents. Basically, the latter is a major challenge since they may sabotage attempts to move to a new mode of operation. Also, they may feel unequipped, and moving to a project with such a mentality is amongst the easiest ways of facilitating its failure. The best way through which there can be is that every person agrees to the shift by showing them the success levels, especially in the pilot project undertaken. Most people have an intrinsic desire to be associated with successful practices, and showing them such success is the best way of ensuring that they are on board.

Common Hurdles in the Adopting of the Agile Methodology

There are some hurdles that a company must be prepared to face in the course of transitioning from traditional to agile project management. It is important to always keep in mind that with any change or developments, some obstacles ensue and the organization must be prepared to overcome all of them for the transition to be successful. Some of the key hurdles that are expected when attempting to shift include:

1. Lack of Agile Acceptance

As much as agile project management has a track record of success, some stakeholders and team members may be unwilling to shift from the traditional methods. Agile project management cannot be successful without the cooperation of all the other stakeholders, which makes a lack of acceptance a major problem. Depending on who is unwilling to accept the change, the organization is bound to act in different ways. Where it is their ordinary team members who are unwilling to accept the change, dealing with them is relatively easy since they can be replaced with people who are more cooperative. Where the top management is involved, it becomes a bit harder to overcome the challenge, since they are the ones who are supposed to instigate the change. The only reason as to why the top management may be unwilling to shift is due to the fear of losing their place as the managers and leaders of the organization. In such a case, the sabotage of the methodology becomes imminent.

2. Insufficient Experience and Knowledge of the Agile Methodology.

Agile project management is undoubtedly very popular in the current business environment. Some companies may be willing to shift to the methodology, but lack the minimal unexpected skills and knowledge about the knowledge area. In the case where the company may not have sufficient resources to hire experts to guide in the transition, it becomes a major hurdle since they are bound to fail in the process. This hurdle can also be caused by a rapid shift to the methodology, without getting all the facts that pertain to the new system. Not all companies and organizations can benefit from going agile, and the companies must evaluate where they lie. The shift, therefore, becomes problematic since the management and the team members may not know what they are doing.

3. Changing the Complete Traditional Office Environment

Amongst the biggest challenges of the transition process is the complete change of the traditional office environment. Most traditional offices have cubicles and even offices where the staff members operate in. Each person is required to conduct various activities alone which warrants such privacy. The major giveaway in agile project management is the conducting of activities as a team, which means that none of the people are required to work alone. There is, therefore, they need to change the office environment from the cubicle setting to an open plan office setting. This shift is uncomfortable, as some may be used to carrying out the activities in privacy. Getting the people to accept such a change without having them feel violated is a major obstacle in this case. When the team does not appreciate the consequences of a shift, they may become biased and opponents of the change.

Strategies to Undertake for the Transition to be Successful

Once all the factors have been determined, the company is ready for a transition. The next step after the decision to go agile is the undertaking of all relevant strategies to ensure that the methodology becomes a success. There are some strategies that can be adopted by a company, the key of which are:

1. Securing Management Commitment

Management commitment is the first item that must be secured before the undertaking of any project. Transitioning from traditional to agile project management practices is a major project that must be seriously planned for. Each major organizational project normally has a program sponsor who also doubles as the champion of the program initiative. Normally, the sponsor may be amongst the top management or is outsourced, either of which requires management commitment. The identification of a sponsor is the first sign that the management takes the initiative seriously, consequently resulting in its success. According to the United Kingdom National Audit Office (2013), lack of clear management ownership and leadership is an illustration of a project bound to fail and must be avoided at all times. Some of the major benefits that accrue to an initiative with a program sponsor include:

a) They help in the identification of distinct stakeholders and communicating their needs. Project sponsors are ideally people who are extremely knowledgeable about the selected objectives/initiatives. Therefore, they can identify stakeholders who would be affected by the shift, and addressing any concerns that may ensue.

b) They help in the securing of resources and monetary support. Transitioning to agile project management requires distinct resources, which range from the human, intellectual to the monetary resources. When the management is committed to the transition, they can identify the sources where they can be able to obtain such resources, consequently facilitating the success of the initiative. As previously stated, there need to be experts who guide the transition process, and the management must be on the forefront to identify such persons.

c) They serve as the project champions and help remove any

roadblocks. Just like the undertaking of any project, transitioning from a current mode of operation to a new one is bound to be faced by numerous challenges. Where the management has not identified forerunners to deal with such setbacks, there is always the risk of being tempted to do away with such programs. The project sponsors play a major role in sticking to the plans and reminding all stakeholders why they wanted to shift in the first place. Ultimately, they help ensure that the plan stays on board until it is completed.

d) Worth noting is that sometimes key resources may be unavailable. Even where the project sponsors have been selected, they may fail to live up to the financing expectations. Therefore, there is always the need to identify proxies/deputies, who help where the project sponsors are unable to. The deputies are also important since they may be required to take over in the cases where the leads are unavailable for extended periods.

2) Empowering the Team

The nature of agile project management is such that all team members have an equal role in the carrying out of activities. Further, the nature of the agile methodology prompts the fast delivery of services in sets of predetermined iterations. The fact that the team is not used to such practices means that they may have a relatively hard time adjusting to the changes. Further, the fact that the traditional methods require them to follow instructions from the top management means that they may still be inclined to await instructions before doing anything. The empowerment process is, therefore, vital and may be carried out using multiple methods.

First, the management must have meetings with all the staff members and explain the changes that they expect to occur once the transition is over. It is imperative for the entire team to know what is expected of them, and the ways through which it is different from the modes of operations that they are used to. The major point which everyone needs to note is that the project manager is no longer the focal point of the project. After the transition, the entire team is required to take a role to ensure that the project is successful, without awaiting direct instructions from the managers. Even though the project may have some instructions, the responsibility is equally shared by everyone.

To illustrate and depict the changes efficiently, the management should map the difference, so that the team can see what exactly changes. First, the team must be alerted about the aspects that will remain the same, such as time management and the adherence to deadlines. After that, the differences should be clearly outlined. As stated, the major difference is the role of the project manager, where the agile methodology requires everyone to participate in the success of the project. Further, agile project management requires the tasks to be divided into iterations and completed in a much lower timeframe. The fact that collaboration with the stakeholders must be adhered to is also a difference that the team must adhere to.

Empowerment of the team also encompasses taking them through a training program, to enable them to add their skills. Further, when the team knows what is expected of them, they can be able to act accordingly and match the agile values. There are many boot camps that train on agile project management, and the organizations can choose a cost-efficient one to participate in. Where such training is not possible due to the costs involved and other restrictions, an expert can be hired for a few days to take the team through the process. In current times, the internet has simplified methods of obtaining content. YouTube and multiple blogs have clear guides about how to transition to agile project management, and the company can select the ones which best suit their needs. Through the latest technological advantages, there is no need for spending large amounts of money.

3) Understanding the Essence of Collaborative Culture

All projects have a particular mission that they are supposed to accomplish. With the traditional project management strategies, collaboration is not of the essence as it is in the agile project methodology. Therefore, there is a need for the entire team to be educated and guided on the ways through which they can foster a collaborative culture.

Cooperation in agile project management occurs on various levels. First, the team must be willing to cooperate with other members and help each other with every aspect of the project. When the team realizes that they all have a similar objective of ensuring the success of the project, it becomes easier for them to cooperate without many problems.

A collaborative culture should also be instilled with the other stakeholders, particularly the clients and potential customers. There is no need for the undertaking and finalizing a project which is unsatisfactory to the clients, hence the need to work with them in each phase. As stated earlier, face-to-face interactions are highly recommended. However, where location becomes an issue, the team can always communicate with the stakeholders through calls, emailing, and video-conferences. Worth noting is that agile project management aims at integrating the various contractors as single teams, to ensure that they work together. When the team understands that such integration is not meant to make them lose their independence, but rather facilitate total cooperation, they are better placed to fully appreciate the agile project management methodology.

4) Embracing the Agile Project Management Methodology

The agile methodology is very specific and different from the traditional modes of managing projects. For a company to fully shift and succeed after the transition, they must stick to all the aspects, no matter how uncomfortable they are. For instance, top-down management must be discarded at all costs. Even though the managerial team may feel a loss of control and leadership, its necessity cannot be undermined. Further, the team must be willing to take an active role in the decision-making process for it to be a success. Embracing the agile project methodology requires everyone to go all in, and act by the laid-down stipulations without fail.

5) Developing a Road Map and Initial Plans

A roadmap is a planning strategy that clearly illustrates how certain functions are supposed to be accomplished. Agile project management is considered to be a component of the overall planning process, which translates the importance of sticking to strategies and plans. According to a 2006 whitepaper that was developed by Hubert Smit, there are five levels of agile project management planning:

i. Product vision, which illustrates the future of a given project, as well as a given process. The product vision represents the ideal state of the end of the project, and the team is obliged to work toward it. Product vision is very important in project management since it gives the team something to work with. For instance, in the case of an architectural project, the product vision is as represented in the initial architectural plan. The team must work hard to ensure that the construction matches the architectural plan for it to be considered a success.

ii. Product roadmap. A product roadmap is essentially a plan which is created to ease the communication of the product plan to all stakeholders. In any project, there are numerous stakeholders who desire to know about the progress and plan for completion of the project. The roadmap is usually presented in the form of a timeline, which all stakeholders can follow at a glance. Typically, the roadmap is updated with each completed phase of the work, to show the stakeholders how the actual progress is ongoing. The major thing that should be upheld in the designing of the roadmaps is that there should be a caveat to inform the stakeholders that there is a chance that what is depicted may change with time. The fact that changes are imminent in agile project management means that no planning can be followed to the letter.

iii. Release plan, where the clients are responsible for the making of decisions about when to release certain milestones.

iv. Sprint/iteration plan. A planning session must be held to evaluate the duration and activities to be done in each iteration. Planning occurs well before the project commences, and it is important since it enables the team to identify what needs to be done, enabling them to plan their activities accordingly. Normally, there need to be a proper estimation of the budget, duration, and workforce required in the accomplishment of a given iteration, and the project managers are charged with this responsibility. The fact that changes may arise in the course of carrying out an activity means that neither the budget nor the required workforce, need to be fixed, to give room to any changes.

v. Daily plan. The daily planning of activities is very important. The three key questions that every team member must answer daily are 1.) what did they accomplish the previous day, 2.) what did they intend to accomplish on the given day, and 3.) the obstacles that they are facing. Once all three questions are answered, it helps in the gauging of progress, and the resultant expectations at the end of a particular period. Further, the identification of obstacles facilitates the finding of remedies, which consequently results in ease of carrying out activities.

6) Incorporating feedback loops.

The best way of gauging the effectiveness of a strategy is the evaluation of the feedback given by various stakeholders. With every feedback given, strengths and weaknesses are noted, which enables the team to devise strategies which would help them improve. Critical feedback loops that the management can incorporate to give and receive feedback are:

a) Standups. As previously stated, there is the need to have daily meetings where performance is analyzed and progress determined. In these meetings, the management should focus on making each session as brief as possible, normally held when the team is standing. Here, feedback is given briefly and alternatives to any issues evaluated and implemented.

b) Service reviews. The service reviews are more detailed and consist of complex meetings held on a weekly or bi-weekly basis. The main aim of these meetings is to review departmental progress and performance, thereby requiring detailed analysis. With such an in-depth analysis, the management is able to gauge how the methodology is impacting the workspace.

c) Review of operations. The review is also more complex and detailed and allows the teams to gather and share the performance data relating to recent initiatives, and the communication of big wins, as well as any challenges that the team is facing. When the operations are reviewed, it allows the project managers to be able to gauge the effectiveness of the method, ultimately helping in the collaboration of solutions by all participants.

d) Use of retrospective. Retrospective involves the looking

back at completed projects and evaluating what went as planned and what did not. When the team looks at all the functions and operations of the previous projects, they can be able to pinpoint what they would wish to retain in future projects as well as what they feel needs to be disbanded. The use of retrospective is amongst the best strategies which project managers can use to prepare for future projects since it has its basis on actual feedback obtained from completed projects.

7) Staying Flexible

The management should foster a flexible practice, which does not hinder the creativity of any of their staff. The excessive emphasis on procedures is extremely detrimental since it stifles any agile methodologies. Therefore, there is the need for the managers and project executives to make sure that all people know their role, as well as ensure that they know that they are free to modify some of the processes as they see fit. Agile project management is all about making conscious decisions about changes that need to be done, and flexibility enhances the practices.

8) Utilizing Relevant and Most Comfortable Forecasting Tools

There are numerous forecasting tools to be used to enable project managers to predict and plan the activities of an organization. The project managers should not be restricted to specific tools, but rather should use the most appropriate and beneficial tools at any given time. There are simple tools, such as Microsoft Excel that can be used by anyone, and complex tools that are used in more complex projects, such as design and architecture. The project managers should be actively involved in the updating of the charts after every sprint so that there can be consistency and proper prediction of future occurrences.

A sprint refers to a defined period whereby a team accomplishes a series of predetermined tasks. To construct a credible and efficient sprint, the following factors must be taken into consideration;

a) The determination of the project owner. The project owner is the person who the work belongs to, and who has the final say over how the processes should be handled and how the final product should look like.

b) A backlog. A backlog refers to a prioritized list of tasks that usually make up the complete project. Normally, the backlog is created by the project owner, and the team must follow all the stipulations laid therein

c) Planning of the sprints. The goals and the workload must be clearly defined and discussed with the team. After that, the activities that need to be undertaken in every sprint are discussed and planned for. Each of the sprints require a different level of financing, human resources and skills, and proper planning helps in the identification of such requirements promptly.

d) The assigning of tasks. There is the need for every sprint within the task to be accounted for by a team member who is responsible for getting it done. The fact that the team chooses their tasks in agile project management means that most of the tasks are bound to be picked by people who are best qualified, increasing accountability.

e) The timing of the stand-ups. As has been discussed, there is the need to hold daily stand-up meetings, which are typically less than 15 minutes. In such sessions, the team gets to refresh its activities and raise any issues that may hinder the successful implementation of the predetermined activities.

f) The finishing of the sprint and conducting a retrospective. The end goal of any sprint is its successful completion, which must follow the clients' stipulations. Once completed, a retrospective is conducted that consists of the analysis of what proceeded as planned and what did not. Further, the team can evaluate what they feel would have resulted in a better outcome. Ultimately, the results enable the making of better decisions in the next project.

Chapter Summary

- Agile project management is amongst the best methodologies proven to facilitate the successful completion of contract works.
- Traditional methods of project management are increasingly becoming inefficient.
- Projects conducted through agile project management are three times more successful than their counterparts conducted through traditional methods.
- The factors that should be considered before going agile are:

1. Organizational goals and objectives
2. Company culture and hierarchy
3. Impact of the transition to customers
4. Resources available in the company
5. Risks and potential shortcomings of the transition
6. The opinions of other stakeholders
7. Feedback about the transition plan
8. Availability of a change management expert
9. Experiences of other companies
10. The results of the pilot project
11. The extent to which everyone is on board

- There are some strategies that can be undertaken to ensure the success of the transition. They include:

1. Securing management commitment
2. Empowering the team
3. Understanding the essence of a collaborative culture
4. Embracing the agile project management methodology
5. Developing a road map and initial plans
6. Incorporating feedback loops
7. Staying flexible
8. Utilizing relevant and most comfortable forecasting tools

SCOPE AND RESPONSIBILITIES OF AGILE PROJECT MANAGEMENT TEAM MEMBERS

Agile project management is very specific about the scope and roles of team members. As opposed to other project management methodologies, the entire team is responsible for ensuring that the processes proceed as planned; and never leave the decision-making to the project managers alone. It is always imperative that all decisions be made based on common sense, and the reactions of the processes and procedures undertaken, and not based on any written policies.

Being a manager in an agile project requires wisdom in the evaluation of the skills and the leadership strategies put forth, which helps in the retaining of a positive spirit and discipline among the team members. An agile project manager is not regarded as the boss of the project, but rather as part of the team. In line with evaluating the scope of agile project management, there is the need to analyze the responsibilities of the project managers and team members, and compare them with the traditional methodologies.

Responsibilities of Agile Project Managers

As previously stated, agile project managers are not considered superior to the other team members in as much as they have a role to ensure that all the functions or the project proceed as planned. There are key responsibilities that every other project manager must adhere to, which are relatively similar regardless of the nature of the project.

1) The project managers must ensure that the added values and practices are maintained without fail. Agile project management has its basis on 12 principles, all of which must be followed for the project to be successful. Therefore, the managers must be privy of the twelve principles and guide their team appropriately. Agile project management entails the following of all the principles to the letter for the project to be a success. Further, the managers must be on the forefront to ensure that none of the values are misconstrued, which would result in project failure. For instance, agile project management is determined to ensure fast delivery of services, which may be misconstrued as the desire for speed over quality. Poor quality and service delivery are not functions of agile project management, and the project managers can refrain from them and ensure that all their activities conducted are in line with what is expected.

2) The agile project manager is the main motivator for the team. Depending on how they interact with other team members, the direction of the overall cooperation is determined. The project manager must always show trust and belief in their team members for cooperation to be achieved. The fact that all people have different skills and talents means that they require each other for the successful completion of the project. Once the project manager shows the team that he or she believes in them, it inspires them to work even harder, so that they can live up to the expectations. Further, leaving the decision-making process to the team members ensures that they leave the comfort zone and

can be able to make vital decisions regarding how to handle different occurrences. The project manager must also always motivate the team to work with each other so that they can give each other ideas. Such interactions are very crucial in helping solve any challenges that may arise in the cause of conducting their activities.

1. Enhancing communication. By nature, project managers are leaders. Amongst the vital capabilities of leaders is to enhance communication among their team members. Agile project managers require everyone to work together, a factor which warrants proper communication. Worth noting is that communication does not only entail talking to each other but rather the passing of relevant information and receiving appropriate feedback. When all the persons know how to communicate effectively, it becomes easier to team up and perform the job, thus facilitating success.

2. Project managers are responsible for spearheading meetings, both the brief stand-ups and complex sit-downs. There is always the need for proper structure to be followed when holding meetings, to ensure that the best is taken out of them. Project managers drive the meetings and determine the direction that each takes. One of the key factors that should be safeguarded is the giving of everyone an equal opportunity to participate so that everyone can feel like they are part of their decision-making process.

3. Finally, as much as the project manager is not a boss in a project, he still has a big responsibility for all the functionalities of the company. Therefore, where the team unable to find proper solutions to any of the problems, they must involve the team manager and seek guidance concerning how to solve such issues.

Further, the project manager is the key motivator, resolver of impediments, and the blocker of issues early enough in the project. With this regard, the project manager can be perceived as a mentor and a protector of his team, rather than the boss.

Activities that Project Managers do not Engage In

The responsibilities of agile project managers differ from project to project. There is a chance that some of the functions can be misconstrued and interpreted differently. Therefore, there is the need to illustrate what the project managers are not mandated to do, as follows:

1. Agile project managers are not the sole leaders and managers of all the functions in a project. As has been widely discussed, agile project managers act as a team with the rest of the members and distribute the decision-making process to ensure that every member has a say in what happens on set. Therefore, the project managers are not the main drivers of the processes and must work hand-in-hand with all the team members until the project completion

2. Agile project managers do not assign tasks to the team members. The team members are responsible for selecting the activities and processes which they feel best suit their talents and skills and are free to help the rest of the team members in the undertaking of the other tasks. The fact that the team members are required to be hands-on and diverse means that they're not restricted to carrying out a single activity, but can take part in all the processes to so long as it is for the aim of facilitating project success.

3. Agile project managers do not make decisions on behalf of the team. Unlike in the traditional project

management methodologies where the project managers are solely responsible for all the undertakings of an organization, the agile methodology is different. Agility encourages group performance and operation of all team members in the fulfillment of the central role of the project. Whenever any issue arises, the team members are free to consult each other and also involve the various stakeholders, ultimately finding the best solution to the problem.

4. Agile project managers are not charged with the responsibility of driving the team to achieve specific milestones or deliverables. Each team member acts independently and is answerable for the various tasks that they undertake. Therefore, they are free to plan their schedules and make decisions which they feel would best help them fulfill their tasks. Aspects such as cooperation, intelligence, time consciousness, and hard work are characters that all team members are expected to have and must not be pushed to showcase them.

5. Finally, agile project managers do not have the mandate to overrule any decision made by the other team members. The fact that all the members of the team have equal opportunity in the decision-making process means that the project managers should listen and allow the implementation of the decisions as long as they are legal and can solve the identified problems efficiently.

Responsibilities of the Team Members

In every other project carried out, there is a unique list of team members. Depending on the type of the project, the scope of the team members may change, although their responsibility to quality and fast-service delivery remains constant. There are some universal characteristics that every agile team member must have. Some of these characteristics are innate, while some must be taught in learning institutions, or in the particular workplace which the team members work. The innate characteristics are the values that individuals do not learn from anyone, but emanate from deep within them. Some of these key innate characteristics are time consciousness, dedication, and a good work ethic. Although they cannot be taught, the company can lay down stringent measures to ensure that every person works as is expected. Some of the vital characteristics that every team member should include:

1. T-shaped characteristics

A valuable and agile team member must showcase a wide breadth of basic skills and knowledge about a subject matter. The T-shaped aspect involves the combination of a wide range of skills and knowledge (Horizontal part) with the specialized expertise in the area of focus (Vertical part), as illustrated in Figure 4.

Figure 4: Illustration of the T-shaped skills required in agile project management's team members.

Source: What Is The "T"? - T-Summit Conference". 2019. *Tsummit.Org.* http://tsummit.org/t.

Workers who employ the T-shape characteristics in their distinct areas of expertise possess skills which are imperative in their various areas of work. As illustrated, there are boundary-crossing competencies on the horizontal spectrum, which includes qualifications such as teamwork, communication, perspective, critical thinking, project management, and a global understanding of some of the vital and unique project factors. The employees are also immensely qualified in many disciplines, which make them assets as they can be able to handle multiple and diverse works. Worth noting is that there are many systems which are imperative in the handling of specific aspects in a project. Employees with T-shaped characteristics are knowledgeable about such systems, which facilitates success in the different endeavors that they are involved in.

This horizontal spectrum is essentially a representation of the team members' ability to contribute to both the creative and innovative processes. There is the need for the team members to engage in a wide array of activities since it is the only way through which they can identify the areas they are best skilled in and the ones they are not.

The vertical spectrum consists of depth in at least one system or discipline. Depth means full understanding and deep knowledge of all the subject matters about the disciplines, which is imperative in the achievement of project goals and objectives.

There are very many advantages that accrue to a company/project which utilizes team members with the T-shaped characteristics. The major advantage is that the team can be able to handle a wide range of activities by themselves, without the need of having to look for other professionals in the field. The T-shape team members also have values, such as:

i. Collaborative culture. The team members who have the T-shaped characteristics are immensely cooperative, both with the management, stakeholders, and other team members. Cooperation is imperative in any project since it forms the basis through which all persons can work together harmoniously and deliver the expected results.

ii. Empathy. The term empathy is used to refer to the aspect through which a person can be able to see, relate, and understand another person's viewpoint. Empathy is normally considered a major basis of respect since the persons can appreciate what the other team members think, and accommodate their viewpoints. Without empathy, some of the team members are bound to feel superior, and require everyone to conform to what they want, which creates strife and lack of proper development of the project.

iii. Enthusiasm. There is always the need for the team members to be highly enthusiastic about a project; so that they can do all it takes to ensure that it becomes successful. By nature, enthusiastic workers are eager to learn and develop in their areas of competence. The agile project management team members are usually required to always be at the forefront of learning new ways through which they can accomplish tasks so that they can diversify their skills. The fact that agile project management requires all the team members to take an active role in the project means that they must be open to listening to each other and coming to an agreement about the best modes of operation.

iv. Vision. T-shaped members have great vision and can predict future occurrences by evaluating the factors that are happening as at a given time in the company. The skills are very imperative in the successful undertaking of a project since the team can predict what would happen, and either work toward making it a reality or averting it.

2. Cross-Functional Characteristics

For team members to be regarded as having cross-functional characteristics, they must have skills outside of their traditional areas. Cross-functional skills include those forms of expertise which are different from what a person was hired to do. For instance, there are some team members who have very fast typing skills, and they would be monumental in the preparation of reports which are time conscious. Through the ability to carry out multiple activities, cross-functional teams can assist each other, particularly where some members have stronger skills which may facilitate the fast completion of the project. In agile project management, the encouraging of cross-functional activities facilitate the continuous flow of features after every sprint. Worth noting is that the use of cross-functional teams reduces four key types of wastes.

The first type of waste is delays, which normally occur due to multiple reasons. First, a team may delay in completing a project due a to lack of clear instructions. Where unclear instructions have been given, the team gets stuck and is unable to proceed. Having a cross-functional team ensures that delays are not experienced, since the team members are diverse, and can be able to find the best approaches for some of the issues. Where delays occur, companies are bound to lose in terms of time, resources, and labor. Agile project managers know the essence of preventing delays, thereby being on the forefront to encourage cross- functionality across the team

Defects are also greatly reduced where cross-functioning is implemented. The fact that the team members showcase additional skills in the course of carrying out the project means that they can identify any discrepancies early enough and work toward resolving them.

In the course of project management, partially done work is amongst the greatest components that contribute to poorly finished and managed work. The partial doing of the work may be as a result of lack of the required skills that would enable its completion, mainly due to insufficient skills. The fact that cross-functional teams can be able to get involved in any work means that they can identify work which is not completed, and an experienced person can undertake the role of completing it appropriately.

Paperwork is also a great function of projects and occurs in every phase of the sprints. A cross-functional team consists of members who are experienced in the conducting of any function, including paperwork. Therefore, there is no need for waiting for a person to perform the task which may result in delays. The major benefit of such an arrangement is that time is saved since anyone can conduct the activity. Further, the team can help each other out whenever any of them is stuck. More important is the fact that, since the team is operating as one, there is no need for a lot of paperwork. The team gets to decide all the activities that are to be done and produce single reports, preventing waste of resources, where individual persons have to produce individual reports.

1. Adaptable Characteristics

Adaptability refers to a function where the project manager can be able to operate in diverse environments without any struggle. In agile projects, a management change is constant and very unpredictable. The fact that change occurs at an exhilarating pace means that all the team members should be ready to handle circumstances as they occur. When the team members are adaptive, they can go into any environment and prosper. Some projects are seemingly more difficult than others; but with an adaptable mentality, the team members can be able to handle all aspects that arise. Also, it is worth noting that projects are unique and ideally never repeated under the same circumstances. An adaptive team views each product as unique and do not attempt to use the previously used methods since the end goals are different. Handling each project in a unique manner ensures that all the requirements are met, in that each client gets what they requested.

2. Curiosity

Agile project management is determined to ensure growth among the team members. For such growth to occur, the team must be actively involved in all the functions and processes of the project and ask questions where they are not sure. Curiosity is very important since it enables team members to seek better ways of performing activities and even solutions to when problems occur. Curiosity also enables learners to catch up with their superiors, since it makes them attentive towards the specific superiors are doing.

3. Commitment to Excellence

One of the key principles of agile project management is delivering quality work within a much lower timeframe. Commitment to excellence pushes the team members to perform the task in the best way possible and refrain from settling for average. As much as project managers do not hang on perfection, they are always dedicated to ensuring that this work is the highest standards possible.

4. Entrepreneurial Characteristics

Entrepreneurial characteristics are very important for project managers. An entrepreneur is a person who is considered to be a problem solver, risk taker, researcher, enthusiastic, and a great determinant of the success of a business. When team members possess the entrepreneurial characteristics, they can run the project in such a way that it becomes cost-effective, with numerous risks taken, as well as highly researched. Such a project is likely to excel as a result.

Chapter Summary

- Each member has a responsibility to ensure that the project runs as was designed to.
- All decisions made are not as a result of any written strategies but by the events that occur during the project performance.
- The project managers are not superior to any of the team members.
- The project managers must ensure that they observe the added value in practices and maintain it within the course of the project.
- The project managers can ensure that each team member is privy to the 12 agile project management principles to prevent any form of misconstruction.
- The project managers act as the main motivator for the team.
- Since the project managers are natural leaders, they must ensure that proper communication takes place.
- The project managers also spearhead meetings, regardless of whether it is the brief stand-up or the complex sit-downs.

- The project managers are perceived to be the mental and protectors of their team rather than the bosses.
- The project managers do not make any decisions on behalf of the team or directly assign any duties. More importantly, they act as part of the team and are not mandated to overrule any decision made by the other team members.
- The team members have the responsibility of sticking to the 12 agile management principles and possessing characteristics which are monumental in the undertaking of the projects.
- The characteristics involved are entrepreneurial, T-shaped characteristics, cross-functional characteristics, commitment to excellence, and a level of curiosity.

4

BASIC QUALITY CONTROL TOOLS IN AGILE PROJECT MANAGEMENT

Agile project management is highly inclined towards ensuring quality output. Therefore, each organization is likely to incorporate the use of various quality tools that will help it gauge the level of performance. As has been discussed, an agile project is usually divided into sprints, and the performance re-evaluated at the end of every sprint. There are some quality tools that a company or organization can use for the main functions of controlling and ensuring that the quality objective is achieved. In as much as the tools are different, they can be used across a wide array of domains field and practices. The quality tools are therefore very generic as they can be applied in any situation. There are eight key quality tools that are normally used in organizations. The tools are fundamental in the provision of information about any problems that are occurring within the organization, as well as deriving appropriate solutions for the same. They include;

1. **Stakeholder checklists**

The use of checklists is amongst the best ways through

which the measurement of the performance of a project is undertaken. Teams which use the agile methodology are sometimes faced with the major setback of the inability to find where they stand as at a particular time. The fact that everyone is involved in a diverse activity, without a leader spearheading it means that there's always a chance that the stakeholders can be unable to track the progress of such a project effectively. Checklists are normally prepared at the beginning or during the undertaking of the project and are different for every stakeholder. Some of the stakeholders whose checklist and monumental include;

a) Product owners. The product owners are the major stakeholders in any project since the end product is theirs. To gauge the level at which quality has been safeguarded, the owner needs to check whether the product backlog is prioritized, whether all the requirements from the major stakeholders are upheld and whether the product backlog is in a manageable size. Further, the owners are interested in the review of the adjustment of the release plan after the previously conducted sprint review meeting. Where the checklist ascertained that the requirements are as planned, it is an illustration of quality performance.

b) Project managers. Even though project managers are not considered as the bosses of a particular project, they still have a role in ensuring that all the activities proceed as planned. Since all the team members are responsible for their actions, care must be taken to ensure that all the activities are proceeding as planned. Among the factors that the project managers look for in their checklist includes the project management plan created, the maintenance of the springbok log created, the iteration plan, and the adherence of the team members to various laid-down strategies. For instance, deliverables such as daily stand-up meetings and a transparent decision-making process must be evaluated. Where the project manager confirms that the team is actively involved in ensuring that the checklist is conformed to, it is a positive sign of quality assurance.

c) Business analysts. The business analysts are concerned with the final product and the level to which it will be profitable for a client. The analysts are also greatly concerned with the level to which the end product fits the description of what was required. The business analysts are mandated to conduct quality checks throughout the various phases until project completion. Some of the factors that are checked include the non-functional requirements, such as the completion of necessary reports and the identification of a feature list. Where a team adheres to the key requirements stipulated, it is a positive sign of working toward quality.

2) **Pareto Charts**

Pareto charts, also known as Pareto distribution diagrams, consist of a vertical bar graph in which values are deduced and plotted in decreasing order. The values are plotted by order of relative frequency from the left to the right. The frequencies help in the analysis of problems that need attention fast to the one which requires the least attention at a given time. Normally, the taller bars illustrate the variables that have the highest cumulative effects on a particular activity or projects.

The basic principle in the use of the Pareto chart is a concept that 80% of the outcome is a result of 20% of the inputs. This 80/20 rule is applicable in many different systems, and the project managers should be at the forefront of identifying each variable. Quality can be highly improved if the factors which affect the most vital functions are handled fast. With a Pareto chart, such identification is simplified, enabling the team to identify which factors they should concentrate on first. A sample Pareto chart is as illustrated below.

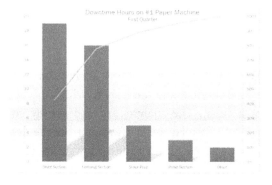

Figure 5: Illustration of a sample Pareto chart

Source: (Wittwer, 2019)

In the Pareto chart depicted, the downtown hours on the paper machine are illustrated in terms of the areas where it affects most. In this case, the Dryer Section is the most afflicted followed by the forming section, the Stock Prep Section, the Press Section, and other areas. With such an illustration, the team is notified that it should handle the issues in the Dryer Section first since that is where the most negative extremity arises. The team can, therefore, be able to coordinate itself and decide on the timelines through which it can analyze all problems. Such analysis ensures that critical problems are handled promptly minimizing the risk of losses in the short and long run.

The Pareto charts can also be used in the analysis of the frequency through which problems and defections affect a process. Through such information, the team members can be able to determine the most appropriate strategies that can be undertaken to permanently eliminate such problems.

The charts also help in the analysis of the broader causes of a particular problem through the examination of its components. For instance, after the identification that the Dryer Section is the most negatively inflicted by downtown hours, the individual components of the Dryer Section, can be an as illustrated in Figure 6.

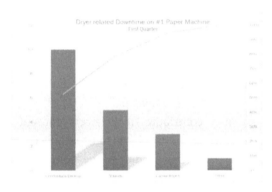

Figure 6

Source: (Wittwer, 2019)

From the illustration, it is clear that there are four factors that contribute to the downtown hours in the Dryer Section. The major cause of such downtime is the condensate backup followed by the stickies, the carrier ropes, and other courses. With such knowledge, the stakeholders can determine the best approach through which they can handle detrimental issues. The ultimate result is the solving of a problem that would have led to quality issues.

Agile project management is highly inclined toward ensuring that the end product not only conforms to the quality requirements but is also problem free. The creation of a Pareto chart is quite simple and involves four major steps.

The first step is the establishment of a purpose. Pareto charts must be deduced to either help solve a particular problem or establish a certain outcome. Most Pareto charts are inclined toward the analysis of customer complaints, as for a service provider. Project managers can also highly benefit from such charts wherever one wants to find reasons that would cause delays and dissatisfaction among the clients. Once the information is obtained, measures can be put in place to prevent a repeat of the same.

The second step is the determination of the causes and coming up with measurement parameters. There are many factors that may contribute to the occurrence of a single problem, and the use of the charts must establish a common measurement parameter. Some of the common measures used are time, cost, and frequency in numbers.

Third, the creators must determine the framework through which they will analyze the chart. A regular timeframe is highly recommended since it helps with the analysis. Data can be analyzed daily, weekly, monthly, or through any of the pre-set timeframe.

Finally, data collection ensues. The collection of data must be done in such a way which will ensure credibility, for the results to be accurate. Basic data can be collected by hand, through the use of a spreadsheet or any other method that the collector is best confident in. The data collected is then used in the analysis process and the plotting of the chart. Once analyzed, the problematic areas are deduced and measures are taken to help eliminate them, thereby helping in quality improvement.

3. The Fishbone Charts

The fishbone chart, also known as the Ishikawa, is a cause-and-effect analysis tool that helps one in the thorough determination of problems and their root causes. In a typical project management task, there are many problems that may be experienced in the course of carrying out the task. Some of the problems are immensely detrimental to the required quality of the end product. In the case some of the serious problems arise it is important first to evaluate all the possible courses that would have resulted in it before starting to think about a solution. That way there is a possibility of all the problems being solved in entirety the first time, rather than partial addressing of some of the problems and ultimately experiencing a rerun. The fishbone charts are unique since they facilitate the combination of brainstorming with mind-mapping, which pushes the stakeholders to evaluate problems in depth and not just the ones that are obvious. The fact that the charts are used in the analysis phase of the six sigma approach means that it creates room for quality and control improvement.

In agile project management, the fishbone charts are very important, since they ensure that any problem identified is solved promptly and in a manner which would prevent its recurrence. The basic steps involved in the construction of a fishbone diagram are:

a) Problem statement. First, the concerned party must write down the exact problems being faced, and in some instances identify the actual people involved and where it occurs. The problem is then written on a large piece of paper on the left-hand side. Once completed, a line is drawn across the paper in a horizontal manner as illustrated below.

Figure 8

Source: (Tech Target, 2019)

The second step involves working out of all the major factors involved that may be part of the problem. Depending on the problem identified, there are some causes which may be unique to a particular project and others universal. Some of the common causes of quality problems involve issues with the systems, equipment, external forces, such as suppliers of raw materials and the people involved in the carrying out of a project. For all the potential causes to be identified effectively, teamwork is highly recommended. The problematic factors are then added to the initial diagram through the drawing of the spine from the first initial horizontal line, as illustrated below.

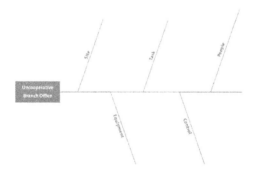

Figure 8

Source: (Tech Target, 2019)

The third step involves the identification of possible causes for each of the major factors identified in the second step. The courses can be as many as possible and are imperative in the seeking of solutions. The identified causes are then branched off from the major factors as illustrated below

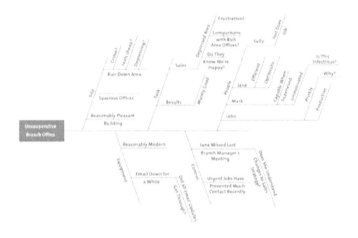

Figure 9

Source: (Tech Target, 2019)

When all the factors have been analyzed and added to the diagram, analysis can then take place. Finding the root causes of major issues forms the basis of finding the best solutions to ensure smooth operations.

The fishbone diagram helps in quality assurance because problems are not taken at face value. The in-depth analysis of the causes of such problems facilitates the resolution process which consequently improves the overall activities in a project and enhances quality performance.

4. **Histogram**

A histogram is a bar chart that includes variables and is used for the identification of root problems in a project.

Histograms can also showcase where certain problems lie about the entire project and estimate how large they appear on the scale. Worth noting is that histograms are among the simplest tools which offer powerful analysis to projects' problems, even though they are often neglected. Data is usually represented by columns in a graph which has varying heights depending on the frequency. Various stakeholders can use histograms in the analysis of multiple aspects of the project and get credible inferences.

Histograms as quality assurance tools are beneficial in the following ways:

a) Data displayed on a histogram is easy to interpret. Histograms are very direct and do not require skilled people to make vital interpretations. Therefore, they enable the direct understanding of concepts and fast identification of problems ultimately facilitating the remedial measures.

b) Histograms show the frequency of the occurrence of various data. Therefore, the stakeholders can tell which of the problems keep arising and the degree to which it affects the project. With such an understanding, they can devise remedial measures which would permanently solve the problem.

c) Histograms also enable the future prediction of some of the process performances. Therefore, the stakeholders can tell whether the project is ongoing in a positive way or whether it is bound to fail. When such an analysis is done, all the people involved in a project can act accordingly so that they can prevent future losses. Consequently, quality is achieved.

d) A histogram can answer whether a process can meet customer requirements. Agile project management is highly inclined toward satisfying its clients who necessitate the identification of instances where such a principle can be achieved and where it cannot. In this case, the results show that if a project will not meet any of the customer requirements, the team makes vital adjustments to prevent such an occurrence.

e) Continuous improvement is also a major factor in agile project management. The nature of a histogram enables the stakeholders to be able to analyze the performance trend, thus allowing them to make adjustments whenever the trend goes downward. The aim is always to ensure that each performance precedes the other in terms of quality.

Plotting a histogram is very easy. Unlike other quality management tools, the collection of data comes first. The data can be collected using a tally chart or recording relevant variables in sheets in such a way that they are easy to deduce and plot on a graph. Once the data has been collected, the stakeholders determine the range of the numerical data to make plotting easy and uniform. The shapes formed to illustrate the trend and allow the stakeholders to make vital inferences about the quality aspect of the project.

5. Charts and Graphs

Charts and graphs are visual components which provide the best way of understanding the quality management processes and how they will function in a particular project. Charts come in various designs; the project managers choose the ones which they believe would best illustrate the project situation. For instance, there are three-dimensional charts and single charts, all of which perform the same function of showing the performance of some processes. Some of the most commonly used graphs and charts include pie charts and line graphs. Just like in the histogram, data is collected first, and then the charts are prepared. Currently, it is very easy to prepare charts and graphs since they are already inputted in Word documents; one just has to fill in the data to get an automatic generation of the visual illustration. The biggest advantage of using charts is that they are easy to understand and construct, preventing any form of misconstruction of data. Also, the charts and graphs are used in mathematical evaluations and can clearly show which areas are using most of the resources, such as cash, as well as the areas which are experiencing the most problems.

In agile project management, all the team members should ideally be on the same page regarding issues that affect the project. Since the charts and graphs are so easy to understand, it helps ensure that all persons understand the data as it should be and helps prevent a situation where everyone may deduce their incorrect inferences.

6. Scatter Diagrams

Scatter diagrams are also known as scatter graphs. They consist of graphical pairs of numerical data which illustrate the relationship between variables on each axis. Wherever the variables are correlated, the points fall along a line or a curve, which can be easily plotted. The better the correlation, the more the data points fall along a line. Ideally, scatter diagrams are beneficial when trying to identify the potential root causes of problems. When a problem is linked to several factors, the more the correlation, the better the illustration, that such problems are factors of the identified root cause. The scatter diagrams are also used after the construction of a fishbone diagram, with the main role of objectively trying to determine whether the particular causes and defects identified are related in any way.

To be able to draw a proper scatter diagram, there must be a collection of data where a relationship is expected. A graph is drawn with the independent variable on the horizontal axis and the dependent variable on the vertical axis. Just like other graphs, a point or a symbol is indicated where the x-axis value intersects with the y-axis for a particular component. Then, the symbols which closely correlate have a line plotted through them to showcase a relationship. Scatter diagrams are not that common in agile project management, but they come in handy where immense numerical data is involved.

7. **Control Charts**

Control charts are agile project management quality control tools that enable the measurement of any form of variation, defect, and unstable processes. Project managers analyze the control charts periodically and find areas which need changes or modifications. Through the analysis, the managers are able to make credible rectifications, changes, and acceptable reviews. Normally, the process variations in control charts are analyzed before any process improvement can begin. There are common causes of variations in the data in various types of control charts, which help in the identification of elements that are beyond human control. Once identified, they are either modified or changed in entirety, to enable the continuity of the project.

Control charts are widely used in the software spectrum. Amongst the major benefits incurred is that they help in the identification of how many times the software exceeds the acceptable error as well as how many times it exceeds what is acceptable. There are lower and upper limits that govern the acceptable region and any statistics and data that falls beyond the parameters need intense scrutiny. Software developers affirm that without control charts, some of the unacceptable fluctuations would go unnoticed.

In other projects, the control charts are majorly used to illustrate the lead times for the products, versions or sprints. The charts, therefore, help in the identification of whether data from a current period can be able to predict future performance. The lower the variance, the more accurate the analysis of future performances. Further, using current data, the project managers can be able to see how a change in a process affects the overall team's productivity. In this case, the control charts are the best control tools for a repetitive process/project.

There are a number of components that are basic in a control chart

i. The center line. The center line in a control chart illustrates the ideal capability of a process. The values are normally obtained through the calculation of the mean value of the parameters being investigated. As stated, the charts work best for repetitive work. Therefore, repetitive data can be obtained, and the mean obtained.

ii. The specification limit. The limits are normally established after the analysis of customer expectations, which are sometimes mentioned in agreements. When data exceeds the set limit, fast modifications and changes are imminent

iii. Control limits. The charts contain upper and lower control limits, which are identified after statistical analysis from historical data/records. When the current data exceeds the limits, adjustments must be one.

An illustration of a control chart is as represented in figure 10

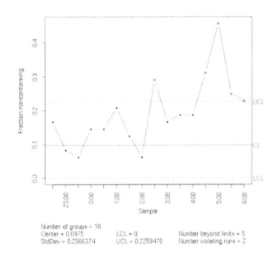

Figure 10

Source (Scheid, 2019)

In the diagram, the dotted lines represent the upper control limit and the lower control limit. The points marked in red are beyond the parameters, and the project managers must re-evaluate and modify the processes.

Chapter Summary

- Agile project management is highly inclined toward ensuring quality output.
- There are some quality tools that a company or organization can use for the main functions of controlling and ensuring that the quality objective is achieved.
- The quality tools are, therefore, very generic as they can be applied in any situation.
- Some of the quality control tools to be used include:

- Checklists
- Pareto charts
- Fishbone charts
- Histograms
- Charts and graphs
- Scatter diagrams
- Control Charts

5

AGILE PROJECT MANAGEMENT
TOOLS/METHODOLOGIES

Every company involved in agile project management has its own set of tools which it uses to make the activities run more efficiently and strictly. In light, selecting the best agile methodology tool, it is worth understanding why an agile tool is required in the first place. While agile project management can be managed through a plethora of old-school methods, such as Microsoft project, spreadsheets, and index cards, the strategies do not provide for collaboration. The identified methods may come in handy in the tracking of the project progress, analyzing the iterations, listing requirements, and gathering data on developmental efficiency. The functions are important in the overall project management process, although they do offer the high efficiency required of agile projects.

Agile tools are beneficial in that they integrate all of the project's functions into a single resource and improve overall efficiency. Burndown charts, user case storage, iterations, backlogs, and collaboration are all distinct functions that can be integrated into a single resource through the use of an agile tool. When the stakeholders know where to look every time, they can stay on top of their roles within the scope of the project.

Since the inception of agile project management, the approach has become amongst the most sought and used in the management environment. With response to the increased popularity of the methodology, software development companies have been at the forefront in the designing of agile-specific tools. As discussed, each of the tools has its benefits and shortcomings, and the selection of the best tools is specific to the needs of an organization. The fact that all the tools promise good results makes the decision-making process relatively challenging. The decision-makers must ensure that they consider all the functions that they want the selected tools to solve so that they can make the best decision.

Some of the most common tools are Scrum, Kanban, and Scrumban. Since it may not be easy to determine the best approach at a glance, the decision-makers are better suited to read and analyze online reviews, enabling them to eliminate some tools right away. Online reviews comprise both positive and negative commentaries and are from people who have used the tools. Once the decision-maker analyzes the strength as well as the weaknesses that the previous users are criticizing, they can determine whether the tool would be beneficial for their operations. The major setback that the decision-makers need to consider in such an approach is that some of the reviews are fake since it might be a strategy from the developers to promote their products. However, there are some sites which are very strict and credible, and their reviews can be relied upon as being authentic.

Upon the identification and selection of the most appropriate tool, the decision-makers can then compare the individual characteristics of the tools and choose from which of them would be the best. While the characteristics and project requirements may point to a certain tool, there is always the need to ensure that, at the very least, the tool serves as a complete resource for the management of agile functions. The key functions include tracking tasks, storing of searchable data, and discussion processes.

Depending on the nature of the project, the tools used differ significantly by the ability to solve the needs of a project. That notwithstanding, there are some tools which are used across different projects, regardless of their nature, and have proven to facilitate the fulfillment of the 12 agile project management principles. As stated, the three major tools used are Scrum, Kanban, and Scrumban (a hybrid of Scrum and Kanban)

Scrum

Scrum is one of the most popular frameworks used in agile project management. This tool has its basis on the belief that transparency, collaboration, adaptation, and frequent iterations are the best practices for success. The Scrum project tools enable users to visualize the overall amount of work given by the client, to make them effectively divide the entire project in iterations and individual work. Through the Scrum framework and strategies, the team members can handle and address complex problems witnessed in the course of carrying out the project while being productive and creative in the ultimate delivery of the project. Worth noting is that Scrum is usually used in software development, although its benefits and uses can be implemented in any kind of project.

Some of the benefits that accrue to projects which have adopted the use of Scrum cannot be underestimated. The Scrum tool has its sole basis on the belief of leaving all the activities up to the development team, instead of providing complete descriptions about how everything is to be done in a project. Scrum, just like agile project management, is also inclined to the belief that the team knows how to best solve problems as they present themselves, and do not need step-by-step guidance. The tool relies on a self-organizing and cross-functional team, who ensure that the project proceeds as planned. That notwithstanding, the teams are supported by two key figures the first of whom is the Scrum master, and the second whom is the product owner.

The Scrum master can be thought to be the coach for the team and helps the team members' hold the Scrum process in the highest regard. On the other hand, the product owner's represents the business, the customers and their users and they guide them towards producing quality and efficient products. The Scrum model suggests that projects should progress through a series of sprints, which have a defined start and completion date. The methodology, therefore, advocates for the planning of a meeting at the start of a specified sprint, where the team members discuss all aspects about the piece of work, and at the end of the sprint re-evaluate what was achieved. Some of the factors that must be considered are how many items a person can commit to, the resources required to satisfactorily complete the milestone, and the overall list of tasks that must be performed during the sprints.

In projects such as software development, the Scrum team takes small sets of coded ideas and features and tests their functionality. At the end of the sprint, the features are experimented and integrated into a product or evolving system to enable the study of their suitability. The main idea behind the experiments is the belief that in an agile environment, business and technical sides are not recognized since the most important factor is value delivery. The best results are undoubtedly obtained where diverse talents are incorporated into activities since efficient problem-solving skills and creativity are encouraged.

Worth noting is that people may often think that Scrum and agile methodology are the same things because of their philosophy of being centered on continuous improvement. However, Scrum is usually the framework through which work is completed, while agile is the mindset. For that reason, a company cannot go agile without the dedication of the whole team and their willingness to change the way they think about value delivery to customers. That notwithstanding, a Scrum framework can help in the mindset changing process and the incorporating of agile principles into everyday communication and tasks.

Also notable is the fact that Scrum is undoubtedly structured, although it is not entirely rigid. The execution of some of the crucial works is done and tailor-made with regards to the needs of the individual organizations and clients. Project managers should note that, even though they are required to act differently with regards to the needs of the unique projects, transparency, communication and the dedication to quality should always remain constant.

Philosophy Behind Scrum

The earlier advocates of Scrum were inspired by its empirical aspects and agile feedback loops, which would help cope with complexity and risks. Scrum always insists that decision-making from the real world is more important than speculation

Scrum Artifacts

There are three artifacts in a Scrum framework. The artifacts are ideally something that is made like a tool to help solve a problem. Scrums' artifacts play a major role in the solving of project management problems. The artifacts include a product backlog, sprint backlog, and an increment.

The product backlog refers to the master list of work that needs to get done and is maintained by the product managers and respective product owners. The backlog contains a dynamic list which involves aspects such as features, requirements fixes, and enhancements. In simple terms, the backlog is the to-do list which is prepared at the beginning of a project or sprint. The product owners must constantly revisit and reprioritize the list as the project continues.

The main problem solved by the product backlog is the lack of clear instructions since the list contains everything that needs to be done. The most popular and successful ways through which a product backlog is created is there populating it with user stories which consist of short descriptions described from the perspectives of other stakeholders. The key stakeholders, in this case, are the users and their customers, and getting their perspectives to help in the quality delivery of the final project.

The sprint backlog contains a list of items, user stories, and bug fixes which are selected in a current sprint cycle for development and implementation. Before each sprint commences, a meeting is held, and the team gets to choose the items which they feel would best work for the particular phase. Normally, the team outlines what they would wish to achieve and cannot compromise under any circumstances. That notwithstanding, a sprint backlog is mainly flexible and is free to evolve as the project develops.

The increment is also referred to as a sprint goal and is essentially the usable end product at the end of a sprint. The increment represents a completed milestone or goal based on the definition and the characteristics which need to be fulfilled for it to be considered done.

Agile project management serves multiple areas of interest, and there is the need to remain open to the evolutions within the artifacts.

Scrum Roles

Scrum has three major members of interest

1. Product Owners

The product owner is ideally the client, who is bound to get the end product. Product owners should be people with vision authority and who are available to answer any questions that may arise in the course of carrying out the project. The product owners continuously communicate their visions and priorities that the development team must adhere, as well as answer any questions that may arise. Sometimes it is hard for the agile methodology to strike a balance with product owners, especially since Scrum values self-organization amongst its team and does not require anyone to micromanage any of the activities. The product owners are normally champions for their products. Further, they have a major emphasis on trying to understand the business, the customers' market trends, and the overall profitability of the products. Some of the major characteristics of effective product owners are:

a) The ability to build and manage the product backlog without necessarily acting or taking managerial roles.

b) Forming a close partnership with the business and the team members, and ensuring that everyone involved in the project understands their work specification and what they are supposed to do.

c) They can give clear guidance on which features they require to be delivered after the completion of each sprint. This gives the team members an idea as to what is expected and enables them to work toward fulfilling it.

d) Effective product owners are humble and realize that they are not project managers. They, therefore, refrain from undertaking any managerial roles over the other team members and respect that every person knows what they are doing.

2. The Scrum Master

The Scrum master is ideally the project manager who acts as the connection between the product owner and the team. Worth noting is that the Scrum master is answerable to the project manager and is responsible for informing him about the progress of the project and any other issues that arise therein. That notwithstanding, the Scrum master is ideally part of the team and does not manage any of the functions, but rather works with a team to remove any impediments and obstructions that may hinder proper service delivery. The Scrum master also coaches the team, as well as the product owners, about the Scrum processes and helps find a middle ground through which the practice is fine-tuned.

An effective Scrum master helps the team optimize their transparency and product delivery flow without acting as the boss. They deeply understand that the work should be done in teams and encourages all people to cooperate throughout the project lifecycle. Since they are the facilitators of the project, effective Scrum masters ensure that all the necessary resources are provided as and when required, and ensures that they are of the best quality possible. Resources such as human labor must be carefully selected, and the Scrum masters undertake background checks for every one of the employees to ensure that they are well-qualified to carry out the processors.

3. The Scrum Team

The Scrum team consists of the people who get all the work done. They are considered as the champions for sustainable development practices, and the more open they are to cooperate and work with others, the better the results of the project.

The Scrum Values

There are five key Scrum values that must be followed by every person taking part in a Scrum project. The values are focus, commitment, respect, openness, and encouragement. With these values, the Scrum team is assured of living up to its expectations and succeed in the project.

Benefits of the Scrum Methodology

There are various benefits that accrue to companies which use the Scrum agile methodology.

1. Better Quality of Products

Projects exist so as to fulfill a specific goal or vision. Scrum provides a framework through which continuous feedback and exposure are guaranteed, thereby ensuring that the quality is as high as possible. The fact that the methodology requires the elaboration and definition of all the requirements before a project begins helps in ensuring that all the product features and needs are fulfilled

Further, the incorporation of the periodic tests and obtaining the owner's feedback ensures that any areas of concern are handled promptly. The team gets to review the product after every spring, identifying mistakes when they are still fresh and preventing their progress to the other phases. Conducting sprint retrospectives also helps in the prevention of mistakes that were previously witnessed.

2. Decreased Marketing Time.

Scrum's capability of delivering output 30-40% faster than the traditional methods is proven. The decrease in time is normally as a result of earlier development initiation, due to the fact that the upfront documentation phases are fore-gone. Also, the separation of the high priority and low priority items enables prompt delivery of products and services that are urgent. Since all the projects are releases sprint by sprint, the product owners have something that they can begin marketing, making the obtaining of customers easier when the final products are released. The ability to market the product while it is being completed concurrently is amongst the factors that make scrum highly sought.

3. Increased Return on Investment

The ability to market the products sooner results in higher returns on investment. The fact that the revenues start coming earlier from the finished sprints adds to income. Further, some of the buyers are bound to make advance payments as they await the final products, enabling the marketing teams to seek more clients. Ultimately, the clients make more than they would have they waited for the final products to begin advertising.

The products also have little to no defects as a result of the rigorous scrutiny by the owners at the end of every sprint. Therefore, the chance of losing income when defective prod-ucts are returned is minimal, ensuring that the owners gain revenue as well as reputation. Most companies capitalize on a good reputation since customers are more likely to refer their friends to purchase similar products, which increase the returns.

More importantly, the use of scrum ensures that when a project is bound to fall, it does so earlier and faster, saving the owners losses from additional investments. The fact that the failure of a sprint can prevent the completion of a product means that the owners have a chance to modify the products or processes early enough, ultimately preventing losses

4. Higher Team Motivation

Working with happy people who enjoy their jobs is immensely fulfilling. Scrum helps improve the morale of the team members by enabling them to be part of a self-managing and self-organizing group, which promotes creativity and innovation. The Scrum teams also make decisions which are tailored to provide a balance between their professional and personal lives. The fact that the organizational barriers are broken down means that the team members are more comfortable, and can approach the management from the same level. There is always a big self of fulfillment when one is trusted to perform a service, which is what the scrum methodology aims to do.

The use of Scrum as a tool in agile project management is, therefore, very monumental since the end goals, responsibilities, and practices are similar.

Kanban

Kanban is a popular framework commonly used both in the implementation of agile software development, as well as other projects. The Kanban methodology has its basis on lean development practices, which are based on lean methodology successfully used in the manufacturing processes. The Kanban management tool is not only applicable in software development and can be applied where other projects, such as marketing or construction, are ongoing. The tool facilitates the scheduling system for lean and other just-in-time processes from start to finish. The just-in-time projects are unique undertakings that are custom made for specific clients on demand. Kanban is very important in software development since it utilizes the stages of the development life cycle to represent diverse stages. The main aim of such development is to control and manage the features developed so that the number of features which enter a particular process match with those is being completed.

Worth noting is that even though the Kanban management tool is agile, it is not necessarily iterative. Kanban allows the software to be developed in one large development process without being broken down into sprints. Despite this fact, Kanban is considered to be a vital tool in agile project management since it fulfills all the 12 principles behind the agile manifesto, and also follows an incremental basis.

Also notable is the fact that the principle behind the Kanban methodology is limited throughout, despite being incremental. With no iterations, the project which adopts the Kanban tool has not defined a beginning and end and has no predetermined duration through which the project is expected to run. Instead, each piece of the development life cycle has a limited capacity for work at any given time. The work item cannot move on to the next phase until some other capacity opens up a hand, thus controlling the number of activities that are conducted in each phase as at a particular time. Such control of the number of active tasks gives the opportunity for agile principles to be applied.

Kanban Boards

It is a fact that the overall work of the Kanban team members revolves around a pre-constructed Kanban board. The boards are typically used in the visualization of work and the optimization of workflow among the team members. It is important for the Kanban boards to be physically and readily accessible by each team member since they illustrate where particular job functions are and whether they can move to the next phase. The Kanban boards can either be physical or digital, so long as they serve the vital functions of ensuring that the team's work is visualized and that the workflow is standardized. Kanban boards have three major steps: to-do, in progress, and done. A sample Kanban board is as illustrated in Figure 10 below.

Figure 10: Illustration of a Kanban Board

Source (Wittwer, 2019)

As illustrated, the board showcases the activities that are to be done; the ones that are in progress; the ones under review; and the completed projects. In the illustration, the section for the activities in progress is already full, and their team members cannot undertake any other task before they move one of the activities to the review section. The review section has an available space, which means that activity in progress can be moved to this section so that it can be marked as complete or incomplete. The board is clear, and every team member can deduce what is happening and consequently plan on the activities which are to be done. The use of cards ensures that all the team members track the work's progress in a highly visual manner. Each of the cards contains simplified information about the various tasks, and the team members can be able to understand the messages at a glance. Worth noting is that the Kanban management tool has its basis on three principles: limiting the amount of work in progress, visualizing what is done daily, and enhancing the flow of the tasks.

Benefits of the Kanban Agile Management Tool

Kanban methodology is among the most popular software development tools adopted by agile teams today. In addition to the major advantage of task planning and simplification of the product life cycle, there are some other benefits, which include:

1. Flexibility in Planning

The Kanban team always has its major focus on the work that is actively in progress. When a certain piece of work is completed, it is part of the board, and the team can concentrate on the other uncompleted pieces of work. Since the product owners have a say in the works that they want to be prioritized, they can do so without disrupting the activities of the team.

Any changes outside of the current work framework do not impact the team, ensuring a serene workplace. The product owners just need to ensure that the priority items are kept at the top of the backlog and the delivery team takes up the job to deliver as required.

2. Short Time Cycles

The time cycle is a key metric for the Kanban teams. A cycle is defined as the amount of time taken for a piece of work to travel through all the processes until completion. Through the optimization of the project time cycle, the team can be confident in forecasting the delivery of future work. Kanban teams are people who have overlapping skill sets which, therefore, make them able to handle a wide array of activities. This is a major factor in the shortening of the time cycle since the activities are not left to one specific person.

The Kanban agile management tool encourages the constant holding of review and mentoring meetings to help spread knowledge. Also, if there is a backlog of what that needs to be done, the entire team can work on it and get the process flowing fast again. For instance, when it comes to a task such as testing, the involvement of the developers, as well as the engineers, ensure that the work is conducted promptly and in a much lower timeframe.

3. Fewer Bottlenecks

The Kanban agile project management tool is highly inclined toward limiting the amount of work in progress. By definition, work-in-progress refers to uncompleted tasks that are on the way to completion. It is a fact that when the team members undertake roles that require a lot of multitasking, efficiency might be reduced. The more the pieces of work in progress as at a particular time, the more the team members are inclined to shift their focus, resulting in many uncompleted tasks.

4. Visual Metrics

The improvement of team efficiency and effectiveness is a core value of Kanban project management. The visual charts provided in the system provide a clear display of the activities as they occur and the mechanism through which the team can be able to gauge performance. One of the major teams' goal is the reduction of the amount of time that a task takes to move across the entire process. When the team members observe a drop in the average time cycle in the control charts, it is regarded as an indicator of success which is a great motivator.

5. The Kanban methodology is very responsive to change, which means that the team can be able to select the best approach to handling an unexpected problem. Further, since they're always new technological advancements that occur daily, a Kanban methodology ensures that the team stays on top of its game in the use of the latest technological devices.

6. As previously stated, the Kanban management tool ensures that the average time cycle of the project is greatly reduced. Therefore, the project is delivered much faster in line with agile project management principles.

7. The Kanban tool requires little organization/room set-up changes to get started. Depending on the project that is being worked on, the team only requires very few resources, since software development takes place online. Unlike other projects, such as in the construction industry where a lot of raw materials are required, software development requires the purchase of tools that help with a coding process, for use in multiple projects.

8. The Kanban tool is highly inclined toward concentrating on activities that add value to the team and overall stake-holders. When the work in progress is illustrated in the boards, the team can be able to tell which activities should not be given attention as much and eliminates them to reduce wastage of time.

9. The Kanban tool enhances a rapid feedback loop, which improves the chances of the team becoming more motivated, performing better, and empowered. Therefore, the team is

bound to grow in their careers and engage in activities, which guarantee value in the output.

10. Kanban is considered to be a mindset in addition to being a project management tool. As a project manager, the tool ensures that one gets to choose the right things at the right time, and shift focus on what should be done as at a particular time. This enables the team to work on the urgent tasks and leave the ones which can be conducted at a later date. The fact that the major focus is on the floor of work ensures that none of the team members becomes burdened since they are only required to handle what they can.

Scrumban

Scrumban Agile development methodology is a hybrid of the Scrum and Kanban management tools. The integration of the two methods is warranted by the varying needs of the different companies and organizations. Scrumban emerged to form a middle ground and meet the needs of the teams who are concerned with minimizing the batches of work, while at the same time adopting a pull-based system. The hybrid involving Scrum and Kanban allows flexibility in the conducting of activities and facilitates the adoption of changes to suit the stakeholder and production needs. Normally, agile project activities can't make the team members feel overburdened by their project methodology, and Scrumban offers away out since the team gets an integration of the two common methods.

There are various components of Scrum and Kanban which are incorporated into the hybrid system to enable a balance to be stricken. Some of the elements of the Scrum that are incorporated in the scramble methodology are:

1. The iteration planning which is synchronized with retrospective and reviews at regular intervals. The Scrum agile

project management methodology insists on the conducting of activities at regular intervals known as sprints. On the other hand, the Kanban methodology is not big on iteration planning, which results in disadvantages such as the lack of a regular structure. The hybrid methodology integrates the iteration planning, thereby creating a balance

2. The decision about how much work can be put into a sprint with regards to the complexity of the work and the length of this print is also greatly considered. Since the Scrum methodology does not follow such a structure, the hybrid enables such decision-making regarding the length of the work to be input.

3. The prioritization on demand. Scrum agile management greatly prioritizes demand, providing the team with the best thing to work on. The Kanban methodology has no such priorities, and the teams are required to work on what they are provided with by the schedule laid down on the board. When the two are integrated, priorities are put first, which enables the conducting of activities by the overall needs of the different stakeholders

The Kanban methodology also adds visualization process improvement in the number of value metrics to the Scrumban methods. The key elements that are incorporated into the hybrid are:

1. The pull system and continuous workflow. The Kanban methodology operates in such a way that once an activity is finished, it is moved promptly into the other phase. The performing of work outside what has already begun is not recommended; it disrupts the continuous workflow which contributes to the faster completion of products. The system is very fundamental in that it ensures that every activity which begins is completed within the shortest timeframe possible. It is different from the Scrum methodology in the

sense that activities in the latter are carried out depending on the skills and talents of the team members. When a balance is achieved, important tasks are prioritized and undertaken until completion within a very short time.

2. The work in progress limits. The Kanban methodology has a limit on the amount of work that should be undertaken as at a particular time to ensure that full attention is given to each task. The limit also helps in the utilization of the incremental changes of a project. The integration of this characteristic is important since it prevents situations where work is handled incompletely, causing confusion. Once a limit is determined, each task that is begun must be completed before the team members move to another task.

3. Short lead times. Lead time refers to the time taken after the completion of a task at the beginning of another task. Where there is short lead times, the team members can get involved in other activities as soon as they finish what they are working on. In so doing, a lot of tasks are accomplished in a short period, resulting in greater productivity. The Scrum methodology has not defined lead time, and the hybrid helps solve the problem.

4. Individual rules not specified. This function is similar to the Scrum methodology, where the team members have no defined roles, but rather work on what is available as long as they have the required skills and expertise.

The use of a Scrumban methodology is highly recommended in cases where the teams need a Scrum structure, but with the flexibility available is a fine based method. Also, teams and project which are looking for a transition from a Scrum to Kanban or the other way around should adapt the methodology to ease the movement.

Scrumban is also highly beneficial in projects which have

achievement milestones. Projects managers have difficulty in predicting the amount of work to be done over a large period. The methodology can be adopted to ensure that the team members carry out their work in an effective and quality-oriented manner. The Scrumban methodology combines the best aspects of both Scrum and Kanban agile management tools ultimately helping in the proper carrying out of a project.

Chapter Summary

- Each company involved in agile project management has its own set of tools which it uses to make the activities run more efficiently.
- The three major tools used are Scrum, Kanban, and Scrumban.
- Scrum tool has its basis on the belief that transparency, collaboration, adaptation, and frequent iterations are the best practices for success.
- The Kanban methodology has its basis on lean development practices, which are based on lean methodology, and successfully used in the manufacturing processes.
- Scrumban Agile development methodology is a hybrid of the Scrum and Kanban management tools.

6

AGILE PROJECT MANAGEMENT ESTIMATION TECHNIQUES

E stimation of work is regarded as being amongst the most difficult aspects of project management. Before the undertaking of a project, the clients normally have an idea for the products and how they want the final product to be. In most cases, the clients do not have complete clarity about the requirements needed and can never be able to fully define the said requirements without the help of qualified stakeholders, such as the project managers and the project partners. Getting a budget estimate is normally very important since it allows the clients to gauge their ability to pay for such processes and prepare themselves accordingly. In agile project management, the fact that changes are imminent in the course of carrying out a project makes estimation very challenging. Without a reasonable estimate, project planning becomes very difficult. There is, therefore, the need to carry out estimation activities at the beginning of projects. There are three main levels of agile estimation:

1. The Proposal Level

This is the estimation that must be done when the project is still being reviewed. Normally, this level is finalized when tabling a proposal.

1. The Release Level

This level includes activities such as the assigning of the story points to the users and defining the order based on the priority concepts.

1. The Sprint Level

In this level, stories are broken down into tasks and estimation of hours assigned to every task depending on its complexity. This level also identifies some of the team members that might be the best in carrying out of the project due to their skills and expertise.

The information retrieved in the three levels is later used in the calculation of the overall budget so that the client and the team members can start preparing themselves accordingly. When a budget is created, there is always the need to try and work with it. Working over the budget is detrimental to the organization, as it results in excess unprecedented costs.

Estimation of a Budget

There are two ways through which a budget can be estimated, the use of a bottom-up or top-bottom approach. In traditional project management techniques, budgeting takes a lot of time since the stakeholders spend several weeks/months before the commencement of a project, defining every little detail and requirements and estimating the costs that would ensue. Once all the requirements are documented, a Gantt chart is produced. The chart illustrates all the needs and requirements that are necessary for the completion of tasks and involves the assigning of resources to each task. This is known as the bottom-up method since all the details regarding the project are clearly defined before the project begins and all costs estimated therein.

In agile project management, the bottom-up methodology cannot work since there are immense changes that occur in the course of carrying out activities and tasks, making the estimates inaccurate. The changes are immensely common, especially in the software industry where new development tools and access to new knowledge often occurs, necessitating a change. The biggest danger accrued as a result of not adhering to the changes is the delivery of obsolete products which cannot be used in a current market. For that reason, a top-down method is highly recommended in agile project management.

The top-down level uses information which is available to provide gross level estimates. The fact that the estimates are gross means that there is always room for adjustments where changes occur.

Agile Project Management Estimation Techniques

As stated, the values given in agile estimates are gross-level and are used in most agile approaches, such as Scrum. There are some estimation techniques that come in handy during the estimation process, and they include:

1. Planning Poker

One of the most popular gross estimation techniques is the use of the planning poker. This technique is also referred to as the Fibonacci sequence, and it is used in the assigning of point value to a featured item. The mathematical sequence was introduced in the 13th century and has a major use in the explanation of certain formative aspects such as nature.

The series is normally generated by adding numbers together to guess the next value in the sequence. For instance, 0,1,1,2,3,5,8,13,21….. In agile project management, the sequence has been changed, resulting in numbers with the order 1,2,3,5,8,13,20,40,100. The numbers are presented in a set of playing cards, to form a point value for each of the items. The following steps ensue:

Each of the team members is given a set of cards. The business owners do not get to estimate the value of the items under investigation, and they are only required to begin and control the discussion. Each of the team members selects a card privately representing their estimates, and when everyone is ready, the cuts are revealed at the same time. In the case where all the team members select a similar card, it is regarded as the point value of the estimate. Where the cuts are not the same, the team is involved in a discussion about the estimates with emphasis placed on some values.

First, the member who selected the lowest values gets to explain why he selected the low-value card, while the member who selected the highest value gives their explanation. The selection process is done again until an estimate is converged. The poker system is regarded as one of the best methods of estimating a large backlog of items since the exercise goes relatively fast and the team spends roughly two minutes on each item. The sequence also provides an almost right level of detail for the smaller and better-understood features, preventing a false sense of accuracy for the higher estimates.

2. Affinity Grouping

The use of affinity grouping is an even faster way to carry out estimates, and it is normally used where the number of items to be estimated is large. Therefore, it comes in handy in situations where items cannot be estimated individually.

In this strategy, the team members group items that are similar together and judge them as a group. The method is relatively simple and very fast and proceeds as follows:

The first item is normally read to the team members and placed on a wall. A second item is consequently read out, and the team is asked whether it is smaller or larger than the first item. Depending on the team's beliefs and perceptions, the placement on the wall is done concerning their perception of the different values. The third item is read, and the team is asked if it is smaller or larger than the first and the second item. Depending on the responses, it is strategically placed on the wall. The process goes on until the control of the placement is turned over to the team to finish the grouping of the remaining items.

Estimation Units

Estimation units are abstract tokens of measurement widely accepted as a norm. For instance, the use of t-shirt sizes XS, S, M, L, XL are widely accepted measurement terms which are understandable to every person. The different teams are free to create their own estimation unit, which provides a fun way of estimating critical units in a project. The fact that the teams take an active role in the determination of the estimation units to be used means that they are highly likely to adhere to them and effectively analyze the performance which results in credible estimates.

Worth noting is that agile estimation is regarded as a team sport. The estimation includes everyone ranging from the designers, testers, the developers, and every person on the team. The major advantage of using the estimation methods discussed is that every member brings a unique perspective on the product and the work, which is required to deliver quality products. The team provides vital input regarding the design changes and the development of each aspect of the product. The fact that the team sets the standards means that they are highly inclined toward fulfilling them.

Story Points in Agile Estimation

The traditional software teams give estimates in a time format which may include days, weeks, and months. Agile project management, on the other hand, does not use such parameters, but rather uses story points. The story points are used in the rating of the relative impact of work in the poker-like method. Just like the Fibonacci format, the story points are rated in the 0,1,2,3,5,8,13,29,40,100 format. In as much as it sounds counter-intuitive, the obstruction is immensely helpful as it pushes the team to make risk-oriented and diverse decisions where work is difficult. Some of the advantages that accrue to our team using the story points are:

1. The dates do not account for the non-project work, which inevitably creeps in the course of conducting the project. There are some activities that take place that is not related to the project which includes emails, interviews, and meetings. Team members who get involved in such activities need to account for all of them systematically.

2. The use of dates has an emotional attachment which is avoided in some of the projects. Using relative and abstract estimation methods helps to remove such attachments.

3. Using story points is also incredibly fast since the assignment of points without much debate is enhanced where the persons agree on the relative effort of each story point.

4. Finally, the story points help reward the team members by facilitating problem-solving based on the level of difficulty and not time spent. This aspect

helps keep the team members focused on the overall shipping value and not time spent on each activity.

Purpose and Benefits of Estimation in Agile Project Management

Agile project management has continuously helped in the attempt to solve the problem of successful project delivery. There are three dimensions of the project management that estimation helps to solve. The dimensions of scope, schedule, and cost are interdependent, but greatly affect a project where proper planning and estimation is not done. Even though each of the dimensions affects the project individually and differently, it can result in the failure of the project even where the other two dimensions are successful. Therefore, they are better handled as one to facilitate that successful completion of the project. Notable is the fact that since the three dimensions are interdependent, it is possible to make one of them constant. For instance, where a project has to strictly adhere to predetermined costs, the scope and the schedule must be kept variable. This is because the cost is not supposed to shift at any particular time, requiring the scope and the schedule to be kept variable in a way which enables the cost to remain constant.

Similarly, if the schedule is constant, it means that the deadline must be adhered to at every cost. Therefore, the costs and the scopes are kept variable since the need for a faster service delivery may result in the need for additional resources which add to the estimated costs.

Chapter Summary

- Estimation of work is regarded as being amongst the most difficult aspects of project management.
- Getting a budget estimate is normally important

since it allows the clients to gauge their ability to pay for such processes and prepare themselves accordingly.

- There are two ways through which a budget can be estimated: the use of a bottom-up or top-bottom approach.
- In agile project management, the bottom up methodology cannot work since there are immense changes that occur in the course of carrying out activities and tasks, making the estimates inaccurate.
- The estimation techniques mostly used are the planning poker and affinity grouping methodologies.
- Estimation units can be customized by the needs of the people.
- Agile project management insists on the use of story points as opposed to time formats.

Future of Agile Project Management

Just like any other discipline, project management is subject to constant change. New techniques and methodologies continue to be established and will continue being developed just like any other innovation program. While agile is not alone in changing the technological business landscape, it is one of the major forces in the digitization of the current business environment. The proponents of the agile methodology predict that in the future the traditional methods of project management will be replaced in entirety with the agile methodology. A comprehensive approach to studying agile project management has already established its positive ability in a wide array of projects, which makes the prediction possible.

Further, the education system is constantly changing to modify the way through which students perceive a work environment. Agile project management requires all the members to work as a team and fast decision-making ability so that the project can be handled effectively. The equipping of such skills ensures that once the students are already in the job market, they can be able to adapt the agile methodologies effectively. It is apparent that the future of agile project methodologies is bright and its suitability will be spread to even more practices.

CONCLUSION

It is a fact that agile project management is amongst the best methodologies of running a project in the current times. The approach involves a process where the projects are managed and implemented in small chunks known as sprints. Normally, every project has a predetermined deliverable, and agile project management has proven to be amongst the best ways through which such deliverables are achieved.

Agile project management's foundation was an article published in the Harvard Business Review in 1986. During this time, there was widespread concern about the new approach and methodology of running projects that was increasingly becoming popular, and the authors were determined to find out more about it. Traditional project management methodologies were proving to be highly inefficient, especially due to the reason that most products being developed became obsolete even before they were presented to the clients. The developers had noted that the reason why the occurrence was so prevalent was the fact that the team always had to follow a strict set of rules in the development process, and had no communication whatsoever with the clients. This led to a lack of brainstorming, ultimately resulting in the development of products which were not required as at this time. The traditional methods were also opposed to flexibility, which meant that they had to stick to a plan despite the knowledge of better ways of running projects. Therefore, the agile methodology was developed to help offset such problems

Agile project management is guided by four key foundational values and 12 principles. The fact that the two components were created during the launch of the methodology means that there is the need to follow them to the letter for benefits to be realized. Even though some of the tenents may be misconstrued, they are relatively straightforward and are easily understood by anyone. Any company which would wish to shift from the traditional to the agile methodology must be privy to the said tenents, for proper and full transition to occur.

Agile project management is immensely specific about its scope and the roles of the various team members. The team is normally responsible for ensuring that all processes proceed as was planned, and the undertaking of the project management tasks. The major difference between the agile and the traditional modes of operation is the fact that in the former, the project managers do not act as bosses but rather mentors and part of the team members. Further, they allow the team members to take part in the decision making processes, which is proven to be very beneficial. Other stakeholders such as the project owners, Scrum masters, and customers have a major say in the development of the product, making the output more value-oriented.

Agile Project management can also be handled through the use of various tools, which simplify the overall processes by the needs of the organizations. Amongst the most common tools are Scrum, Kanban, and Scrumban. Depending on the scope of an operation, one can choose the tool which is better suited to carry out the functions of the organization effectively.

Agile project management is undoubtedly very widespread and popular in the current times, a situation which is expected to keep improving into the future.

AGILE PROJECT MANAGEMENT

THE ULTIMATE INTERMEDIATE GUIDE TO LEARN AGILE PROJECT MANAGEMENT STEP BY STEP

INTRODUCTION

Agile project management (APM) is a methodology that continues to positively impact the management arena in the world today. Initially, the methodology was widespread in the software development sector. Currently, APM is used in literally all projects, ranging from engineering, construction, education, medical, and all other sectors whose work can be divided into distinct deliverables. By now, I am sure that you are not new to agile and its constituents. You already know the history, tenets, benefits, shortcomings, future, and ideally all the basics of agile project management. Since you are not a beginner anymore, this book will delve into the ways through which the project managers can use the basic information learned to not only ensure that they succeed in their projects but to also give them an advantage over all other competitors. There are many instances where projects end up operating at losses, particularly when clients reject completed works. Through agile project management, such occurrences are mitigated, ensuring that all parties are satisfied at the end. The information contained here will ensure that you are well on your way to become an expert. Your basic agile knowledge will also be polished, reaffirmed, and improved to ensure that the agile skills help you achieve undoubted success.

1

BASICS OF AGILE PROJECT MANAGEMENT

E xperienced project managers know the essence of applying the agile methodology in their daily undertakings as the benefits realized are incompa-rable to any other methodology. As you learned in book 1, agile project management has not always been in existence. There are many traditional methodologies that are in place, some of which are used even in the current day. As project managers continued using the traditional methods of opera-tions, the outcome was always the same. Some of the prod-ucts were either considered obsolete upon completion or the team had trouble completing the project altogether. Upon the realization that instances of project lag and outdated products were widespread, professionals came up with a solution; agile project management

Agile project management highly encompasses the develop-ment of the team and human labor over the tools and processes used. Therefore, the whole essence of the method-ology is the development and improvement of the efficiency of people who are involved directly in the conducting of the activities. Collaboration with the other team members and clients is amongst the factors that result in the development of the team since they get to have access to the client's brain and discover what they want and what they do not. This strategy helps in character development over time as the team becomes more confident in their work. When work has been done right and is approved by the clients, there is always a sense of satisfaction and fulfillment, which boosts morale and motivation.

By now, you already know the tenets of agile project management. Just to reiterate them, some of the expected outcomes are:

1. The continuous flow of value, which ultimately results in increased return on investments.
2. Delivering reliable results to the clients since they are involved in every step of the project.
3. Immense creativity and innovation since the methodology is not rigid and allows the team members to come up with ideas about how to best conduct the project.
4. Enhanced team efficiency and accountability since all the responsibilities are shared across the members.
5. Improved reliability and effectiveness since the team utilizes specific strategies, practices, and situational processes.

Agile project management has continued to prove its efficiency in the achievement of these expected outcomes, and many industries have already adopted the system (see chapter 2). The methodology has continued to prove its efficiency in the fulfillment of the basic APM principles, which are:

1. Constant and fast delivery to ensure customer satisfaction
2. Enabling the customer to gain a competitive advantage through the finished products
3. Taking the least time possible to deliver the goods and services
4. Enabling collaboration between the clients and the agile team
5. Ensuring that the team is motivated
6. Ensuring that face to face communication is fostered
7. Ensuring that the final product is an embodiment of success
8. Promotion of sustainable development
9. Fostering technical excellence and proper design to enhance agility
10. Quality over quantity mentality
11. Fostering a self-organizing team
12. Adoption of efficient and fine-tuning behavior by using regular intervals

2

AGILE PROJECT MANAGEMENT
ADOPTION ACROSS INDUSTRIES

Agile project management was initially developed for the software industry. For a long time, the methodology has always been regarded as an exclusive component of Information Technology, since that is where it was originally adopted. However, the narrative has changed in the last 20 years that the methodology has been in existence. Numerous industries have shifted to APM and continue to enjoy the benefits that accrue to its usage. Proponents assert that APM can be used in literally any industry. Any work can be broken down into segments, and all that is required is getting the team on board and guiding them towards its successful implementation. Many industries and individual companies have been using traditional management methods with unsatisfactory results for too long. The shift to agile is undoubtedly worth it and the benefits are indisputable as evidenced by the permeation of industries to date.

Project managers operate in different capacities and in different industries across the world. Notably, some of the managers do not know that they can successfully implement agile project management in their industries. While some managers are reaping the benefits of APM, some are still stuck to the traditional methodologies. This chapter will delve into the different industries that can benefit from agile project management and analyze ways in which the project managers can utilize the methodology to their advantage.

- **Software Industry**

To understand how agility has revolutionized the project management industry, it is worth revisiting where it all began. The inception of agile project management in software was discussed in detail in book 1. Agile project management was developed at a time when there were immense issues in the software development industry as the products ended up being further from the customer specifications and in some cases obsolete. The major cause of the issue was recognized as a lack of proper communication and interactions with the client, and agile project management helped streamline all the issues. Currently, the larger section of the software industry has shifted from the traditional methods to full agility and continue to benefit from it. it is estimated that over 90% of the reputable software firms use APM, and more companies follow suit as they learn about it. Just to reiterate the benefits of agile project management over other traditional methods, some of the aspects that only exist in agility and are not in the other management methods are:

1. *Use of backlogs*. The backlogs are agile concepts relating to the functions and features which become the final part of the deliverables. Backlogs can be viewed as a large collection of scope items described in terms of what they will mean to the end users. This concept is not available in any other project

management strategies, which makes APM revolutionary.

2. *Use of Sprints.* A sprint is a timeline given to complete a particular iteration or story. The latter refers to the various divisions given to different projects; each of which is assigned a particular completion timeline. Depending on the particular work, the iterations can take as little as a few hours or several months. That notwithstanding, all iterations have designated sprints which the project managers strive to work with.

3. *Cross-functional teams.* The concept of the cross-functional teams relates to the aspect of having a good team that knows the value of proper communication, togetherness, and co-operation. As much as the project managers are the ones who may control the project, the rest of the staff are responsible for its actual creation. Therefore, they can either make or break the company. When togetherness and unity is fostered, the employees are likely to make the projects personal, ultimately making the best out of them. The overall effect is a good performance, which ultimately results in customer satisfaction and increased efficiency.

4. *Iterative and incremental development.* In the traditional methods of handling projects, evaluation is done after the entire project is completed. In agile project management, the projects are handled incrementally, which means that analysis is done after the completion of every iteration. As much as the traditional methods may argue that the process results in a wastage of time, the truth is that it helps the stakeholders save valuable time and resources. Notably, whenever there are issues in a project, the use of iterative helps in the identification of the

issues early enough, which prevents them from moving into the next phase. Ultimately, the costs of re-doing the projects and analyzing to find the problems are reduced, and the clients develop more trust in the team.

5. *Scrum Agile Meetings.* The scrum meetings devised by the agile methodology are not a mean feat. While the traditional methodology identifies the project managers as the leaders and requires all employees to follow their lead, agile project managers encourage all the staff members to express themselves and give them a say in the overall happenings of the project. Through the scrum meetings, all participants are able to give their views and address any issues they may have.

In the software industry, agile project management is widespread. Since the inception of the methodology, the management's practice was adopted in the industry and continues to be used to date.

- **Healthcare Industry**

Healthcare is the core of any government function. The healthcare leaders are always on the forefront to attempt to work hard towards the improvement of patient care, reduce costs, and ensure that the patients' experience and satisfaction are taken into consideration. Efficiency, customer satisfaction, and improved services are all agile tenets, which explains why the healthcare industry has shifted to the process.

Notably, the healthcare industry has for a long time relied on the waterfall approach to carry out most of its functions. Due to the sensitivity of the industry, the managers always believed that there was a need for the employees to follow requirements and deliverables as was mapped out without any modifications or questions. A Gantt chart was used to illustrate all the deliverables, and the project participants had to execute it as it was. While the waterfall approach is still widespread in the industry, agile project management is continuing to gain recognition and is slowly taking over the industry.

The realization that the industry needed to shift from the rigid waterfall approach to the more flexible agile approach was a result of multiple needs in the industry. First, the health boards popularized the Plan-Do-Study-Act (PDSA) approach in most of the healthcare functions to ensure efficiency. The PDSA approach relates to all the activities within the industry, ranging from service delivery to the identification of new ways of handling different patients. As it turns out, the PDSA approach conforms to agility in the sense that all of them use iterations. Therefore, the industry has already started using APM unknowingly and it was working for them.

There are key elements of APM that are of immense benefit to the healthcare industry. Effective communication, removal of obstacles, and fulfilling commitments in a given time frame as well as teamwork are all agile components that the industry needs. When one looks at a typical hospital setting, the probability of quality services is determined by how well the team conformed to the stated principles.

Let's consider a scenario where a patient is rushed in after suffering from a massive stroke. Once the patient is taken to the hospital, he or she becomes the project which the medics must work on to bring back to health. As soon as they are taken into the hospital, teamwork begins. Depending on the gravity of the illness, the medics handle the patient as they see fit. If the patient is unconscious, the first thing to do is often to find the cause and attempt to restore consciousness. As the emergency team is working on the person, another person has to get the medical records and history of the patient either looking for the records online or interviewing their family members. Knowledge of the medical history is often important before any medications are administered since it helps to identify any issues that may relate to allergies or other complications. Evidently, everything is done systematically; with the completion of one phase leading to the other.

Timeframes are also very important in hospital settings. Some patients' medications are very specific and must be administered at specific times throughout the course of the day. Therefore, the hospital team must work together to ensure that all the patients get their medications and food on time, so they can heal promptly.

The best part about the adoption of APM in the hospital setting is that it gives the doctors the chance to illustrate their efficiency when handling different patients. Doctors study for many years before they qualify to handle patients, and it is safe to say that they realize the best approaches that must be undertaken for any patient. It is usually not right to constrict the doctors and other medical personnel to one mode of performance as not all patients' needs are the same.

Since agility is all about trust, giving the medics the leeway to make the best decision pertaining to how certain cases should be handled makes them take the cases more personally. This is not to say that the medics are allowed to do whatever they want, but that their preferred approach gets a voice. In many instances, multiple medics work on the same person. These days, the team of medics assigned to a certain person can in most cases be seen in scrum meetings where everyone brainstorms particularly when the patients are not responding to medications. When a senior medic tells the other team members *"give him 10 ml of a medicine"* and when he says, *"what should we give him?"* results in two different reactions.

In the first case, the member commanded will just do as they are told without question. Sometimes, it may not even be the best option. In the second scenario, everyone involved will give their suggestions, and at the end of the day, all the pros and cons will be identified. The unity will also make every team member take the case personally and may even prompt research from the medics. When every team member goes the extra mile in educating themselves, they become more resourceful which is beneficial for the latter projects.

Having a single goal and working towards it as a team empowers each and every individual to do their part and deliver a positive change to the problem. Ultimately, the decision made will be the best one for the patient. When every one of them has a voice and has their opinions respected, they are usually able to improve their efficiency, ultimately providing more quality services.

In a 2015 review of 60 articles published under the *International Health Care Quality Assurance,* agile's potential in serving as a guiding principle in the improvement of healthcare was widely scrutinized. The results showed that the larger percentage of the writers believed that APM was the best bet towards quality and cost-efficient healthcare. The writers also believed that agile was particularly helpful where the organizations and departments wanted the participation of stakeholders in developing solutions to identified problems. Mostly, the stakeholders refer to the government when considering public healthcare and hospital board of directors. Private hospitals also have their own stakeholders, ranging from investors to medical representatives. Either way, all the stakeholders are collectively concerned with the well-being of the patients and all decisions made was because of this concern. Some of the success stories involving agile project management in healthcare are as follows:

i. Massachusetts General Hospital

The Massachusetts General Hospital was concerned with the increased levels of opioid administered after C-sections. Most of the women developed complications after the surgery, which resulted in the need for opioid administration. The hospital selected a team of competent healthcare personnel who decided to incorporate an iterative analysis of the discharge data. Since agility pertains involving all the stakeholders in a certain project, the personnel began by offering patient counseling and began by telling the patients what they could expect, and all other aspects related to pain. As the hospital continued to select the best course of action, the team held meetings and decided to test other medications, which are not as harmful as opioids. As a result of the commitment of the team and co-operation with patients, the researchers were able to find an alternative for the opioids.

The determination of the effectiveness of the alternative was concluded after close analysis of multiple women after the C-sections. Follow-ups were also done to test how efficient the medication was. In the end, the researchers found that acetaminophen was as effective, and had lower side effects compared to opioids. As at 2018, the hospital had reduced the administration of opioids by 35 percent and increased acetaminophen prescription from 33 to 92 percent. The initiative credited agile tenets as it followed them promptly and was able to benefit from what it stood for.

ii. Software Development at a Teaching Hospital

Researchers at a community teaching hospital decided to try out APM in software development. The hospital wanted to develop an electronic clinical and collaboration platform, and they adopted the agile methodology. As a result of close working with the product developers, the hospital benefitted from 36 software releases in a record time of 24 months.

The agile methodology is finding its place in the healthcare industry and the benefits expected makes it the best choice among the stakeholders.

- **Manufacturing Industry**

Agile adoption in the manufacturing industry has been immensely widespread and easier compared to other industries. It is actually ironic that agility, a central concept of competition, began in the software industry and not in manufacturing. Manufacturing industries provide some of the greatest opportunities for project management and agility has been undoubted of major help. Also, it is in manufacturing industries that the sole goal usually is efficiency, consistency, and striving to meet the needs of clients. For that reason, the adoption of agile in manufacturing was inevitable and the industry is one of the highest-rated users of the system.

Agile manufacturing is regarded as the 21st manufacturing paradigm. With the many advantages that have accrued to the users of the system, it is difficult to fathom that some industries still prefer to use the traditional methods. While a considerable number of companies fear giving up control to employees are still inclined to the traditional methods, the competitive advantage obtained by their agile counterparts continues to compel them to shift.

Most of the companies that are inclined towards customer satisfaction are in the manufacturing industry. The manufacturers get into the business for the sole purpose of providing goods, which are required by the general public, so that they can make sales and earn a living. Every single thing that can be found in shops and supermarkets is a subject to a highly thought out process since there are always competitors and similar companies which provide complimentary products. The necessity of change in the business environment has always been a topic in the manufacturing arena, and agile manufacturing is one of the greatest changes that are occurring therein. The fact that agile is currently considered as a key driver in all organization means that it undoubtedly affects the firm's ability to thrive and survive in the uncertain and turbulent market.

Worth noting, there is the need to distinguish between agile, lean, and flexible manufacturing. Some of the companies have been known to adopt the latter two strategies believing that they were actually adopting agile manufacturing. The three strategies are similar in some instances but differ in most of their operations. They include:

Lean manufacturing is a production process with the intention of achieving a perfect first-time quality of the final products. The methodology also seeks to eliminate as much waste as possible through the removal of all the processes that do not add value to the company. The process seeks to achieve continuous improvements, achieve flexibility, and enhance long-term relationships.

Flexible manufacturing is highly inclined towards ensuring that the production lines are not rigid and that they can be reconfigured and re-structured to produce different products whenever needed . Therefore, the strategy is highly inclined towards uncertainty since it is based on the belief that it may be necessary to change the entire products in the future.

Agile manufacturing incorporates some aspects of lean and flexible manufacturing, although it offers an entirely different approach to doing business. The agile manufacturing process allows the businesses to respond with a high level of flexibility to the customer needs since they are the target group at the end of the day. The method is concerned with relationships between the stakeholders since unity is the best bet for proper service delivery.

Basics of Agile Manufacturing

The adoption of agile in the manufacturing industry has seen the individual companies split the projects into smaller modules, which are known as iterative. Once divided, it is the responsibility of the company to ensure that each of the divisions is running smoothly. The basic trademarks of agility in the companies are:

1. *Focusing on smaller teams to ensure better cooperation.* When agility is adopted, the staff is divided into groups depending on their level of expertise and the managers ensure that all teams work together for the benefit of the production. Once the teamwork ensues, the managers then device parameters, which they can use to measure and quantify the efficiency of the teams, thus helping in the determination of whether they are on the right track or not.
2. *Ensuring that the teams have a clear vision of what they are supposed to do.* Since the project is broken down to phases, the management must ensure that every team knows what exactly they are supposed to be doing. There are a number of agile strategies that can help

the team to keep up with the tasks, and the company chooses what works best for them.

To adopt agile methodology in your manufacturing company, the first step is usually the change in mindset. Re-designing the company operations and requiring everyone to work with each other is mandatory and is the only way the other aspects of co-operation can be achieved.

- **Construction Industry**

The construction industry is considered to be amongst the global economic giants worldwide contributing an estimated 15% of the total global GDP. As of 2017, the industry was estimated to have a net worth of $1.18 trillion, a figure that is expected to increase over time. It is worth noting that the construction industry is known for its continuous applica-tion of traditional project management methodologies such as LEAN, waterfall or the critical chain method. The water-fall methodology is perhaps the most popular and is based on a simple model of the management governing the junior team members to ensure that they develop products and services, which are exactly what the managerial team dictates. An illustration of the waterfall methodology is as represented in figure 1.

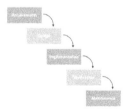

Figure 1: Illustration of the waterfall methodology

As illustrated, the instructions are very straightforward. Once the requirements are determined, a design is drawn, and the team implements it exactly as it is indicated. This means that there is no room for modification and the clients are only presented with the end results. In the construction industry, the waterfall methodology has prevailed for a long time. Normally, the clients hire contractors, provide them with a construction plan, and expect the final construction to be exactly what was in the architectural design. While this aspect cannot be changed, there are a number of processes that can successfully shift into the agile methodology.

Over time, the waterfall and other traditional methods have had their fair share of benefits and shortcomings. Initially, the concept of agility was seemingly not welcome in the industry since most people believed that the methodology was related to IT or software management. Currently, the belief has changed considerably, and project managers continue realizing the effectiveness and efficiency of APM across their scope of work.

Typical construction is divided into phases and sections. Each of the phases and sections can benefit from agile project management principles. Construction industries, which have adopted agility assert that shifting to APM makes the work easier and has resulted in an array of more satisfied clients. The construction phases are:

1. Design and delivery phase

Since we have agreed that the stipulated construction design cannot be modified or changed, it is evident that there is the need to evaluate all the processes that precede the drawing of the final design to ensure that the client gets value for their money. The first segment of the design phase is programming. In this segment, all the requirements of the client are reviewed to enable the construction team to know what exactly they are building and for what purpose. In the traditional methods, the review of the requirements is done by the managerial team only. In some instances, the laymen do not even know what they are building as they are just instructed on what to do and where to do it. In agile project management, every participant in the project is notified about what is being built, why it is being built in the location, and all other information that pertain to the project. Through the involvement, the team is likely to feel more trusted, motivated, and have a sense of ownership for the project. This increases the likelihood of better performance.

2. Schematic design phase

The second step is referred to as the schematic design segment where the actual design of the project ensues. Where the design has not already been developed, the team works on different designs and presents them to the client for approval. It is worth noting that traditional methods do not question the client's design when it has already been developed. The main goal is getting the work done and the management work with the design as it is. In agile project management, the supervisors review the plans, research on its efficacy, and engage the client with any modifications that they believe would be necessary before the actual groundwork begins. This step is very important as it allows the clients to work with different viewpoints and select the one they believe would work. If the owner is not satisfied with the concepts presented, they actually point out to where the adjustment should be made, consequently ensuring that everyone is on the same page.

When all of the designs have been prepared as per the clients' specifications, the last step is signing off the documents, which include contractual agreements and financial agreements.

3. Delivery phase

The delivery phase involves the interaction of the stakeholders regardless of whether they are from the same company or not. The delivery method phase usually explains how the entire process is managed and the steps involved in the management. In some cases, the clients may choose the delivery method which they believe would suit the project better. In some other cases, it is the responsibility of the contractors to choose the delivery method that best appeals to them with no client intervention.

In many instances, clients often prefer to have everyone working together. Therefore, where persons such as architects are separate from the construction company, the clients would rather have them working together, to ensure the successful completion of the project. Agile project managers know the essence of involving all stakeholders, as it is the cooperation which ensures that all the activities conducted are as planned.

Agile project management in this phase is therefore very beneficial. As illustrated, some of the key benefits that would accrue to the adoption of the agile methodology are:

1. Increase in client participation, which helps in the development of the final deliverable.
2. Reduced rate of uncertainty since the project managers can be able to know what exactly is needed and when. Some of the information is obtained from the clients while some can be obtained from external parties such as independent architects.
3. Since agile project management breaks down the entire process into phases, there is increased

accuracy when determining the expected construction costs as well as the complexity of the construction.

4. When multiple stakeholders are involved and given a voice, there is always a high likelihood that the people involved can help in the identification of factors that were not planned for. For instance, construction projects are usually long term taking a few or numerous months to complete. Since it is highly likely that a local member may be involved in the construction, the team benefits from information pertaining to the weather conditions as well as any other local factor that may affect them.

4. Construction Phase

Agile project management is particularly beneficial during the actual construction phase of a project. There is often the need to integrate manpower, labor, and the budget to ensure that they all follow the tenets of agile project management in order to be able to benefit. Once all the paperwork is complete, the first step is to align the deliverables with the customer requirements. This means that agile project managers determine the deliverables and the timelines of the milestones so they can be able to plan accordingly.

Most of the determination of the milestones are done using a Gantt chart. Using visual representation is important as it simplifies the process of identifying what needs to be done and at what time. Once the milestones have been determined, the project managers determine what is required for each milestone in terms of human labor, resources, and machinery. The managers thereafter seek to find all the requirements and ensure that they conform to the needs of the client.

Agility in the construction industry really comes to play during this construction phase. In contrast to the typical construction industries where the managers control everything, agile construction industries are represented by the staff working together as well as involving the clients in every step of the project. The fact that there is no superiority makes all the difference, and an amicable working environment ensues. Also, since the construction industry is quite complex, the team members can be able to give their varied suggestions pertaining to what they think is the best approach and the managers can get information that they were not privy of.

Factors to Consider Before Adopting APM

There is no doubt that agile project management is very beneficial and can revolutionize any working environment. The system has garnered more proponents tat opponents, and it is obvious that anyone would benefit from the use of the system. Despite the advantages, potential users must know that there are some factors that they must put into consideration as well as potential pitfalls that may accrue to the adoption of the process. Agile project management is quite easy and straightforward but also necessitates the potential users to put some thought into the process and learn as much as they can before implementation. Some of the factors that must be considered are:

1. What to adopt and what not to

Agile project management has many strategies and operation methods, and the project managers must decide on what to adopt and what to discard. Each project is unique in its own way and varies in line with multiple parameters. Some projects have big budgets while others have small budget and the scope level also differs. Project managers who jump into the agile bandwagon and just adopt everything are misguided and they are highly likely to face issues when they begin adopting the system. Knowledge of the management system is very imperative, and the managers must be guided on how to correctly adapt to the agile methodologies before implementation is done.

2. *Ease of Transition*

Some companies have been in operation for years on end. People who have been loyal and stuck to the company for long periods are undoubtedly accustomed to particular processes and operation methods. While change is good, some of the people may be opposed to the adoption of the methodology due to various reasons. For instance, some people in authority derive satisfaction from commanding people around and may be opposed to teamwork. Therefore, the shift to agile methodologies may not be taken kindly. Managers must ensure that they can be able to control the situation and get everyone to adopt the system since lack thereof ultimately results in more chaos and confusion. For this reason, potential agile companies may consider challenges in three levels:

3. **Management level**

Senior management and executives play a great role in the determination of whether a potential strategy can be successful in the company or not. As it has been stated, there are some senior-level employees who may feel that agility is depriving them of the command and prestige that they are accustomed to. Therefore, they may attempt to sabotage the implementation of the same, which is disadvantageous to the company.

4. **Team Level**

The core tenet of agile project management entails the need for skilled team members to work together toward the overall good. Not only should the teams be willing, but they should also be highly motivated and well-trained in order to handle all the challenges that come about with ensuring customer satisfaction. Whenever the team members are not willing to adhere to these stipulations, a problem is created.

5. Client level

The end result of engaging in any project whether through the provision of tangible goods or services is to satisfy some level of need that the customers have. However, some customers and clients may be problematic, making the adoption of APM difficult. The specifications of agility assert that the clients must work hand in hand with the project management team, and lack thereof results in the failure of the system.

6. Knowledge of the agile methodology

Agile project management is bound to work when implemented correctly. The knowledge should not only be available to the top management but to the entire workforce as well. Agility is all about teamwork and so, all people must be privy to work the system entails and what it does not. Resisting the big bang change (drastic change) is very smart, and the management must ensure that they slowly roll out the system to their employees. Currently, there are numerous resources online and seminars which teach about the system. Investing in such programs is highly recommended, as it helps prevent erroneous adoption of the system which will not be beneficial to the company. The step by step strategy that can help in the transition is:

1. *Providing agile training.* As it has been stated, there are currently a lot of resources online that can help anyone learn about agile project management in its entirety and with minimal difficulties. However, a

serious company cannot leave the learning to be entirely handled by the employees. Training must be provided ideally on a face-to-face basis. There are many willing trainers who are certified to provide quality training and the companies can benefit from that. Once the training is complete, it is imperative to gauge how much each of the employees has learned. The company can engage in a quick Q&A session or give a small test where possible. The better the personnel internalize the system, the better the adoption.

2. *Assessing the readiness of the team.* Once training is complete and the result test is done, it is important to put the staff through an actual test. This means that the management will have to roll out the system and observe how the team actually handles the work on the ground. There are a number of criteria that can be used to assess the team readiness, which includes:

i. The team's ability to make quick and independent decisions.

ii. The team's commitment to collaborating with each other.

iii. The ability of the team to solve problems and come up with new ideas.

iv. The team's ability to use the APM tools and resources to project results.

The better the team performs the more ready they are to shift to the system.

Evidently, agile project management is reigning in industries beyond software successfully. It is impossible to address each and every industry where agile project management has been adopted. However, it is clear that agility is monumental for any business regardless of its distinct operations and needs. If you are still wondering and skeptical about the benefits of the system, you would benefit from a popular 2013 Ted talk by Bruce Feiler, who illustrated how the system could also be used in household management and even raising children. The talk can be viewed at http://www.ted.com/talks/bruce_feiler_agile_programming_for_your_family.html

3

BUDGETING IN AGILE PROJECTS

S ince the inception of the agile manifesto in the early 2000s, the mastering of agile project management is a key concern for many project managers. One of the key aspects that the managers must get accustomed to is effective budgeting. Amongst all the questions that clients and other stakeholders will have for the agile projects, the most prevalent is "how much will this cost?" Budgeting for agile projects requires a much different approach than costing in traditional projects.

All projects operate on a budget. In an ideal situation, the project is supposed to spend a lower cost than the estimated cost. However, some projects end up spending even more money, which means that either the clients or the contractors operate on losses. In most instances, the clients receive a quote from the customers and agree on a price. If the project uses more than the quoted price, the liability rests on the contractors. For that reason, project managers work hard to ensure that the budget is adhered to without compromising on the quality of the output.

Poor budgeting is considered to be the primary reason as to

why over 75% of businesses fail over the last several years. Generally, projects with big budgets have a higher chance of failing than those with low budgets, particularly due to the differences in scopes for the two. The more the activities and resources that a project uses, the harder it is to control them. A budget is considered to be a proxy for project planning. Since agile project management always aims to result in satisfied clients, the managers take budgeting very seriously. When the monetary aspect has been set, they can basically walk through the entire project with ease and provide proper services.

By definition, budgeting is the process of creating a plan on how the money available for a project will be spent. The budget includes all costs regardless of how trivial and minor they may be. Usually, there are two types of costs that must be accounted for:

1. *Direct costs*. These are the costs that can be traced back to specific cost objects. These costs are involved in the making of the final products and include costs that relate to raw materials, direct labor, commissions, and supplies. For instance, the direct costs of a construction project are raw materials, such as cement, metals, and wood. Employees hired on the project, whether exclusively or for an assigned number of hours, wages are identified as direct costs.

2. *Indirect costs*. These costs are necessary to the production, although they cannot be traced back to the final product. Production cannot be complete without these costs, hence their importance. Some of these costs include aspects such as rent, electricity, water, security, food and any other overheads needed. The office equipment such as laptops, desks, and chairs are also indirect costs in addition to the

supplies required in the company for purposes such as cleaning and designing.

In both the direct and indirect costs, there are fixed and variable costs. Fixed costs remain the same regardless of the output while variable costs fluctuate depending on the resources used. Some of the fixed costs that accrue to a project are premise rent. The rent is usually predetermined, and the managers must pay the amount owing whether they use the premise or not. Variable costs include aspects such as salaries and some bills, and these are usually the costs which are manipulated when the managers want to keep the project running as per the budget.

To properly budget for agile projects, all stakeholders must identify all the direct and indirect costs that are imperative to the project. Once identified, it becomes easy to quote the project amounts, and the project managers can begin to allocate the funds.

Notably, some of the agile projects have a clearly defined scope while some do not.

Budgeting for projects with a clear scope

Projects with a clear scope are very simple to budget for. For instance, a project entailing the building of a room at a particular place is an illustration of a clear scope. Also, most software development jobs have a clear scope, which makes budgeting immensely easy. There are four key strategies that immensely help with the establishment of the accurate project budgeting:

- **Ensuring that all of the key elements are identified in the project scope**

Project managers are expected to ensure that the project

budgets are realistic and that all requirements have been factored in the final expenses. Sometimes, the clients may require potential contractors to bid for the project with the least quoting contractor having a high chance of being awarded the project. For that reason, the project managers may attempt to reduce the costs as much as possible so that the clients can be impressed. While managing costs is imperative, the managers must ensure that the final budget presented is realistic and that they can actually be able to complete the project with the quoted funds. Since the main aim of a business is to make profits, the managers must also factor in their profits within the project to ensure that they get value for their service. Identifying the overall project scope is, therefore, fundamental as it simplifies the identification of all the costs involved.

One of the best ways of ensuring that the scope is identified is the development of a mind map. The mind maps are ideally a plan of the entire project, which identifies what needs to be done, at what time, and the importance of the project . Since the mind maps are visual, they help with the logical planning of the project, which then ensures that all the vital details are identified. Mind maps also help in the identification of gaps as well as factoring in of any uncertainties, such as extreme and destructive rain as well as heat periods. A sample budget mind map is as illustrated in figure 2.

Figure 2: Illustration of an agile mind map

When the contractors devise a mind map, they are essentially illustrating everything that they believe the project needs. Due to the probability of missing out on some functions, it is always important for the mind map to be shared with the clients so that they can be able to identify any missing parts. In the case the contractors have never undertaken a particular project before, there is always the need to seek guidance from project managers who ever had to ensure that the budgeted amounts are realistic.

- **Establishing a method of refining the budget**

Once the scope of the project as well as all the requirements have been identified, the team then has to refine the budget. In the first step, the project managers are responsible for the determination of the expected costs of some of the processes. In this step, refining is done to ensure what was predicted is actually in line with what will actually be used in the course of the project.

Many agile projects follow the same system of refining the budget, which consists of three phases.

The first phase is known as the **product definition phase**.

Here, no prices are provided but the project concept is usually established.

The second phase is referred to as the **detailed requirements phase**. The team usually estimates the general cost of product development in this phase. The cost of development is usually determined by the client's ability to pay, as well as the expected difficulty of the project.

The final step is the **design phase**. This step applies to some of the projects and is not used in others. Where software development or manufactory of certain materials is the project scope, the team first creates a prototype. The prototypes are replicas of the expected final product and they help the stakeholders know what they can expect.

- **Using a Collaborative Solution to Enhance Feature Prioritization**

One of the agile principles is concerned with fostering collaboration amongst all the stakeholders to ensure that the final product is as desired by the client. The process is known as feature prioritization since the stakeholders give their input as the process is ongoing. Collaboration is immensely cost effective since it ensures that what is developed is in line with the needs of the clients. Therefore, instances of rejection and the need to repeat are reduced, which ensures that the contractors do not end up spending more money than was anticipated.

An example of collaboration and feature prioritization in the construction industry is checking the quality of cement before construction begins. Constructions serve different purposes and it is a fact that there is always the necessity of the buildings to be of the expected strength. When the wrong materials are used, it may result in the buildings becoming uninhabitable, which means that the amount invested is lost in entirety. Preventing such scenarios across the different industry is necessary and the major strategy through which the mistakes can be avoided is if the stakeholders operate together from the onset of the project.

- **Using the project as a means of creating a refined product**

Once the preceding steps have been followed, a clear scope is defined, and a budget can then be adequately prepared. Normally, the budget determines the level of detail in the project with large budgets being expected to result in better output. In some projects, the leaders consider the feedback given for similar products to deduce what exactly the market wants and what would be redundant for them. For example, if a project involves software development, the stakeholders can be able to actually be able to find reviews for similar products whether online or through an actual survey. The feedback helps with eliminating unnecessary features, which ultimately results in saving more money.

Budgeting for Projects without a Clear Scope

Budgeting for projects without a clear scope can both be frustrating and highly inaccurate. Depending on the length of the project, it is always better for the agile team to work hand in hand with the client and have milestones approved as work continues. The agile team should handle each iteration as a separate contract to ensure that they are in line with what the client wants, and it is also safe to ask for milestone payment for each iteration before the next one ensues. Lack of a proper scope may result in stalling of the project or failure at the Ultimate end, and the project managers must protect their team from it.

Also, it is worth noting that any successful endeavor in the world today is a function of either science or model. Science is represented by math while an individual person devises the model. Without a proper scope, science cannot apply since the stakeholders do not have the parameters needed to estimate the components of the project. Therefore, devising a model is the only alternative.

In project management, one person cannot do the creation of a project budget. Therefore, the project managers may require the help of both the stakeholders and the team members. Asking help from a qualified external person is also a good option, as it increases the successful development of a good budget. As is known, the experience is undoubtedly the most valuable resource that any project can benefit from. Where no external experts are involved, the manager can follow the following steps to ensure that he develops the best budget:

1. The first step is involving the rest of the team members and asking for estimates considering how they view the work. Without a proper scope, the team may be unable to formulate the estimates. However, their experiences in prior projects can be imperative in enabling them to get close figures. The management should not be choosy as to which of the team members should be involved and which ones should not, since the knowledge levels may differ. In such a case, coming together as one is the best option.

The management should also dig into their records and identify a project which is relatively similar to the one in question. Thereafter, they can compare the team estimates with the actual amounts that were spent in the previous project and reach a consensus. The main advantage of this approach is that the leaders get to review projects that have already been completed, which means that they are able to identify all the aspects that are required in the project.

2. Once the estimates have been confirmed, the management must ensure that the budget is calculated on the higher side. Slight overestimation is important since it helps prepare for uncertainties that are not anticipated. The budget must be continuously monitored as the budget progresses, and all the stakeholders must be involved. The standard deviation must always be studied, so that mitigation strategies can be adopted when the deviation is too much.

Handling a project without a proper scope requires utmost transparency, and the clients must be involved in every step of the way. In the case the leaders and the clients cannot come to an agreement requiring the addition of funds where necessary, it may be best to forego the project. When the clients are on board, the project managers must renegotiate with the contractors, and inform them early enough about the possibility of the scope changing, and how they expect to be handled.

Best Agile Practices to keep the Projects under Budget

As was prior stated, it is always ideal for a project to be under budget than for it to exceed the pre-set budget. All projects face immense challenges when it comes to staying on budget; an occurrence which has resulted in the stalling of many projects. To avoid the extra costs, the following strategies can be adopted:

- **Require the team to do the budgeting**

Agile project management is known for its key characteristic, which is the involvement of the entire team in key decision-making processes. When it comes to setting a budget, it is a fact that the management may not know as much details as the actual team performing the task. Therefore, the team is better qualified to prepare an inclusive budget than any other person. Agile project managers usually ask the team to come up with a range of budgets ranging from low-high cost; most of which is determined by the materials used. Once the budget has been made, the stakeholders can then be engaged so that they can decide on which one they are most comfortable with.

- **Begin with a Realistic Figure**

Producing a realistic figure from the onset is very important as it shows the true value of the project at a particular time. To get the proper figure, research and in-depth planning must be done. The stakeholders are always advised to take into consideration all the risks involved in the carrying out of the project so that they can come up with a more credible figure.

While we understand that clients desire to spend as little money as possible for some of their tasks, the fact remains that it is not always possible. Unrealistic expectation results in stalled and incomplete projects, which all stakeholders strive to avoid.

- **Using the right tools for tracking the project**

For project managers to be able to ensure that the project stays within budget, they must account for where every cent goes. The use of comprehensive and accurate time tracking systems allows all the stakeholders to know whether they are staying within their budget or not. Notably, the tools should not only track aspects such as time and work completion levels, but there must also be the adoption of communication tools to ensure that the team shares information as they should. Luckily, agile projects are based on a system, which supports daily meetings and teamwork and makes the analysis of any issue very simple.

The major advantage of proper communication is that it ensures that any issues witnessed are discussed promptly and solutions implemented. Also, the team can be able to brainstorm on which of the practices are bound to cost the least amount of money rectifying the mistake. At the end of the day, the agile team members recognize that any issues that befall on the company directly affect them, thus prompting fast mitigation strategies.

- **Continuously monitor the estimations**

The budgets created at the beginning of a project are all estimations. Since each iteration has its own budget estimation, the project managers must be actively involved in evaluating the estimates against the total costs once the iterations are complete. Through the analysis, they can be able to identify the deviations. In some instances, the deviations are positive while in some instances it is negative. If the project managers realize that the deviations in each iteration are too material, there is a high probability that the deviations will extend to the other iterations. Ultimately, the project is bound to run out of funds. Mitigating this probability is easy as the project managers only need to involve the clients and discuss potential modifications of the same. In instances where contracts have already been signed and the cost liability has shifted to the contractors, the project managers can always involve the team to identify the ways through which they can be able to cut down on costs.

In some projects, the managers have had to cut down on human labor. If three people can be able to work on a project effectively, there is no need having 10 people on the team.

The additional people represent additional costs and the fact that service delivery remains the same means that it is just an unnecessary cost. Also, costs relating to electricity and water can be cut down by switching to energy saving bulbs and using natural light in the daytime. When it comes to water bills, the team must be taught on the measures, which can help reduce wastage such as not leaving the water running.

- **Analyze the hidden costs from the start**

In any project whether big or small, there are always hidden costs. Project managers must work with the team and all the other stakeholders to ensure that the hidden costs are resolved before the actual work begins. One of the best strategies of identifying some of the costs is the consideration of the extent to which you rely on third parties for the provision of some of the commodities. Whenever a project relies heavily on third parties, there is always the probability of risks and shortcomings, which must be mitigated and prepared for before they arise. For instance, managers must ensure that they know multiple people who can deliver the same commodities. That way, if one of the suppliers fail, they can always use others to fill the gap.

- **Creating a contingency plan**

Project managers know that risks are imminent in any project. Therefore, there is always the need to expect the unexpected and always plan for any instances of failure. Mistakes are also inevitable and some of them may be so material that they result in the disruption of the entire budget. The obstacles within the project may be caused by:

- Delays caused by 3rd parties that are beyond the project stakeholders. For instance, if a key supplier suddenly goes bankrupt and cannot be able to provide the supplies as was promised.

- Unexpected rework. In some instances, something may go wrong within the course of executing a project and it must be repeated. For instance, if the project developers do not code correctly, there is bound to be a bug, which then must be fixed when it is realized.
- Wastage of time and involvement of a higher number of human resources also results in additional costs. For example, a team may be unable to conduct some of the activities in a project, requiring the employment of additional persons. This scenario is prevalent across different industries and the team always has to use extra money to find a human resource that can help them out.
- External cost shocks, such as fluctuations in currency. Currency values are never constant. Sometimes, the currency strengthens while it weakens at times. The currency valuations normally affect international companies to a large extent since they deal with the gain and loss in value by themselves. The increased decrease in the value of the currency may result in lack of sufficient money for the continuity of the project resulting in under-budgeting.

Projects going Over Budget

Instances of budgets going over the predetermined values are rampant. To prevent this occurrence , it is worth noting some of the reasons that result in the problem. Some of the key reasons that may cause the budgets to go overboard are:

- **Lack of a clear scope**

In a study conducted by the Advanced Electronic company and the Missouri University of Science and technology, 70% of failed projects in healthcare and information technology were as a result of unclear scopes. If the project managers could not be able to set a clearly defined scope for their projects, then it was highly unlikely that they would be able to stick to the budget. Unclear scopes cause a myriad of issues, most of which relate to the occurrence of unprecedented costs. When the managers do not know how to proceed and what exactly to do in iterations, they end up spending more money than was anticipated, ultimately ruining the budget.

- **Working with the wrong people**

Agile projects are all about teamwork and moving together to deliver the best products to clients. The team members must be on the same page and agree to the scope and functions that must be met for the project to be deemed as successful. More importantly, the entire team must be qualified, which means that the project managers must be sure of each individual's' skill set and what they can offer to the company. According to the project management institute, building an effective team is more than just a group of people willing to work. An effective team is made up of high performers who personalize the project and make it their own. The team must be committed to excellence and following all the guidelines to ensure customer satisfaction. More importantly, an effective team brings its own ideas on board and can, therefore, help identify budget cutting techniques that can be adopted. Working with the wrong people deprives the management such benefits and it is highly likely for the project to go overboard since laxity and non-performance would be prevalent.

- **Failure to execute**

It is one thing to believe in yourself and it is an entirely different thing to commit to something that you can't handle. Yes, we are all always told to challenge ourselves and take on new milestones and learn on the job. Some contractors take on projects that they absolutely have never dealt with before even though they may have a few ideas about how to accomplish it. For instance, an engineering company may take on a bridge construction project while all they have ever dealt with is road construction. As much as some of the processes remain the same, it is a fact that the two are not comparable. Where the contractors do not involve people who have previously succeeded on working on such projects, there is a very high chance that they may not be able to execute. The ultimate consequence is a lot of money being used to mitigate errors and even more unprecedented costs surprising the management.

- **Indiscipline**

Two things are imminent once a contractor signs the project contract; they either conform to the budget or not. Agile project managers resolve to ensure that the budgets are followed to the letter so that they can use the predetermined resources, time, and money. Where indiscipline is tolerated, the project will undoubtedly end up spending more than was anticipated, causing a strain on the budget. Some of the indiscipline cases that should never be tolerated are:

1. Employee laxity. When the employees do not meet their goals, the ultimate consequence is the requirement of extra time, which means that more money is paid in the form of salaries.
2. Supplier laxity must also be discouraged. The

suppliers are very capable of ruining the project when they engage in activities such as delaying the materials ordered and supplying low-quality materials.

3. Quality is necessary and the project managers must always expect the same for all the staff. Through the tracking tools, they can be able to tell which of the employees are giving their best and which ones are not. Indiscipline on the side of any stakeholder is a liability as it results in increased unnecessary expenses such as increased labor requirements and money required to fix issues with the final products.

Evidently, regardless of how agile a company strives to be, there is only so much that can be achieved if a budget is messed up. Budgeting is essential in any company, and it is only through proper approaches that the stakeholders can be able to realize the entire benefit of the process. As has been discussed, developing and conforming to a budget is actually quite easy and all that needs to be done is a dedication to the process and the realization that without discipline the project is bound to fail.

4

TRACKING AND REPORTING AGILE PROJECTS

Tracking

Tracking is imperative in the agile project since it enables the project managers as well as the teams to understand where the project stands in terms of work completed, pending, and budget-wise. All projects must be tracked continuously for their successful completion. Some of the techniques used to track the various parameters of agile projects are:

- **Using a Task Board**

Task boards are the simplest and most used tools in organizations; both big and small. The boards are normally placed strategically at a place where they are accessible to all team members. The board comprises easy to view items within the sprint that involves the tasks completed and those yet to be done. In small companies, the task board is made up of sticky notes. The projects involved are usually less tasking and their turnaround time is small. This makes it easy for the team to move the notes around and since small projects have few team members, all can be able to view the notes effectively and take note of what is therein.

Task boards may be effective in the case when all the team members are confined to a single room, which can be open plan offices. Where the projects are more complex and involving, the agile teams can shift to the use of digital task boards shared in a common application such as google docs. When task tables are created in such applications, every team member can be able to follow what is happening real-time since everyone is notified of the changes whenever made. Other large organizations, which have to share files after the completion of iterations use Dropbox, which is accessible to all the team members. Either of the techniques works perfectly as long as the whole team is cooperative.

- **Earned Value Management**

The earned value management is a technique that is used to track down the status and progress of a project as well as forecast the expected future performance of the project. The earned value management is known to integrate the scope, schedule, and cost of a project, and answering a lot of stakeholder questions in relation to the performance of the project. The technique is an improvement of the standard comparison of the budget versus the actual cost lacking an adequate indicator of the progress. Usually, the values given are stated in appropriate measurable units such as dollars or hours.

To understand earned value management, there are a number of concepts that are worth learning. The terminologies include:

Planned value, which refers to the work planned to be accomplished based on the budget.

Earned value, which refers to the actual integrated value of work that has been accomplished based on the budget.

Budget at Completion (BAC) is the budget assigned to complete the work. Usually, the metric showcases the number of cents that have been "earned" out of every dollar spent. The budget at completion can also be referred to as the actual cost which the total cost is taken to complete the work at a particular reporting date.

Escaped defects, which refer to the defects not caught at all. Some of the defects are immaterial, which means that they do not affect the final product in the least. However, some of the defects may be material which means that they drastically affect the final product.

The use of earned value is prevalent in software development and not as common in the other industries. When certain iterations in the software are complete, the management can actually be able to quantify the progress in monetary terms. For instance, when half of the software is done, the management can actually be able to determine how much it would be worth at a particular time. Industries such as manufacturing can also be able to use earned value to track their progress. For instance, in companies which develop cars, the expected earnings of the car are only determined when it is completed. Therefore, if each completed car is $10k, the earned value of two completed cars is $20k.

The major advantage with earned value is that it simplifies tracking to a very large extent. Each company has its own milestones. If a car manufacturing company wished to earn $100k per month, then it has to make 10 cars. Lack thereof, results in failure of hitting the milestone, which then prevents the companies from making their dcsired amount from the project. Such an occurrence allows the management to determine the causes of the project falling behind, consequently enabling them to devise strategies enabling them to fix the problems.

Reporting

Accurate reporting is essential in the fostering of proper communication within a large, complex global company. Agile project managers are particularly communication enthusiasts since agility supports working together as a team. Furthermore, proper reporting facilitates and satisfies the information needs of the key stakeholders. As it is known, agile project management involves the key stakeholders (clients) in all functioning and projects. It is evident that the lack of proper communication may result in trouble determining the important business aspects as well as missing out on deadlines and poorly done work. Therefore, tracking and reporting are imperative as it enables the managers to determine the extent of conforming to the schedule or lack thereof. Reports are, therefore, fundamental because they portray whether the team is doing a good job or whether things need to be changed.

Notably, the reporting can be done at multiple levels. In small enterprises, the reporting can at the company level while big organizations divide their functions into departments. In such a case, the reporting can either be done at the departmental level or at the task level depending on the management criterion.

In agile project management, the basis of reporting is based on the concept that less is more. Therefore, the agile project managers avoid holding complex meetings that are limiting to some people and prefer to address any issues in the simplest way possible. Unlike some organizations, which require multiple reports at each phase, agile project managers prefer to have minimal reports and encourage actual performance. Many reports are a waste of time for both the readers and the writers. Since it is the employed staff that develops the reports, it is a fact that they could be engaging in other beneficial work. Numerous reports also make it difficult to track where certain components of the project were imposed which hinders the measurement of performance.

Many agile project managers require reports to pass the SMART test. SMART is an acronym which refers to Specific, Measurable, Assignable, Realistic and Time-related aspects. Therefore, for the report to be deemed as efficient, the writers must:

1. Ensure that is it discussing a specific part of the project.
2. Have an element of measuring success or lack thereof.
3. Specify who did what, when, and with whom.
4. Be realistic. The issue contained therein must make sense.
5. Have a time aspect such as when some of the activities were done and whether they conformed to the stipulated time frame.

In addition to the reports being SMART, most agile companies have also resulted in the implementation of OKR (objectives and key results). This method is popular among large agile companies such as Google, Uber, LinkedIn, and Twitter, and is considered to be an iterative goal setting framework. Since APM is interested in team performance as opposed to individual performance, OKR works perfectly as it integrates everyone to each other's activities.

One of the most straightforward ways of implementing OKR is using the cascading methodology. Here, the company sets the key objectives and two or three key results, then each of the business units or project divisions set up a key objective and three results that support the company objective. Each team in a business unit sets up a key objective and three key results that support the divisions objective. After, each individual sets up their personal key objectives and three results that support the team's objectives. Graphically, the cascading OKR can be represented as:

An example of OKR for a hypothetical software company is as illustrated in figure

Figure 4: Illustration of OKR at the company and departmental level

The OKR reports are usually accessible to all persons

working together or undertaking a project. Therefore, the individuals can be able to view all the OKRs of the top level management and vice versa. The establishment of the OKRs has been known to facilitate teamwork since all people are working together towards a common goal. Since each person designs their objectives in relation to the upper tier management, it ensures that they work together and actually act as conversation starters since the juniors may be interested in knowing what to do to help achieve the goals.

Where OKR is implemented, another big advantage is that it warrants the development of agile status reports. A status report is a reiteration of what has been happening at a particular period, inclusive of the developments and any challenges faced so far. The reports are held progressively after a short period, say two weeks. The mid-iteration status meetings are very important since they help with the identification of any challenges early, preventing delays and incorrect work at the end of a project.

Some companies require the status reports to be written while others just converge at a meeting point and discuss the milestones verbally. Many agile projects then require a final status report at the end of an iteration. For instance, if the agile project was in construction, a status meeting can be called after the completion of a milestone such as clearing the bushes. When the status meetings are held, they help prepare for the next phase. Usually, different companies have different preferences related to the tracking and reports they wish to be prepared. Notably, some of the companies may require the writers to present multiple types of reports depending on the project at hand. Some of the popular report formats are:

1. **Product backlog report**

To clearly understand the whole aspect of product backlog

agile reporting, there are a few key terms that you must be accustomed to:

1. *Stories*. Referred to as user stories are also referred to as short term requirements which are normally written from the perspective of the end user.
2. *Epics*. The epics comprise of large bodies of work which can be broken down into stories.
3. *Initiatives*. These are a collection of epics, driven toward a common goal.
4. *Themes*. The themes are large focus areas which span the organization.

A visual representation of how the initiative, epics, and stories interact is as represented in figure 5.

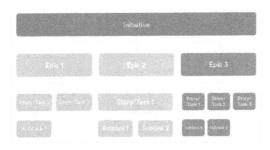

Figure 5: Illustration of Initiatives, Epics, and Stories

A product backlog report comprises of a summary of all the things that need to be done within a project. Therefore, the report is usually inclusive of a breakdown of the particular needs of the iteration, coupled with the deadline of each process therein. Once an iteration is complete, the report writers must include all the information that was provided before the onset of the iteration and indicate whether all the needs have been met. Typically, the backlog is used throughout the performance of the iteration with the team identifying what needs to be done and how from the customer specification. Reporting is therefore simplified since the writers only need to identify what they accomplished and if there is any item from the backlog that was not accomplished. With such a report, the project managers are able to determine whether the project is on the right track or otherwise.

Creating a product backlog report requires skill and keenness. Project managers are better suited to implement the concept of the two "R's" to provide the foundation for the backlog. The two R's represent **roadmap** and **requirements.** Roadmaps help the team determine how they will achieve particular milestones while requirements represent the tools needed to achieve the said milestones.

To develop an effective roadmap, the first step is breaking down the initiatives to epics. In each epic, there must be clear user stories, which enables the teams to identify what exactly needs to be done so that they can mark it as achieved or not achieved when they are developing the report. An illustration of epics and their subsequent user stories is as represented in figure 6.

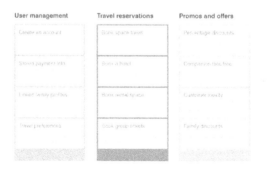

Figure 6: Illustration of epics and accompanying user stories

The illustration is for a website and the initiative is setting up the pages, which will help the potential users navigate easily on the site. As illustrated, there are three epics: user management, travel reservations, and promos and offers. Each of the epics has exact functions that must be set up. For instance, for the user management epic to have been developed in entirety, the website must have a fully functioning "create an account" button, payment button, a button for linking the family profiles, and a travel preferences button. With such a clear roadmap and requirements, creating the product backlog report becomes quite easy as the team only needs to mark the user stories as "complete" or "incomplete." Notably, with projects such as software development, the clients aim at simplifying the user stories as much as possible to ensure that the process is as straightforward as possible to the end users.

2. **Sprint Backlog reports**

A sprint refers to a pre-set period where a specific piece of work has to be completed and made ready for review. Therefore, the sprint backlog report is designed to review the list of works to be completed during the specific sprints. Before an iteration begins, the team members analyze the user stories and determine the amount of time it would take to complete it. For example, using figure 6 as an example, the team may assert that they can be able to create the "create account" function in two days. Once all the stories have been assigned specified timelines, reporting becomes easy since the writers will either identify the milestones to be achieved or not.

A typical backlog report is as illustrated in figure 7.

Figure 7: Illustration of spring backlog visual report

Evidently, the visual representation is quite simple and can be easily understood at a glance. Normally, the product backlog stories are listed in order from what should be done first to the next story. As can be seen in the table, the teams can be able to see the stories which are in progress, in review, in the test, done, and those which cannot be completed due to various problems. Normally, all members of a team have access to the board, which keeps them on their toes when it comes to achieving milestones.

The sprint tables may show daily, weekly, monthly or annual representation depending on the project undertaken. For example, in software development some of the tasks handled are easy and the team can be able to complete even more than 10 stories in a day. In such a case, the task board can illustrate daily milestones. In other projects, such as construction, singular stories such as excavation can even take two weeks, which means that the board can comprise of monthly or even quarter or even semi-annual reports. Some companies may require a written report in addition to the visual report depending on the terms or complexity of the projects undertaken.

3. Burndown Reports

A burndown chart refers to a graphical representation of the quantity of work remaining to complete in a project over versus the time. The outstanding work is normally presented on the vertical axis while the time log is illustrated on the horizontal axis. The slopes or line in the burndown chart runs diagonally from the top left to the bottom right. There are usually four slopes on the chart, one which shows the remaining tasks, the ideal burndown, and the remaining effort. A sample burndown report is as illustrated in figure 8.

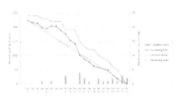

Figure 8: Illustration of a burndown chart

Interpreting the burndown chart is quite simple. The ideal burndown line illustrates the progress that is desired which showcases the planned completion of activities from the beginning. In the case the line representing the actual work done is above the estimation line, then the project is undoubtedly behind schedule. If the actual line is below the estimation line, then the project is said to be ahead of schedule.

The burndown chart is the perfect definition of "a picture is worth a thousand words." Usually, the interpretation is very straightforward and the project managers as well as the team members can be able to see how much work is left at a glance. Normally, the burndown graphs are accessible to all persons in the team, which makes them fundamental in compelling them to act whenever there is a chance that they are running behind schedule. The fact that the chart keeps everyone involved means that it may encourage them to deal with issues early enough before they become problems. The bigger the charts, the better the illustration of the projected velocity. The term velocity is an agile term which refers to the total effort estimated, which is associated with user stories that were completed during an iteration. Burndown charts are usually very simple, which makes interpretation very easy.

There are two variants that exist for a typical burndown chart. There is usually the spring burndown chart, which illustrates the work remaining for a particular iteration as well as a product burndown chart, which highlights the work remaining for the entire project.

Notably, as much as the burndown charts are imperative in the representation of the work remaining, the major limitation is that they do not show everything. For example, the charts show the number of stories that have been completed but does not show the scope of work as measured by the total points. Therefore, it may be difficult to discern whether the changes in the chart are as a result of the backlog items being completed or if they are a function of the increase or decrease in story points. Also, the charts do not indicate which particular stories have been completed. Therefore, the team members have to look for additional information to view which of the stories are indicated to have been completed and which ones are pending.

The major limitation is that the chart is based on estimate. The accuracy is, therefore, questionable. Since the chart does not have exact measurement points, the markers estimate everything ranging from the actual work completed to the work remaining. Estimation is subjective, which means that one person may mark one place while another may mark a totally different place. Instances of overestimating and underestimating are prevalent, which results in the team members and project managers making the wrong inferences. Many agile project managers have since found a way around the inefficiencies, one major one is the incorporation of an efficiency factor in the chart. After the first iteration, the efficiency factor is re-calculated to allow for more efficiency. The efficiency factor is then applied to all of the remaining iterations, making it more credible.

4. **Velocity charts**

The velocity charts represent the amount of value which is delivered in each of the sprints. This enables the proper prediction of the amount of work that the team can get done in future sprints. The velocity charts are useful in the sprint planning meetings, which helps them make a decision pertaining to how much work particular teams should commit to at a particular time. The biggest advantage that accrues to using the velocity charts is that it provides a realistic representation of what can be achieved and what cannot. Therefore, the project managers know what to assign to a team and when to expect the final delivery.

An example of a velocity chart is as represented in figure 9.

Figure 9: Illustration of a velocity chart

To understand the velocity chart, the four key points denoted by the numbers 1, 2, 3 and 4 must be understood.

1 represents the **estimation statistic**. The statistic is on the y-axis, and it displays the statistic used for the estimation of the stories. In the illustration, the company is using story

points. Depending on the company, the story points can be substituted for hours, business values, issue count or any other preferred estimation criterion.

2 represents the **commitment**. This is the grey bar for each of the sprints which shows the estimation of all the issues in the sprint when they begin. After the start of any sprint, any of the stories added are not included in the total.

3 represents the **completed**. The completed tasks are the actual stories or milestones that the team was able to accomplish, and they are usually placed next to the commitment line. Usually, any of the scope changes made after the start of the scope are included in the total.

4 represents the **sprints**. The sprints are indicated in the x-axis, displaying the last 7 sprints completed by the team. The data therein is used to calculate the velocity. Calculation of the velocity is important as it helps in the prediction of how much work can be completed by the team in the future. The calculation involves the taking of the average completed estimates over the last several sprints and dividing it by the total. In so doing, the team is able to determine what values to place on the next projects.

5. Defects Trend Reports

The defects trend report analyzes all the defects that were realized in a certain period. Keeping track and recording all the defects is imperative as it helps the management to devise strategies through which they can prevent the recurrence of the defects as well as helping find the causes and preventive strategies for them as well. Depending on the project, some of the defects are realized within the cause of an iteration and in some companies the defects are realized after the completion of the final project.

There are usually two types of defects: the blocker and

non-blocker defects. The blocker defects are usually real-ized in the course of the sprint and can be rectified before the next splint begins. The non-blocker defects are consid-ered to be the most damaging as they are rarely realized, and most of them proceed to the final iteration. In this case, the defects are either realized when the testing phase ensues or when customers complain after purchasing the defective goods.

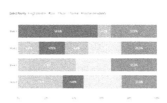

Figure 10: Illustration of a defect report

Incorporation of the defective trends is very beneficial in agile project management due to the following factors:

- The agile managers are able to track down how well or bad the project is performing. Through the analysis of the reports, readers can immediately tell which sprints are doing well and which ones are not. This facilitates the taking of drastic measures to reduce the risks involved in the sprints as well as the devising of strategies which will help in the rectification of the defects.
- The reports help in the management of the team in a better way, as well as the regular monitoring of the team's progress against goals. When the reports indicate very high levels of defects, it may be a sign that the team is not qualified enough for the job and that the management has to find better options.

- Identify the causes of the defects so that they can be avoided in future projects.

It is important to note that the agile project managers must find a way of independently running the defects report. Many teams would be afraid to be truthful about the defects since that would be subject to questioning their expertise. Therefore, they may under-report the defects, which make it difficult to invoke strategies that would help in the reduction of the defects . When the project managers have an independent test team, all issues relating to the quality of the output is laid out, helping them identify all bugs and issues therein.

Usually, defects tracking and reporting is rampant in the agile software industry. This doesn't negate the fact that all other manufacturing and construction industries can benefit from the reports since it helps solve quality issues. For example, a construction industry can perform concrete tests to determine the strength of the block. Some contractors are known to use low quality cement which then compromises the whole quality of a construction block. Once the quality tests are done, the project managers are able to know when somethings occur as well as how to proceed when the defects are found.

Despite the many advantages that accrue to quality testing and defects revelation, there are a number of disadvantages that accrue to the defect tracking. Many of the disadvantages have more to do with the process overheads, as opposed to the idea of defect tracking itself. Some companies use multiple tools, which cost money. Therefore, there has to be a budget for such tools. Also, where the company uses multiple tools, there is often a chance that some of them may not be able to integrate with each other. Clashing of the tools may cause even more defects, which consequently results in more damage to the products.

Notably, agile project management always insists on promoting individuals and interactions over the processes and tools. Therefore, the best quality tools still remain to be the proper communication amongst the team members to avoid issues. If the team puts too much hope on the tools, they may become careless as they know that the tools will pick up on any issues. The tools are also manmade and cannot be relied upon 100%. Some companies have made huge strides using tools as simple as sticky notes, and some have benefitted from complex tools. Either way, it is up to the management to decide on the best course of approach to use.

Changes report

In many projects, changes are inevitable and required. The changes may be as a result of requests from the clients or modification of the team based on their belief of what is best for the team. Examples of changes across different industries are:

1. A client who paid for a website may request a change of the background theme of the site.
2. A manufacturing company may require a certain raw material to be changed due to multiple factors.
3. A construction client may want a change of the finish, location, tiles, etc.
4. A software client may want a change of one of the functions in the end product etc.

Agile teams are usually receptive to any of the changes requested by the clients or the management, to ensure that the end product is as satisfactory as possible. Whenever any addition is made, the team must always note on what exactly has been changed when it was changed, who changed it, and who authorized it. Authorization is always mandatory since it helps prevent issues as some clients may be problematic in the end. When the changes are instigated by the management, they always have to ensure that the client is privy and in agreement with the changes. When the clients order the changes, the management must be privy so that the entire team can discuss on how to make the changes as beneficial as possible.

Team capacity/Load Report

At any particular time, the project managers need to know what everyone is up to. In as much as agile project management is all about teamwork, some people are natural performers while others are non-performers. When the employees are operating as a team, it may be difficult to identify the non-performers since the iterations are submitted by the entire group. Agility entails each and every person working at optimal capacity and refraining from taking advantage of the others. Therefore, there is the importance of reports and tracking strategies which can help expose the sloths and deal with them. team capacity or load reports entail various information which includes:

1. *Total hourly capacity*. The capacity section reports the total amount of time that each team members is able to dedicate to the project. Most projects multiply the hours by the number of days allocated to the project, to find the total amount of time dedicated.
2. *Assigned hourly capacity*. This section entails the number of hours (story points), multiplied by the average number of times per story point for the team's skill set.
3. *Available capacity*. Entails the total capacity minus the assigned capacity.

Normally, uncooperative team members are highly likely to

miss hours since they do not want to work. Whenever a report shows immense missing hours for some of the team members, it should be treated as a red flag and the project managers need to engage the afflicted to understand what is going on. Also, when the team members have all the hours present and still fail to deliver on the predetermined deadlines, it is a red flag that must be investigated.

It is worth noting, some of the reporting techniques can also be used as tracking techniques and vice versa. Depending on the approach taken by the different companies, the techniques can be used interchangeably and successfully.

Reporting using Statistical Analysis

Many projects in the world are subject to an array of statistical data that must be evaluated. Through the analysis of the data, various inferences can be deduced, and the stakeholders can be able to make informed decisions pertaining to some of the functionalities of the organization. Whenever statistical information is derived from a project, there are two key questions that the stakeholders must ask themselves:

1. What can be deduced from this information?
2. How can we ensure that the statistical data is not flawed?

First, it is important to get a description of what statistics refer to. According to the six sigma institute, statistics comprises of a series of data and information which can be used to make conclusive inferences. Data refers to facts, in particular numerical facts, which are collected together for reference or to showcase a particular piece of information. Information, on the other hand, refers to communicated knowledge which concerns particular facts. The statistical information form key aspects of reports, especially the ones which have mathematical elements in them. For instance, most engineering, science, and research reports have statistical reports, which are easily understood by both the project managers and the team which prepared them.

The statistical reports can take two forms:

1. Descriptive Statistics
2. Inferential Statistics

Descriptive Statistics

Descriptive statistics represent a method of organization, summarization, and the presentation of statistical data in an informative manner. There are many methods that can be used to present the data and project managers select the one which is most efficient for them. Depending on the report in question, the report writers can present the data using measures of central tendency or using the measures of dispersion and variance. The measures of central tendencies are the most common, and can be described in the form of:

1. Mean

The mean is an important arithmetic average that sums up all of the values under study and divides them by the number of the data values. The mean has multiple uses and can be used to calculate the averages of any process. For instance, when the project managers wish to know the average time spent to complete an iteration, the mean is the best average to be used.

2. **Illustration**

Assume that there are five team members working on a project. The first team takes 30 minutes to complete, the second 45 minutes, the third 50 minutes, the fourth 55 minutes, and the fifth 60 minutes. For the project managers to determine the average time taken to complete the project, the calculation will be:

= (30+45+50+55+60)/5

= 48 minutes

Once the mean figure is determined, the project managers can be able to use it as a base for the next iteration or future projects. The teams would be given a maximum of 84 minutes to finish up on the iterations and the managers will have used a very objective measure to arrive at the number. This helps in planning as the managers have figure that they can work with.

3. Median

The median is the middle number in a given set when arranged in order. By itself, the median does not really reveal a lot about the project but when used with the mean it can be used to illustrate the degree of skewness. Using illustration 1 as the example, the first thing would be to arrange the data in an ascending order. Therefore, the order would be:

30, 45, 50, 55, 60

In an odd number, getting the median is simple as it is the middle number. In this case, the median is 50. If the data had an even number, the median would have been derived by adding the two middle numbers and dividing by two. Therefore, if the data was:

30, 45, 50, 55, 60, 65

The median would be: (50+55)/2

= 52.5

4. Mode

The mode is the data point which has the highest number of

repetitions or frequency. In projects, the mode is very important, and it can help the project managers make a series of decisions. Assuming that you are a project manager and you are contemplating changing the arrival time of the employees. You can conduct an analysis of how early thy arrive. For instance, if the arrival time of the employees is:

7:00, 7:30, 7:45, 7:30, 7:30, 8:00, 7:15 it is clear that most of the people arrive at 7.30. Therefore, the management can set a restriction that the last employee should be arriving at the workplace by 7:30. The fact that most people are comfortable with that time means that the larger number of the company will be favored, which is an advantage.

Inferential Statistics

The inferential statistics are used as a method of drawing conclusions or inferences about the population characteristics from a set of data used as a sample. Inferential statistics is therefore drawn from sampling. In projects, sampling is done most of the time. A typical project has so many constraints, ranging from time, cost, resources, and others. Therefore, it would not be possible to study 100% of the population and the managers need to use samples.

An illustration is where a company with 1,500 employees wishes to sort employee dissatisfaction issues noted. Since it is not possible to listen to all 1,500 of the employees, the project managers tell the disgruntled employees to summarize their concerns with their heads of departments and the heads ultimately meet with the owners and come up with improvement and developmental strategies.

Another illustration is where a client has given a company a project to manufacture 1,000 cars in lots. When the project is done, the project managers cannot be able to test all the cars one at a time. In most cases, they would select a random sample of say 15 cars and test them. In this case, all the sample cars selected are of excellent quality and it would be correct to assume that the whole batch is perfect. However, if 6 cars in the batch have serious flaws, the managers would re-consider sending out the products to the end consumers and would have to take time and examine where the issues are. Sampling is usually beneficial in the managing of projects, thus highly popular in the agile project management industry.

5

AGILE ESTIMATION AND PLANNING

Estimation

You must be familiar with the love-hate relation-ship that defines the estimates, particularly in the business arena. Most business ventures demand the use of the estimates while agile teams are more or less against them. Agile project managers and enthusiasts confess that using the estimates makes them feel like they are confined to a strict commitment, which feels like a stranglehold. As much as the opinions of the different project managers differ, it is a fact that the estimation of work for stakeholders and developers is not easy. Amongst the challenges that most project partici-pants confirm to having with estimates are:

1. The struggle to make accurate estimates. Where proper estimation parameters have not been defined, it is very easy for the project managers to over or underestimate the scope and budget, which then results in execution difficulties.

2. In some instances, the stakeholders may demand the scope and cost of the project to be locked down even in cases where the requirements are vague. Some of the stakeholders

want to work with a particular budget that must be provided well in advance, and the fact that the estimates rarely provide the true value of the processes means that locking down the scales can be disastrous.

3. Depending on the person making the estimate, everyone always strives to ensure that they benefit more in the contract. For instance, as much as the clients have the desire to get quality output, they always wish to do so at a low price. Therefore, they may present an unrealistic estimate with unrealistic timelines. On the other hand, the project managers may wish to get more money from the project; therefore, prompting them to set higher estimates relating to cost. Agile project management is never about extortion, and the fact that the stakeholders work together means that such incidences are prevented.

In agile project management, there are two key estimation methods. The methods are:

1. *Capacity estimation method*. This method analyzes the total number of hours available for the team to successfully complete a print. Each of the sprints has its own user stories, which are broken down into tasks. Each task is highly scrutinized, and the team knows the potential amount of time that can be taken to complete it. In the case the task is finished before the estimated time is over, the next sprint is taken up.

2. *Velocity estimation method*. The method takes into consideration the number of user story points that a team completes in a sprint. The average number of completed stories is referred to as the team's velocity. Normally, the velocity is revised after every successful undertaking of a sprint to ensure a certain level of stability. For example, if a particular team is

able to complete 10 user stories every sprint, then its velocity is 10. Where the team realizes that there is a lot of time left after the completion of the assigned stories in a sprint, they can add the workload. The converse also applies and it all has to do with the unanimous agreement to do more by the entire team.

As much as agile project management is not really inclined towards the reliance of estimates, it is clear that the velocity estimation method is preferred in relation to estimation by capacity. Some of the advantages that accrue to the use of velocity estimation are:

1. *The general uncertainty is taken into consideration*. The size of a user story is often a combination of effort and complexity. Even if distinct projects may have the same number of stories or iterations, it is a fact that the level of effort required to handle the stories is different. Some stories are intensive while others are less involving. The velocity method considers the level of involvement required, enabling the estimates to be a little more realistic.

2. *The estimation method considers waste as a user story*. There is no project which does not have some level of waste. In some cases, the velocity is usually hindered by waste. Typically, waste may refer to the period where no one is working due to various factors. For example, heavy rains and storms may cause a halt to a project that was taking place outdoors such as construction. Also, some countries experience constant power shortages and where backup generators are not available their results to a halt in the activities. It would be inaccurate to assume that the staff would always have favorable occurrences in their workstations, which makes accounting for waste beneficial.

3. *The method builds a meeting commitment culture*. Using

velocity as an estimation method has a psychological effect on the employees. When determining the velocity taken to complete the splints, the management directly involves all the staff to enable them to come up with a number. Since agility strives to form motivated employees, there is an extremely high chance that with the right push, the team can be prompted to improve its efficiency. Also, recognizing waste helps the team members to be able to identify the causes of inefficiency, prompting them to change, improve, and increase the velocity speed.

The capacity estimation method is known to have more drawbacks than benefits. Some of the key disadvantages that result in the discouragement of the methodology include:

1. *The assumption that all the estimates are perfect.* Capacity estimation methodology is quite rigid and provides no room for risks and uncertainties. As much as the proponents of the methodology argue that rigidity is necessary for the enhancement of performance, the fact remains that the system is often crippled by the constant missing of the deadlines and inefficiency as a result of the unsettling expectations

2. *The assumption that all the tasks will be handled in a parallel manner.* The capacity estimation considers the number of human labor available in relation to the hours available for work for each of them. For instance, if a company has 5 people working 10 hours a day, then the capacity is calculated as the total hours available which are 50 hours. Capacity estimation then gives out tasks enough for the 50 hours without taking into account that the personnel rarely works in a similar mode to each other. People are different and so is their work ethic. Therefore, while some of the staff can indeed accomplish their tasks in the 10 hours, some

cannot. In the end, the deadlines are highly likely to be missed.

3. *Assuming that everyone is equal.* This is a reiteration to the previous point. People are different and so is their motivation levels and their work ethic. The management would be wrong to assume that everyone would give in the same effort and energy to a task. Sometimes, inefficiency may not be on purpose, and some of the staff can actually be in the middle of retrogressive events such as stress or illnesses. People are different and should be treated as such.

Estimation is undoubtedly necessary in some companies while it can be overlooked in others. Despite the love-hate relationship that estimation has with agile project management, it should be noted that the decision concerning whether to use it or not is dependent on the specific project.

Planning

Agile planning can be conducted in a multitude of ways. The most used strategy is through the use of the SWOT analysis. SWOT analysis is a popular tool that is used to identify Strengths, Weaknesses, Opportunities, and Threats to a project, team or organization. The strengths are the positive traits, which have contributed to the success of the project. Weaknesses are the internal and external factors that result in the inability to achieve goals. The opportunities are the factors that the management can use to thrive in the industry and the threats are factors affecting the company, which is beyond control.

The use of SWOT analysis in project management is relatively easy and is considered to be highly effective in ensuring that the project becomes successful. The analysis majorly helps the project managers to identify the areas, which need improvement and implementing the correct methodologies for the same. The analysis further helps with ensuring that all the requirements of the project are met on time and that the job is completed on a timely and efficient manner. Therefore, the project managers' end up improving the whole project at both the individual and company level. Usually, a SWOT analysis should be carried out at the start-up phase of the project, to prepare the team for any eventualities. A well-planned SWOT analysis is known to bring both structure and robustness in the strategic process, promoting prompt thinking about the positive and negative sides of the internal and external environment.

Conducting the SWOT Analysis

Before beginning a SWOT analysis, it is always important for project managers to have clear objectives. The stakeholders must understand what is expected of them so that they can effectively identify all the constituents of the analysis. In any project, the managers are better suited to devise a series of questions in line with their key objectives. These questions act as a guide for the analysis session and the participants can be able to properly identify their scope and what they're supposed to study. From what has been described, SWOT analysis encompasses the strengths weaknesses opportunities and threats of processes or parts of a project.

Strengths

The strengths are in most cases internal, which means that the project managers must look within the organization to be able to identify the aspects that they would consider helpful to the overall productivity and continuity of a project. Normally, the project managers have to ask themselves a series of questions inline to what they would consider a strength to be. Some of the key questions the stakeholders as themselves are:

1. Does this organization have all the necessary talent required to successfully complete the project? If the answer is yes, then the skills and talents our strengths to the organization. However, if the answer is no, the organization is devoid of a pivotal strength and the project managers have to go out of their way to bring people who can bring the skills to the organization.

2. What is the nature of the budget given? A budget can either result in the success of a project or lack thereof. If the budget is not sufficient, then there's a very high chance that the project will be completed efficiently. A proper budget ensures that the project managers can be able to get labor resources and materials required for a project, thus ensuring that it runs as expected and is completed with minimal delays. Whenever a budget is questionable, the team is better suited to refrain from beginning the project altogether and working on ways to reduce the budget or get the clients to add more funds.

3. Have we handled similar projects before? Experience is undoubtedly a major strength to any organization since they are able to use the lessons learned in the past to ensure that the present project runs as efficiently as possible. The project managers have never undertaken similar projects, which means they have to learn from scratch. The nature of not knowing what to expect can be extremely detrimental since it results in more instances of mistakes and challenges.

4. Are the team members experienced? projects are only likely to succeed if the team members know what they are doing without relying on others. Where the team members have handled similar projects in the past, there is undoubtedly experience,

and the project managers can be sure of a quality job. However, experienced team members and likely to make a lot of mistakes which may result in defects or errors that ultimately make the clients lose trust and faith in the work.

Weaknesses

The weaknesses consist of aspects of the organization or the project, which the project managers are not well equipped. To identify the weaknesses, the stakeholders can ever ask the questions identified above in the strengths and where they realize negative answers, it is an illustration of a weakness in the company. In Agile Project Management, some of the weaknesses that are prevalent in projects are:

1. *Unrealistic schedules.* The project managers are undoubtedly warranted to provide the best services possible to the clients. In the course of attempting to impress the clients by fast service delivery, the project managers can set unrealistic schedules and put pressure on the team members to conform to the set schedule. In such occurrences, the team members compromise quality to achieve the speed or fail to deliver, which then makes the clients lose faith in the developers. The project managers may end up losing the potential long-term clients, which is a miss to their company. As much as the project managers may want to prove themselves, it is always good to set realistic goals so as to ensure that the job performance is as required.
2. *Unskilled team members.* The team members are responsible for carrying out the project and they cannot do so without the necessary skills and expertise required in the specific projects. There are

a number of reasons why a project may be carried out by unskilled team members. First, some of the projects managers may not be willing to pay the cost of having skilled employees since it translates to higher salaries. To reduce the overheads, the managers may decide to use employees who are in a semi-skilled or unskilled since they will generally request lower payouts. The major disadvantage with doing this is that the overall quality of the project is compromised and there's a very high chance that client satisfaction would not be achieved. Also, some projects may be new, which would mean that none of the team members may have engaged in conducting a similar Project thus rendering them unskilled. This is a major weakness, and in most cases, the teams are not able to deliver.

Opportunities

Opportunities present the chances that the project managers have to make the most out of the project and subsequently identify the trends that can be exploited. To get a clear picture of the opportunities available, the project managers must understand the economic factors, competitor analysis, and customer preferences. To identify the opportunities, the project managers must consider:

1. *What they can do to take advantage of the competitor weaknesses*. If the project managers can be able to identify the weaknesses that their competitors have, they can be able to use such weaknesses to their advantage and ensure that they gain a competitive edge. The identification of competitor weaknesses can be done in multiple ways. First, the company can engage previous clients and attempt to get as much

information as they can about how such clients interacted with their competitors. Also, the company can invest in the observation of the activities of the competitors and attempt to find gaps in their processes and procedures. Once the discovery has been made, the company can begin working towards ensuring that clients do not face the same problems as they have in their competitors' companies.

2. *The latest technological improvements.* The company should ensure that they are always privy of the latest technologies that emerge in the market. With technological advancements come more efficient processes and strategies of excelling in the projects. Since the technological advancements are always inclined towards efficiency, their use results in better quality products and overall service delivery.

3. *The emerging trends in the market.* Trends change over time despite the industry one is involved in. For instance, the modes of construction and even construction materials have changed drastically over the last five years. Therefore, project managers have to keep in touch with the current trends so that they can be able to give the clients the best output possible.

Threats

Threats are to a larger extent considered to be part of the external factors that affect a project's ability to prosper. There are very many threats that face a typical organization, depending on their operations and even geographical location. Some threats are universal and are experienced by almost all projects. Some of the threats include:

1. *The difficulty of finding skilled employees.* This is particularly a major threat in the instances where the project managers

are involved in a project that they had no prior knowledge of. Sometimes, the managers may be unable to find employees who can be able to carry out the project successfully resulting in the inability to execute the project.

2. *Competitors. In any undertaking, the threat of competitors often supersedes all other threats.* Project managers are often faced with the threat of their clients moving on to their competitors, which ultimately causes a loss of income. Since project managers offer services on numerous occasions, the threat of competition is high since the clients will ideally choose the people whom they feel will execute their projects as per their desire. New entrants to the market pose as part of the competition and the project managers must always be ready to devise strategies which would give them a competitive advantage.

6

AGILE AND SIX SIGMA (AGILE SIGMA)

Project managers and other organizational leaders are always looking for ways through which they can improve the business process. Adopting the agile project management methodology is not enough to ensure that the company runs at its utmost efficiency. The Six Sigma methodology is proving to be a beneficial bonus for agile industries, and its advantages have resulted in its undoubted popularity across industries.

Agile methodologies have undoubtedly dominated in the software development domain since its inception. The methodology has since been adopted across various industries as has been described in depth, and it is expected to continue dominating. The agile teams usually focus on incremental completion of milestones, which entails dividing the entire project into small deliverables. While the short term improvements fostered result in better chances of project success, sometimes the agile teams lack the bird-eye strategic approach, fundamental in problem-solving, and process improvement. This is the gap that the six sigma methodology can help fill.

By definition, Six Sigma is a philosophy as well as a measure for problem solving and improvement of company processes. According to Jack Welch, Six Sigma is a program that helps facilitate customer satisfaction, helps lower the total costs of operations, and helps build better leaders. The methodology strives for a near-perfection quality of perfection, hence, works towards zero defects, customer perfection, and operational excellence. Six Sigma uses a data-driven review, which emphasizes of cycle time improvement while reducing the manufacturing defects to near zero. So strict is the measure that the system strives to realize no more than 3-4 defective occurrences per million units or cycles. Through the inclusion of the Six Sigma approach to agile project management, the companies benefit from the successful fulfillment of its values as well as better conformation to the agile principles. Simply put, using Six Sigma helps achieve faster output with fewer mistakes.

To further understand the Six Sigma approach, it is important to evaluate its history. The concept of the Six Sigma was developed by Motorola in the late 1980s. Bill Smith is considered to be the father of Six Sigma and developed the concept as a result of the need to ensure that the customers would be fully satisfied with the end products and that there would be minimal if any, complaints. After the success of the system, top companies such as Toyota adopted the system and achieved massive success. The methodology continued receiving the wide accolade and has since gone global.

As a professional agile project manager, you need to know everything that pertains to the Six Sigma approach, so it can be easy to integrate the system to the agile methodologies.

Six Sigma Approach

What is Six Sigma? An in-depth analysis of the question reveals that there is no single definition that can truly explain what the Six Sigma approach entails. Figure 11 gives an analysis of how Six Sigma can be explained.

Figure 11: Illustration of Six Sigma [14]

Six Sigma can be described as a business strategy where businesses can align their plan of actions to ensure that they achieve cost reduction, process improvement, and revenue increment. The strategy aims at improving all areas and sectors of the business to ensure that success and benefits accrued are all around the company.

Six Sigma is also a vision where the management aims at ensuring that the companies' outputs are perfect and free from defects and any kinds of errors. When the attitude of the company shifts to excellence, the management can often envision a positive environment which yields success.

Most companies describe Six Sigma as a benchmark. The methodology aims at ensuring that the companies and all processes are operating at an optimal level and that stability is attained. For instance, where the cycle time for pizza delivery is 60 minutes, the methodology aims at improving efficiency. Ultimately, the company can be able to deliver the same for 45 minutes or less.

Six Sigma is undoubtedly a goal. The organizations are able to develop and achieve certain goals for themselves and ensure that they work towards achieving them. Whenever industries and companies correctly use the methodology, they are often able to achieve any of the goals set.

Six Sigma is also a statistical measure, which is data driven. The methodology effectively identifies the root causes of some of the problems and helps in finding ways through which the problems can be resolved. Usually, the approach uses its own metric units, which helps in uniform calculations about any of the issues as well as process performances.

Finally, Six Sigma is identified as a robust methodology. Currently, the process is the only methodology, which is documented for its effective problem identification and problem-solving ability when it is used in the right manner. Companies which have adopted the methodologies have continually boasted of its benefits and its ability to prompt high yields.

As it has been stated, Six Sigma highly advocates for quality and the meeting of customer requirements. Whenever the quality aspect is met, customer satisfaction always prevails. According to the Six Sigma, there are three key activities that ensure quality:

1. Understanding customer requirements

There is always the need to know exactly what the customer wants, and it also helps to know why they want specific products. In agile, conforming to the customer requirements is also the end goals and the use of Six Sigma helps give more ways through which the customer requirements can be achieved more easily. In any business, customers are the final authority. The clients not only determine the value of the products and services that they offer but also whether to accept the products or not. Value is often determined by the final cost, quality, features, and availability. If a product is favorable in the four aspects, then the value is said to have been given to the clients. The stated values can only be achieved if the project managers:

a) *Listen to the customers*. Listening does not only entail leaving the client to talk about what they want in the final products but to also attempt to get into the mind of the client and try to get an idea as to what exactly they require. In the case, the clients are not clear about their needs and the project managers must conduct follow up interviews so that they can ensure that everyone is on the same page pertaining to the requirements.

b) *Accept feedback*. In some instances, the team attempts to do the best job possible for a client and it may not always pay off. Some of the clients may not be impressed with the work, which results in negative feedback. Despite the work that you put in a job, always listen and empathize with your client's feedback regardless of whether that is what you would want to hear. Once you allow the client to state their genuine feedback, you can be able to learn a lot from the information given, which will help you in future jobs.

c) *Learn about competitors*. No single company operates in a vacuum. All businesses in all industries have competitors. Therefore, a good team goes beyond what they are instructed by the clients and conducts research on the client's competitors. With the information, the project managers can be able to determine how to ensure that the products surpass those of the competitors in order to give their clients a competitive edge. Agility is all about customer satisfaction and developing a product that gives the clients an edge is undoubtedly a means of ensuring customer satisfaction.

d) *Give clients options*. In some instances, a client may want something, which the developers are sure is not the right fit for them. For instance, the team may have better features in mind than what the clients may want to be developed. As much as the customers' requirements should be followed, it is always vital to give the client options as they may not know about better alternatives. Agile project management advocates for effective communication between the clients and the team and this is part of the information that should be handled in the course of the communication.

e) *Re-assuring clients*. The assurance that you will do a good job is what every client wants. There are a number of ways through which you can reassure the clients, one of which is offering an exchange policy and money-back guarantee. Through agile project management, the fact that the clients are involved after every iteration means that there is a very small chance of making extreme mistakes. With that being said , re-assuring the clients always helps.

2. Designing the products to conform to the requirements

The end products designed must always meet the specification requirements. Once you understand all of the customer requirements, designing the products becomes immensely easy.

3. Developing processes to ensure proper product delivery

The development of a process is not straightforward. Every business and institution are unique, and each has their own distinct needs that are not similar to any other businesses'. As much as projects may be in the same industry, it is always necessary to note that they cannot be similar to other businesses. Before the analysis of which processes a company would like to develop, the first step should be the identification of key performance indexes (KPIs).

The agile methodology is one of the processes that many project managers highly advocate for and it can be combined with other approaches to ensure that the clients get the best. When agile project managers involve the Six Sigma methodologies in the development of processes, they usually have the option of choosing between process improvement or continuous development. Agility is inclined towards continuous development as part of ensuring success in its iterations. However, some companies can pick some strategies from process improvement and adopt them in the agile methodology if they deem them effective.

The continuous development methodology is applied where the project managers wish to instigate changes and it is considered to be much effective as well as easier. According to a Harvard review, the companies which implement continuous development benefit from:

a) *Faster marketing time.* Marketing time applies where the product in question is meant to be used by end customers which are the general public. Some software, such as websites is an example since they are often meant to be used by outsiders. Using the continuous development process ensures that marketing begins even before the final product is available, which means that people get an idea of what is being developed way before it is even implemented. Also, some applications undergo continuous improvements, evidenced by the constant updating that is generally done on most of them from time to time. Whenever a popular application such as WhatsApp requires one to update, that is a form of continuous development as the updates are meant to give the users access to more features and uses.

b) *Enables the running of more experiments.* Continuous development is effective since it gives the developers a chance to witness how people respond to certain changes. Sometimes, clients may not know how people are going to react to some changes. Therefore, they implement them briefly and based on the response given determine whether to keep the changes or discard them in entirety. To use the example of

WhatsApp updates, there was a time when there was serious outrage over the permanent status feature that can been replace with the temporary 24 hour feature. When the developers got wind of the outrage, they actually returned the initial feature ensuring that customers were satisfied. Using continuous development, the developers can actually run experiments and determine what is good for the general public.

c) *Fix errors faster*. Mistakes are imminent in any project. As much as the six sigma methodology aims at achieving least error rates, they are not able to fully eradicate such occurrences. Through the use of continuous development, the organizations are able to find the errors in each iteration quickly, which ensures that the end product is not ridden with errors.

d) *Maximizing employee productivity*. The continuous improvement methodology does not only target the end products but human labor as well. When the employees observe how much effort is made to the products, there is often a motivation that compels them to work even harder and becomes part of the causes of success.

Process improvement is defined as an effort directed to the identification of high-priority in projects and finding a way to mitigate all of the problems. Usually, process improvement uses a methodology known as Define, Measure, Analyze, Improve, and Control (DMAIC). The processes are as illustrated in figure 12.

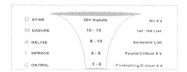

Figure 12: Illustration of the DMAIC process

In the define phase, project definition is achieved. This involves identifying all factors that pertain to the project and identification of all the requirements and client specifications. The define phase is followed by the measurement phase, which involves the collection of data and validation (lack thereof) of the existing performance. The third phase is the analyze period where the root causes 0f all the problems in the project are identified. Once identified, the improve phase ensues, which is governed by the creation of new solutions which are bound to help solve the situation. Lastly, the control phase follows and is characterized by the sustaining of new performance.

For the DMAIC process to be deemed as having been successful, the following characteristics must be imminent:

- The project must be manageable within the pre-set time frame.
- The project must align be aligned with the business goals and results.
- The customer requirements must be fully met.
- All issues met must be solved promptly by the management.
- The solutions implemented must be long-lasting.

Process improvement also ensures that the companies are able to effectively meet the changing market demands. Whenever the Six Sigma approach is implemented in agile projects, another key advantage that accrues is that the project managers are able to identify the process capabilities. The capabilities are usually defined by the baseline, entitlement, and process benchmark.

The process baseline is defined as the average long term level of performance when all the variables are running in a fashion that is unconstrained. The baseline, therefore, showcases how efficient the overall process is when there are no issues or hindrances to proper project execution. Process entitlement is slightly different from baseline since it analyzes the short term performance of a process in the case all of the variables are centered and controlled. The process benchmark usually entails the performance level of a process in comparison to the best performance possible. Therefore, this capability evaluates the current performance in comparison to a performance that is considered to be the best that was ever done.

Advantages of Six Sigma

To understand how Six Sigma will benefit agile project managers, it is worth evaluating the advantages that accrue to its usage on its own. As has been stated, the six sigma methodology is highly inclined towards ensuring zero defects on any of the processes. Therefore, processes and products are said to be in line with the Six Sigma when they do not contain defects outside of the customer specifications. The Six Sigma methodology works with two sub-methodologies; DMAIC (Define, Measure, Analyze, Improve, Control) for existing processes and DMADV (Define, Measure, Analyze, Define, Verify) for new processes. Some of the key benefits that accrue to the use of the methodology include;

1. Improvement in time management

The implementation of Six Sigma in organizations helps the employees to manage their time effectively. When time management in a company is improved, all the other processes are highly likely to fall in place since efficient and productive employees are capable of achieving more. Normally, the employees are usually asked to set smart goals and apply the principles of Six Sigma on them. To effectively set the goals, the participants look at three key areas: learning, performance, and fulfillment.

When it comes to learning, the employees are usually required to look at how efficiently they are able to sort their various tasks and the factors that hinder them from achieving the said tasks. For instance, the employees can evaluate how often they are interrupted and how often the interruptions mess with their ability to complete their daily tasks. When the employees identify such shortcomings, they can be able to learn about how to control such occurrences and prevent future disruptions.

Looking at performance, the employees are required to consider how their practices are helping them reach their professional goals or lack thereof. The creation of an action plans helps with such identification and the employees can be able to analyze where they spend most of their energy in and the resultant inferences. It is said that efficient employees are happier in the job environment since they derive satisfaction from achieving their goals and even setting up more. The better the performance, the more confident the employees

Finally, the evaluation of fulfillment is pivotal. The employees derive fulfillment from a multitude of factors, which range from working on a job that is their passion and being helpful in the said job environment. Having a work-life balance also results in fulfillment, and the employees are supposed to evaluate the extent to which they have been able to achieve the balance.

When the employees learn that the three key areas correlate, they can be able to plan their time efficiently so as to derive satisfaction from productivity. Also, work-life balance is achieved, and the employees are able to plan their time more efficiently to achieve it.

2. Improved customer loyalty

The aim of any business is to make profits and retain its clients. Project managers know the value of happy and satisfied clients as they are not only highly likely to involve them in future projects but are also more likely to refer them to other clients. When a business fosters a good working relationship with their clients, they are sure of customer loyalty, which is a pivotal measure of the success of any organization.

There are a number of reasons that may result in customer dissatisfaction and their lack of returning the business to a particular organization. The major cause of dissatisfaction is defective products, which do not meet the standards and requirements ordered by the clients. Also, the attitude that the organization and its team have towards the clients greatly determines their future interactions. When the clients are dissatisfied with the attitude given, they are seldom likely to give any other business to the team and would rather look for other developers.

Through the implementation of Six Sigma, the customers are put first. Therefore, all their needs, requirements, and demands are taken seriously, and the result is fewer complaining customers. Six Sigma ensures that the end product is as perfect as possible and there is no greater satisfaction to the client than providing them with output that exceeds their expectations. Also, since the methodology advocates for one-on-one interaction with the clients, there is a sense of respect, and the clients are sure that their needs are seriously taken into consideration. Ultimately, a perfect working relationship is fostered, and client loyalty is imminent.

3. Reduced Cycle Time

Deadlines are important in any project. Usually, the time-lines are set before the project begins and the project managers are charged with the responsibility to ensure that they conform to the set deadlines and an ideal situation is where the project managers work towards reducing the timelines. When the clients are presented with the final products before the set deadlines, they are likely to be more content and satisfied with the services.

Through the use of Six Sigma, the employees are given a chance to identify all of the factors that may result to the failure of adhering to the deadlines, enabling them to come up with ways through which such occurrences can be prevented. Six Sigma advise the employees to look at the factors which cause delays ranging from the departmental levels to the entire organizational level. Once identified, solutions can be recommended and the team will work towards reducing the prevalence of the problem. Whenever the companies actively pursue the problems that lead to the delays, they are often able to create shorter cycle times, which results in lower cycle times.

4. Employee Motivation

No businesses can prosper without its employees. As it is well known, it is the employees who take care of the clients and any of their actions can either lead to client satisfaction or lack thereof. Six Sigma realized that their success relies on the ability of their employees acting in the right way. Notably, sufficient motivation must be available for the employees to act right. Studies show that organizations, which fully engage the employees have continued to demonstrate an increase in productivity with a 25-50 percent increase.

Six Sigma has a myriad of tools and techniques that ensure that they achieve employee motivation as well as create an enabling environment for them. Some of the techniques range from involving them in all aspects of the project and giving them a voice. Whenever the employees feel valued, they are usually motivated to give their all. The results are evident in the performance where constant improvement is realized.

5. Strategic planning

Six Sigma is known for its ability to help in the various planning stages and strategies for a company. There are a number of planning techniques that can be used with the SWOT analysis being amongst the strategies, which are advocated for by the methodology. Usually, the identification of weaknesses and threats enables the team to be able to come up with mitigation strategies. The Six Sigma methodology can even help convert the shortcomings into strengths, consequently resulting in the development of a competitive advantage over all other competitors.

When we consider the advantages obtained from Six Sigma, it is clear that they are centered towards client satisfaction just like in agile project management. The advantages are to a very large degree similar to the principles of agile project management, and what the project managers strive to achieve. Therefore, there is evident synergy between agile and Six Sigma. The two are clear on their need to deliver more value as well as ensure that the processes are as efficient as possible. Usually, Six Sigma is inclined to the provision of significant and sustainable results with the major disadvantage being that it takes too long. On the other hand, agile is fast and effective, which means that integrating the two systems will help one make up for where the other lacks.

Disadvantages of Six Sigma

Despite the many advantages that the Six Sigma methodology has, there are also a number of shortcomings that must be considered by project managers. One of the major drawbacks of the methodology is that it has the potential to create immense bureaucracy and rigidity. The methodology attempts to take over all of the company processes, resulting in the imposition of stringent rules. Notably, since the methodology is mostly aimed to improve processes, it may be ineffective for companies which are more about relationships than the processes. Also, there may be some complications in the implementation of statistical and empirical data generated during the analysis and shift from other processes to Six Sigma. The processes can be quite complicated thus rendering them inefficient to project managers who do not have the arithmetic capabilities.

Evidently, the shortcomings of Six Sigma are immaterial and can be overcome easily. Therefore, the benefits outnumber the shortcomings by far; making the methodology credible and effective on a larger scale.

The best of the agile and Six Sigma methodologies has been combined to a single strategy, dubbed Agile Sigma. The development of Agile Sigma is quite recent as it began in 2016. The development and efficiency witnessed in the synergy is causing waves across different industries, and has continued being adopted throughout the world

Agile Sigma

Through the ease through which agile and Six Sigma complement each other, there is the development of the agile sigma concept. Basically, agile sigma combines all aspects of agile and Six Sigma that can coexist with each other and develops it into a single functioning methodology. The synergy between the two processes undoubtedly delivers more value to the users and results in long-lasting and sustainable results. Agile sigma is slowly finding its way in a number of industries and professional agile professionals continue to benefit from the synergy.

There are a number of benefits that accrue to project managers who implement agile sigma in their various work institutions. The major advantage is that the projects get to realize all the benefits of six sigma while they retain the delivery benefits of agile. With the combination of the two, the project managers benefit from:

1. Improved processes which result in faster delivery of the iterations.

2. Ensures that all decisions made are backed up with data, which affirms its authenticity.

3. Since all the tools and metrics are customer-centric, delighting the customers is achieved.

4. Ensures that the project managers get financial account-ability since all the actual benefits are in the books.

5. The method banks on the team's knowledge and skills to deliver the improvements more quickly.

Current studies show that the use of agile sigma can be monumental for a project than simply using agile or Six Sigma on their own. Figure 13 provides an illustration of how the different methodologies compare against each other.

Figure 13: Illustration of the widely used process method-

olologies and their attributes

Agile Sigma is ranked higher than any other of the processes. Most of the other methodologies lack in one or multiple functions while Agile Sigma performs in all of the KPIs. The closest to Agile Sigma is the Six Sigma, which apparently lacks in delivery speed compared to Agile Sigma. The cooperation is undoubtedly impressive and professional agile project managers can consider implementing the system so as to ensure that they can enjoy all the benefits that accrue to the users.

Phases of Agile sigma

Agile Sigma consists of a four-phase adaptation that is derived from the DMAIC process in Six Sigma and a multitude of other processes in agile project management. Figure 14 provides an overview of agile sigma.

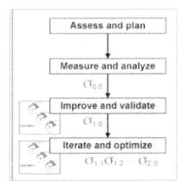

Figure 14: Illustration of constituents of Agile Sigma

As is illustrated, the four Agile Sigma phases are:

1. Assessing and planning

This phase involves the assessment of the current environment and effective planning for the project. To be considered to have achieved proper planning, the team needs to identify the problem, objective, scope of work, team, approach, and the timeline required to complete the project. Typically, Agile Sigma advocates for the use of a control plan in this process. Depending on the project and its complexity level, the control plan may include few or multiple items. Some of the basic constituents of the control plan are:

a) *The process flowchart.* A large number of control plans are inclusive of a visual illustration of the process workflow where the decision-making stages are highlighted. The flow-chart is considered to be a high-level process overview and allows easy references by the stakeholders.

b) *The process steps.* Some tasks are usually continuous, and there is a need to ensure that the team does them right. The control plan can include a reiteration of some of the steps for some processes, which allows for quick reference by the team members. For instance, in a car assembly company, there can be a control plan which outlines the order in which the machinery in the bonnet should be fixed. Inclusion of the process steps ensures that minimal mistakes are done.

c) *Specifications of some of the processes.* In any project, there are processes, steps, and equipment that must be properly specified. The plan must include the units of measurements to ensure that the team does not end up misconstruing some of the information. For example, "the tube must be 4 cm in diameter" is a specification and the team is obliged to follow it promptly.

d) *Standard operating procedures (SOPs).* Each process of performance in a project is governed by SOPs, which are mostly devised by government officials. Certain require-ments must be met for the project to be deemed as both legal and operating as it should. For instance, there are very clear guidelines about the disposal of waste and every team member must be privy of the specifications. Whenever any of the team members does not conform to the practices, there is often the possibility of legal action being imposed.

2. Measuring and analyzing

Measuring and analyzing involves the key output process metrics, which analyze the current productivity and estimate the future state processes. The measurement criterion differs in accordance with the specific projects. Some use duration in months, weeks or days. For others, the ideal period is as dictated by the stipulations of the project and its level of difficulty. With time analysis, the project managers are often interested in finding out where work was mostly spent. When the managers can be able to track the time, they are often able to gauge if the employees are operating at optimum capacity or whether further action needs to be taken to avoid wastage of time.

The determinant of the parameter used to carry out measuring is the actual values that are important in the project cost and cycle time as well as the working features to be delivered. There is often value in story points that can be seen, and the project managers often use them in the determination of the parameters used to measure performance.

Notably, time spent well should add value to the company. The team may spend time making efforts that may or may not yield to anything, unused work, excess processing or on any other activities. Scorecards should be developed to account for each minute spent as illustrated in figure 15.

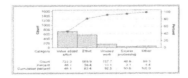

Figure 15: Illustration of an analysis of time spent in a company

As it has been discussed, Six Sigma aims at reducing defects to the minimum level possible. Therefore, most companies are known to use the level of defects as a measurement metric of the efficiency of the personnel and the processes set in place. The more the defects, the less efficient the processes are deemed to be and vice versa.

It is worth noting there is often a misconception of what the term "defects" refer to. To be clear, the defects refer to anything that may be unacceptably missing, wrong or extra when the project is handed over to the clients. In this case, the missing or wrong items are discovered and rectified before the project is handed to the client or customer, then the correct term is a mistake or error. Defects only occur when the mistakes and errors are not realized well on time and proceed to the final stage. The mistakes are usually realized by the clients or customers, which gives rise to the concept of defective goods.

3. Improving and validating

Improvement and validation consist of the use of the iterative sprint approach to enhance productivity and confirm the statistical significance of the improved processes. In order to determine how to improve productivity, there has to be a measure of the current productivity measures. There are a number of ways which can be used to measure productivity, which includes:

a) *Ideal time rate*. The measure uses the iteration process and experience to illustrate the way through which the ideal time actually worked as a percent of the calendar time. An increase in the ideal time rate showcases an improvement in efficiency while a decreased number can be a sign of wastage at an overall company level.

b) *Delivered features rate*. This scope measure evaluates the rate at which working completed features are delivered. Depending on the scorecard being used, the working features may be evaluated per iteration or per the completed project. Usually, the measures that are mostly used can range from velocity to the standard performance per day or per person. Clients usually care about velocity for the simple reason that it relates to what they get at the end of the day. When the standard performance per person is analyzed, the project managers are usually interested in the rate at which each person is contributing to the team efficiency as some people are known to drag others behind.

The two methods are not exhaustive and the project manager's view of Agile is different across different companies. In the development of the same, the goal is usually to ensure that the parameters considered have illustrated useful ways through which the agile projects can progress.

4. Iterating and optimizing

Iterations are the small divisions that make up a project. The iteration and optimization parameters largely deal with the team sizes and assessment of available resources and schedules. When the available team size and iteration length is combined with the analysis of the base productivity, the project managers can be able to tell the maximum capacity for the project to be scooped. Using this parameter ensures that the project managers can be able to establish the small pieces of work based on what they can see and actually accomplish it more effectively compared to the big bang methodology.

Agile Sigma Model

Agile Sigma model is also regarded as an important component of the synergy between the Six Sigma methodology and Agile project management. Figure 16 depicts the standard agile model whose use continues to grow in the project management environment.

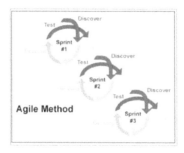

Figure 16: Illustration of the agile sigma model

As per the illustration, each iteration is handled independently. In each of the iterations, the design stage begins and is followed by the development stage which ultimately leads to the final test phase. In this case, when any defects are realized, the process begins again. The design is re-evaluated, development is re-done, and the test is undertaken again. This cycle continues until the project managers are convinced that the end process is perfected. Once the product is moved to the next iteration, the cycle begins all over until perfection ensues. The iterative process in Six Sigma plays a major role in improving overall process performance. Since each cycle has an identifying component which helps distinguish properly completed events from those which are not, the managers ensure that the products have a credibility aspect when the process is completed.

7

VALUABLE RESOURCES FOR AGILE PROFESSIONALS

C urrently, information about Agile project management can be obtained from multiple sources both online and in hard copy. In addition to the sources, there are also hundreds of companies and websites which exist to provide information and support for agile project management. As a professional, there is a need to ensure that the information obtained is genuine to prevent instances of misconceptions and misconstrued facts. Since you are no longer a beginner, the following resources will be fundamental in your further learning of agile project management and will ensure that you achieve undoubted success.

The Scrum Alliance

The scrum alliance is an organization that provides resources, education, and support to scrum enthusiast. As you know by now, scrum falls within the Agile methodology. The company is considered to be the biggest professional organization that involves membership in the agile community. The key role of the organization is to ensure that the participants have a clear understanding of Scrum and its usage and achieves this goal through the promotion of training and certification classes. The organization is not limited to a particular locality and is open to membership from all parts of the world. The fact that the company has its footprint on all materials ensures that people can learn in multiple ways either through its various websites and blog posts, which contain relevant information or through gatherings where the founders address potential scrum users on a personal level.

On the surface, the scrum alliance can be viewed as a mere organization which provides the education and training to the scrum and agile practitioners. Digging deeper, people often find that the scrum alliance is part of a movement and mindset, which makes it more than a study topic. The alliance enables the participants to change their approach towards project management in entirety, therefore ensuring that Agile users are on one track. Since the inception of the alliance in 2001, more than 750,000 scrum practitioners have been certified worldwide, a number which keeps growing annually. Users of the alliance assert that through the information and guidance offered, they have been able to create a workspace that is prosperous, joyful, and sustainable. To help achieve the breakthrough in the job environment, the scrum alliance strives to accomplish three key functions:

1. Inspiring the participants to adopt the agile mindset as they lead their various organizations. The organization ensures that the transformation is supported through the continuous training and sharing of change and innovation stories.
2. Enabling the participants to accomplish their needs through the creation of a global network of agile trainers and peers. The network allows the

participants to interact with each other and ask questions whenever they need any clarifications and guiding each other towards the successful implementation of Agile.

3. Guiding the participants through the transitioning process and helping affirm the knowledge that they have. The community of trainers and coaches focuses on providing knowledge, skills, and experience, which goes beyond what simply reading would achieve.

The scrum alliance undoubtedly provides the participants with pivotal information which enables them to deliver value to their clients. However, the prospective agile project managers need to ensure that they are indeed comfortable with revolutionizing their work environment and give up total control over the project. Amongst the guarantees that the agile alliance coaches promise the participants of the program is that:

1. They will benefit from a step by step analysis about how they can revolutionize their working environment by properly monitoring the projects and keeping tabs on the priorities and making sure that the clients get the best work done possible.

2. As a scrum expert, you will find it much easier to deliver the projects using the incremental strategy. Project management does not have to be difficult and confused, and scrum mastery helps simplify the process.

3. Your expertise in project management can be a huge asset for potential participants and you can even undertake the role of a tutor in addition to managing your projects.

4. Most importantly, being a member of the alliance

guarantees you total support from the tutors and you can access them directly at any time in the case of any help needed.

The Project Management Institute (PMI); Agile Community

The project management institute (PMI) is also amongst the largest non-profit project management associations, located in over 200 countries worldwide. As at 2018, the institute has an overall membership count of around 400,000 and continues to grow each year. The institute supports the agile community and seeks to establish a community of well-versed project managers worldwide. Many professional project managers confess that the information and knowledge provided by the institute was monumental in their fully understanding of APM, thus highly recommended if you want to move to the next level of agility.

According to the founders of the institute, all organizations need to understand how important and impactful the adaptability to APM is to the company's success. Whether the organizations in question are big or small, the effect of the decisions made remains the same. Signing up as a member of PMI allows you to learn how you can benefit your organization and help it embrace the opportunities, which will put in on the forefront to achieving transformation with minimal disruptions.

One of the key benefits of being a member of the PMI is that it seasons you to be a better manager through building up on the information that you already know. Before the tutors get into the learning process, they usually first take their time to identify what the participants really know about project management. The tutors assert that when each participant is asked what they know, their answers always differ. This means that each and every person analyzes the concept from their own viewpoint. The checklist that helps one identify if they are on the right track is if their ideas are in line with:

1. Effectiveness of communication
2. he facilitation of meetings
3. Documentation and management of the project tasks and schedules
4. Identification of potential risks and issues in the project environment
5. Management of the scope changes
6. Creation of a status report or dashboard

The more one works as a project manager, the more necessary it is for them to learn about the true nature of agile project management and how it can be achieved. The institute enables the managers to understand the nature of the work as well as the culture and structure of their different organizations. There is always the need to understand these aspects, so that the work to be performed is accomplished successfully.

One of the aspects which the Project Management Institute advocates for is learning all the areas of agility, so the participants can be well versed with all of their different options. Some of the areas which fall under the study topics are agile components such as scrum and Kanban, waterfall method in its different forms, and the Six Sigma method. The reason as to why it is important to learn about methodologies such as the waterfall method is because the project managers need to know what exactly those methods entail, so they can be able to compare them with the agile methodology.

Lawrence cooper, one of the members and senior contributors of agile project management concepts in the institute asserts that there is always something new that one learns in the course of their membership. In a recent member interaction whose topic was on the guiding principles for an adoptive organization, the members produced information that none of the professionals would have on their own. After many discussions, presentations, and analysis the guiding principles that were crafted were:

1. Acting with intent through the clear definition of priorities. The factors subject to review and adjustments must have the collaboration of members both within and outside of the organization.
2. The recognition that becoming an adaptive organization is not a one-time project, and that the company has to adapt it every day until it becomes a way of life.
3. Having a fully engaged and "clear the path" leadership.
4. Recognizing the shared values and principles which are necessary for any company to achieve its goals. Employees must always work towards achieving the same goals.
5. The recognition of the value of acting in relation to realizing true resilience and organizational sustainability.
6. Having a strong focus on the clients and engaging them directly.
7. Creating and promoting a fall-forward safe environment.
8. The provision of a collaborative workspace.
9. Recognizing that the organizational policies are monumental in the achievement of organizational outcomes.

The project management institute is therefore monumental when one wishes to establish themselves as a knowledgeable agile project manager. Meeting like-minded persons is an integral way of not only sharing knowledge, but also gaining insights and solutions whenever problems ensue. The institute also provides certifications, which are an illustration that the project managers are ready to meet the demands of projects and employees across the globe.

The International Consortium for Agile (ICAGILE)

ICAgile is another popular resource center for aspiring professional project managers, which enables people to become agile through awareness, education, and certification. The organization is an international consortium which collaborates with industry experts to define the learning objectives. The agency is currently known for its dedication in advancing the stage of agile learning throughout the world and ensuring that the participants are well on the path towards agile mastery. ICAgile recognizes that the Agile mindset is the game changer in project management. Therefore, the organization does not only seek to transform processes but the people as well. Agility begins with people, and processes can only be modified where the people have already changed their mindset. Through the consortium, a clear path is set for the professionals who intend to solidify their Agile journey.

To benefit from this professional body, the first step that is required is registration and booking of a class. Currently, this resourceful platform is largely available to people from the United States as only a US credit card payment option is allowed. After registration, a confirmation email is promptly sent, and one completes the registration of the classes. In this case, any confusion which may lead to the registration of the wrong classes, corrections can always be done. Notably, group registrations involving three or more people are always given discounts, making it beneficial to organizations which may wish to train more than one person.

Before the enrollment of any ICAgile, participants must always consider the prerequisites required to attend any of the courses. Since the course is divided into levels, the participants need to have passed in the preceding level to continue into the next one. The following summary shows what is taught at each level:

1. **Level one** targets beginners and people who may not be too well versed when it comes to agile project management. Therefore, the tutors focus on:

- Introduction to agile project management
- Agile foundations, tenets, and principles
- Agile experiences
- Agile team accelerator
- Introduction to Scrum and Kanban

2. **Level two** targets people with relative knowledge of APM and is meant to help them scale agile. The set includes a fully scaled agile framework, as well as an additional course that combines the considerations for a holistic organizational transformation. The level also focuses on:

- Leaders as agents of change,
- Teams and team roles
- Program and product management.

3. **Level three** focuses on leadership and business agility to enhance a company's competitive advantage. The key courses offered in regard to this level are:

- Agile project management for executives
- Managing in agile

- Agile leadership

Managing in agile and agile leadership may seem like the same thing, although they are totally different. Managing in agile is actually a one-day resource program that helps explore the fundamental aspects that leaders need to cultivate within their organizations to take hold of agile teams. The topics covered in agile management include ensuring customer focus, improvement of workflow, and rapid impediment removal. On the other hand, Agile leadership involves the changing of the leaders' mindset and approaches to ensure effective leading throughout the agile transformation. The topics of interest include organizational culture, stewarding change techniques, and growth of high-performance teams.

The third level is usually the last step and illustrates the highest level of knowledge achievement for the participants.

INFOQ

INFOQ consists of an independent community interacting online which has a robust agile section offering agile resources in the form of blogs, publications, books, and news flashes. The organization understands that people prefer different sources of information. While some people may find reading books fulfilling, others need more personal teaching practices such as conference meetings and even attending classes. Whichever mode of learning each person prefers, the company provides.

One of the resources that have received wide accolade is the "Agile adoption and transformation survival guide." This book was developed by one of the InfoQ leaders by an educator with the scrum alliance who has experience teaching on a worldwide basis. Reviews on the book are amazing with reputable leaders affirming that the information therein helped them significantly in transforming their work environments. The book focuses on reasons as to why Agile may fail even if the leaders have the knowledge, the proper agile culture, adoption of the transformational, and survival guide as well as how companies can achieve undoubted success. The book has been sold in all parts of the world and has even been translated in languages such as Spanish, Korean, German, and multiple other languages.

One of the major benefits of using the resource is that one is exposed to plenty of information from the different participants. Since the organization does not require anyone to pay for the services, the resource is quite cost friendly and thus beneficial for upcoming agile professionals.

Extreme Programming

Extreme programming is an agile software resource that aims to help with the production of even higher quality software. The methodology is specifically designed for software and information technology-oriented companies which want to follow the effective agile processes. The main goal of the methodology is to ensure that clients get the best value for their money, which conforms to the agile principles of putting the needs of the customers first. The first thing that extreme programming advise is the performance of a test-first strategy as well as code refactoring. The test first strategy test cases require the developers to write test cases before coding while the refactoring practices require constant evaluation and revision of the codes. When the system is adopted, there is often the reduction of cost of changes since any errors are identified early enough.

Agile project managers also learn the values of extreme planning whose efficacy has been proven in software companies. The values that the methodology trains and recommends are:

1. *Simplicity.* Extreme programming always asserts that less is more. Whatever is needed to be done should be done and nothing more. The developers must always strive to create value, and refrain from adding unnecessary functions in the project.
2. *Communication.* Agility is all about effective communication and teamwork. Everyone is part of the team and should be treated as such. Face-to-face communication is particularly highly advocated for since it allows the creation of a connection and a work environment where everybody is comfortable with each other.
3. *Feedback.* This is one of the values that may seem minor at face value but is very important. Since the Agile process is all about working in iterations, every team member must be kept in the know pertaining to the happenings in each of the iterations. This helps in the simplification of work since there is a clear flow of information. All team members must listen carefully to any of the feedback given so that no issue goes unnoticed.
4. *Respect.* This is also another underrated value which is monumental in any organization. Without respect, none of the team members can be able to work effectively with each other. In an Agile environment, respect goes a long way in ensuring that all the employees properly interact and work with each other.
5. *Courage.* The value of courage must be developed in every of the team members. There are many things that could go wrong, and the team members need to face them and tell the management the truth. Developing a system of honesty and transparency takes time, and the leaders must ensure that they

create an environment where the employees are not afraid to admit errors.

In addition to learning about the vital values, Agile project management enthusiasts also benefit from lessons about roles in the project. Extreme programming asserts that there are four key roles which are associated with agile excellence. The roles involve the following stakeholders:

1. The customer

The customers or clients are the owners of the project and they give out the specifications of how they want the project to develop as well as the constituents of the final product. The company teaches the project managers about listening to the client needs and ensuring that they identify:

- The functions of the systems and features which are included.
- How to know when the system is done.
- Amount of money that has to be spent.
- The next course of action.

Singe agility highly advocates for the involvement of all the stakeholders, the team is always advised to work hand in hand with the clients so that they can be able to effectively identify all issues and solve them. Usually, there is the assumption that the XP customer is a single person. However, where the project is complex, the team is advised to work with the entire group of the customer's management to enable the identification of a clearer picture of what they want.

2. The developer

The developers are ideally the people who are involved in the implementation of the project. Every person in the team is usually labeled as a developer and they are responsible for realizing all the stories identified by the customer. Since different projects require different sets of skills, the developers must provide the skills and complete the project as desired.

3. The trackers

Extreme programming teaches the importance of a tracker in the team and how to achieve the tracking process. A tracker is in most cases one of the developers who spend their time analyzing the extent to which the team is achieving their milestones. Different projects have different metrics used to analyze performance and the trackers take time to gauge performance in relation to the various parameters and indicate the results.

4. The coach

Extreme programming and its resultant methodology are not completely easy for professionals who have never used the system before. If the team is just getting started off to XP, it would be immensely helpful to include an external coach who would help in the smooth shift to the methodology. Since the coaches have full knowledge of all the processes, they can be able to help the managers go through them and help the team avoid mistakes that most new users make. Ultimately, the projects have a higher chance of becoming successful.

Platinum Edge

Planning edge is also an independent company that helps companies to maximize their organizational returns on investment. The company was formed as a result of the knowledge that there are numerous companies which begin projects with very high budgets and end up making losses.

Without proper management of resources and budgeting, losses are undoubtedly imminent. Therefore, this program has the major aim of ensuring that all project managers know how to effectively plan all aspects of their project and get a return on their investment.

Other services provided by a platinum edge are:

1. *Agile audits.* The auditing is done to the current organizational structure and processes
2. *Recruiting.* Without a properly skilled and efficient team, there can be no performance. The organization helps the human resource managers and agile professionals to identify the right people for various tasks to ensure that service delivery is safeguarded
3. *Training.* The organization also provides training to both the public and private entities. When the professionals reach a particular milestone, they are usually certified upon request.

8

AGILE PROJECT MANAGEMENT CERTIFICATION AND TRAINING

PMI-ACP

As an Agile project manager, you are always supposed to ensure that your Agile skills are excellent, so you are able to serve the company diligently. PMI-ACP offers a comprehensive certification program, which prepares practitioners for the different management levels in Agile companies. As at 2019, the program has eight certification programs, open to project managers in different levels. It is up to an individual project manager to choose which certification program they want to undertake, depending on their areas of specialty. The certifications offered are:

1. CAPM (Certified Associate in Project Management) certificate

2. PMI-ACP (PMI Agile Certified Practitioner) certificate

3. PfMP (Portfolio Management Professional) certificate

4. PMP (Project Management Professional) certificate

5. PMI-PBA (Professional in Business Analysis) certification

6. PgMP (Program Management Professional) certification

7. PMI-RMP (PMI Risk Management Professional) certification

8. PMI-SP (PMI scheduling professional) certification

All PMI certifications are based on the understanding that there is always the need for impartiality when awarding the certifications. Currently, the PMI certification is known for their global development and application abilities, which makes them transferable across industries as well as geographic borders. Therefore, when one receives the certification, they can use it even when they relocate to other countries. Before a participant is awarded the certification, they must prove beyond a reasonable doubt that they are competent enough to be awarded the certification. For this reason, the institutions take immense measures to ensure that the people awarded are deserving of the certifications. Therefore, the participants are exposed to tests and interviews to determine their proficiency. Therefore, any person with a certificate is a person who has proven beyond a reasonable doubt that they deserve it.

The qualifications of the participants are usually tested using three main measures:

1. *The review of their education and experience.* For the practitioners to be certified, education alone is not enough. The participants must have a track record of success in the actual project management environment. In most cases, the examiners may call the people listed as references to verify whether indeed the participants served in the leadership capacity and the extent to which they succeeded.

2. *Competency testing.* The candidates are required to illustrate knowledge of project management concepts through by applying them in their various capacities. To test the compe-

tency levels, the examiners do not rely on CVs and past work environments. Rather, they present the participants with questions about how they would handle certain scenarios. Depending on how the participants answer, the examiners can be able to tell whether they are qualified enough.

3. *Ongoing development*. The participants need to prove that they are in pursuit of constant development, often through the application of other certifications. In the case the participants fail in one certification, proof of ongoing development is obtained when they re-apply for the certification.

APMG International

APMG international collaborates with government and industry leaders to ensure excellent collaboration and standards among people. Currently, there continues to be an escalating demand for project managers. Many people can easily pass off as qualified project managers while in essence, they are not. The certifications and accreditations are what distinguish the professionals, and each serious project managers should strive to get at least one or two certifications.

Since the inception of APMG international in the early 1990s, the institution has established itself as a credible, reputable, and competent accreditation and certification organization. The organization owns a network of training organizations worldwide, which are responsible for accrediting training organizations and individuals. The fact that APMG is also ISO certified means that it has the authority to not only determine the programs and examinations that should be given for accreditation but also manage any of the programs worldwide. Through the mandate, the organization is known for its quest to guarantee that the accreditation is high quality and also ensure that all due processes are followed before any accreditation is given.

To get the APMG international accreditation, the participants have two options:

1. They can apply for the certification online and follow all the due processes illustrated on the online sites. The online sites mostly comprise of exams, and the professionals have to book and select the option that they feel best appeals to them. Typically, the participants usually have the option of undertaking a classroom-based education and exam or a home or office based exam.

Classroom-based exams are mostly offered by accredited training organizations. The participants may choose this option when they want to supplement the classroom-based training course. This means that the participants get to benefit from actual studies guided by professors before they take their exams. As much as this process may be a bit costly, it prepares the participants considerably by giving them a chance to learn some of the things which they never did as well as ensuring that they are well prepared for the exams. When the participants undertake the classroom-based exams, the results are usually immediate, and the project managers get to receive feedback on all the subjects they covered.

Home-based exams are monitored by software, known as the APMG remote proctor. This option is perfect for self-study students who are confident about the information and training that they have. The best thing about the home-based approach is that the participants are not limited to a particular location. Therefore, they can be able to sit for the exams at a preferred time and date.

2. Paper-based exam options. This conventional method is preferred by numerous training organizations since it results in more credible inferences. The paper-based exams are often offered at the end of a particular training period and

the participants are required to converge at a central point where they can take the examinations. In the exam period, the institution evaluates the location of all the students and comes up with a location which would be efficient for all the participants. The students can choose to either study on their own or undertake training from the institution. Once the exam is done, the institution uses a proficient exam-marking system to analyze the results of the candidates and give them the results.

As with any other examination, the institution has a certain pass mark that the students must attain in order to receive their relevant certifications. The company uses different parameters to establish the suitability of an organization to receive accreditation. When the companies are considered to have passed the required threshold, the accreditation is duly done.

International Consortium for Agile (ICAgile)

ICAgile is an independent global company that is recognized as an independent accreditation and certification body. The major focus of the body is accrediting Agile companies and individuals by ensuring that all the courses align with the learning objectives which are defined by the industry experts. To accredit deserving institutions and individuals, ICAgile runs a series of interviews, course reviews, and matrix assessment. Participants can get certification in three levels: professional, expert, and master in agility. To move to the higher ranks, the participants must start from the lower rank and work all the way to the expert rank.

Usually, the professional level is interested in the knowledge level that the participants have. This means that the participants must be able to describe and illustrate knowledge of some of the essential Agile project management concepts and principles. The expert level evaluates the participants competency, which involves knowledge beyond what they can simply put on paper. Experts can be able to apply the knowledge in real life projects and the examiners evaluate the extent to which the participants apply the concepts. Usually, aspiring participants can be required to submit proof of their competency by compiling a list of the projects that they have headed. In some instances, the examiners may give the participants hypothetical scenarios in the evaluation and determine their competency by analyzing how they respond to the problems. In addition to the proof of performance, the participants must also:

- Pass the standard evaluation which is competency-based.
- Receive credit for various learning objectives within a track.
- Demonstrate experience in their areas of specialization.

The master level evaluates proficiency, which is the level at which the participants can be able to even guide others to achieve success in the agile environment. To apply for the master certification, the participants are required to have a minimum of two expert-level certifications. Thereafter, the candidates are invited by an evaluation panel to demonstrate their mastery in their various discipline levels.

Agile Certification Institute

The agile certification institute is known to offer one of the best certifications in Agile as well as provide the highest standards for the implementation of the Agile methodology. The institute is considered to be amongst the best global professional accreditation bodies, which promotes the best in the agile standards. The programs are offered for individuals as well as professional bodies, enabling them to reach higher heights of excellence. The Agile certification institute is actually considered to be part of the few bodies which actually offer certification for most agile processes such as Scrum and Kanban, which makes it immensely popular amongst the agile project professionals. The Agile certification institute was founded in 2009 and is registered as an education institute since it teaches people the whole essence of agility and gives them the certifications when they pass.

Scaled Agile Academy Scrum Alliance

The Scaled Agile Academy is an alliance that is known to improve the competency of the five core competencies of the participants in Agile project management. The alliance enables organizations and participants to undertake the assessments meant to evaluate their efficiency in Agile project management. Just like all the other certification agencies, the awarding of the certificates is in line with the fulfillment of the requirements outlaid by the agency. In this case, being a recognized scrum certificate holder entails the understanding of scrum as a subunit of agile project management. The academy not only provides the examinations meant to test the participants but also offers training opportunities to enthusiasts. Currently, the academy provides the services worldwide through the use of online education as well as individually taking the participants through the program. The institution is credible and highly acclaimed, and its certification can be used all over the world.

CONCLUSION

It is evident that Agile project management continues to have a positive impact on the users regardless of the industry that they are in. Currently, almost all industries whose job functions can be divided into iterations are adopting the system, ranging from the engineering, construction, education, and the medical sectors. Once a project manager gets to know all details that pertain to agility and the Agile project management, it becomes easy to implement the system in their various industries. For professionals, Agile project management is not merely a practice. The professionals take the knowledge a step further by adding relevant certifications and accreditations, to become recognized and fully fledged agile project managers and educators. Undoubtedly, agile project management will continue to be the remedy that most projects seek, and the management can be sure of success once they implement the systems.

REFERENCES

Agile Modeling with Mind Map and UML. (2019). Retrieved from https://www.stickyminds.com/article/agile-modeling-mind-map-and-uml

Atkinson, R., Crawford, L., & Ward, S. (2006). Fundamental uncertainties in projects and the scope of project management. *International Journal of Project Management, 24*(8), 687-698.

Atlassian agile coach. (2019). Epics, Stories, Themes, and Initiatives. *Atlassian*. Retrieved from https://www.atlassian.com/agile/project-management/epics-stories-themes

Atlassian agile coach. (2019). The product backlog: your ultimate to-do list. *Atlassian*. Retrieved from https://www.atlassian.com/agile/scrum/backlogs

Dart, R. C., Surratt, H. L., Cicero, T. J., Parrino, M. W., Severtson, S. G., Bucher-Bartelson, B., & Green, J. L. (2015). Trends in opioid analgesic abuse and mortality in the United States. *New England Journal of Medicine, 372*(3), 241-248. doi: 10.1056/NEJMsa1406143

Gaffney, T. (2019). Introducing Agile Sigma. *iSixSigma*. Retrieved from https://www.isixsigma.com/methodology/lean-methodology/introducing-agile-sigma/

Ilieva, S., Ivanov, P., & Stefanova, E. (2004, August). Analyses of an agile methodology implementation. In Proceedings. 30th Euromicro Conference, 2004. (pp. 326-333). IEEE.

Ji, F., & Sedano, T. (2011, May). Comparing extreme programming and Waterfall project results. In *2011 24th IEEE-CS Conference on Software Engineering Education and Training (CSEE&T)* (pp. 482-486). IEEE.

OKR - The Ultimate Guide to Objectives and Key Results. (2019). Retrieved from https://www.perdoo.com/okr/

Williams, S. J. (2017). Improving Healthcare Operations: The application of Lean, Agile and Leagility in care pathway design. Springer.

AGILE PROJECT MANAGEMENT

THE ULTIMATE ADVANCED GUIDE TO
LEARN AGILE PROJECT MANAGEMENT
WITH KANBAN & SCRUM

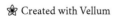 Created with Vellum

INTRODUCTION

The management process is complex. As a manager, it is your responsibility to make effective plans and decisions, organize your resources and projects, lead the execution of activities, and control the process of multiple projects. An error in any of the responsibilities creates a domino effect, toppling all the hard work you have put into your actions and setting you back.

This applies to all forms of management, including project management. It is a tricky matter to try and keep all components of a project integrated and functioning cohesively to reach a specific goal. Projects are like complex puzzles, moving at the right time and ensuring that all participants have made their best contributions. Of course, the technical aspects of project management are rather well defined. You have budgets, risks, tasks, dependencies, and methods, which are some of the components you will be working with. But in order to take a project from start to finish, the manager has to venture beyond the obvious. The manager has to step into the realm of business objectives, human resource management, technology, and various project management techniques. Without having a holistic approach, the project manager will merely be ticking off invisible boxes for tasks without understanding what should be done about the project.

Project management is a business landscape littered with unknown variables that include the demands of the upper management, customers, teams, and the objectives of the project itself.

It seems that project management is a rather complicated subject.

This is why the field of project management underwent some radical and profound changes. Most importantly, agile methodologies began to be adopted on a wider scale. As these changes were expanded upon, they began to dramatically alter the role project managers held in an organization. No more were project managers simply the people who managed a project. Their contributions were recognized to a point where the bar was raised for the very profession of project management.

Project management became such an extensive field of expertise that we now have courses and certificates to impart knowledge and understanding of the field to people. Even Harvard has a special certification course for it (Harvard Division of Continuing Education, n.d.).

While there are many approaches involved in project management, agile is changing the way people think and work, with many applications and in numerous industries. Some of the biggest impacts of agile can be seen in the information technology and software development industries, but one can never say that other industries are devoid of any impacts. The benefit of agile is that it is an adaptive approach to project management.

As the importance of agile grows, it is going to even more dramatically affect the role of project managers, where it might even eliminate the necessity to have certain project managers. This is not because these project managers do not have the skills or experience for the job. Rather, the work in itself might become streamlined to a point where the need for multiple project managers might become obsolete.

The most important thing to note is that agile is not a hype or fad. It is not a process that people are going to adopt for a temporary period and discard in time. People are capable of innovating agile and improving upon it to make it relevant for various scenarios.

With the way projects are being carried out, one can see how relevant agile is today and will be tomorrow.

It is time for us to delve deeper into this methodology and understand it on a deeper level.

Welcome to the world of agile project management.

1

UNDERSTANDING AGILE

O rganizations have come to an understanding that there are more reasons to adopt agile. According to the State of Agile Survey published on May 7, 2019, 71% of organizations who have adopted agile have done so because of its cost reduction techniques (State of Agile, 2019). The same survey also indicates that of all the organizations that have adopted agile, over 92% have reported that their agile projects have been truly successful. More than half the organizations using agile have reported that all the agile projects that they have ever implemented have been successful.

These statistics show something remarkable. They are an indication that agile has not just been improving, but more and more organizations have adopted it for their goals.

However, in order to explore the world of agile, it is important to understand how it reached this point. For that, a little lesson in history.

Early History of Agile

Despite the fact that agile has gained unprecedented levels of popularity, it was not an overnight success story. Rather, our agile had humble beginnings, almost like a rags to riches story.

You would be surprised to know that agile started nearly 20 years ago, establishing its roots when there were increasing frustrations at frequent project failures. Organizations discovered that not only were these failures setting them back months, and sometimes years, but that they were proving to be extremely costly and time consuming. Often, older teams had to be replaced with better ones, but the prospect of getting the new teams up to speed with the projects was an exhausting venture. Not to mention the lengthy delays they had to bear with before they could even notice a modicum of improvement.

Agile project management is truly unique. But that does not become obvious at first glance. In fact, if you too casually glance at its workings, then you might notice the usual suspects: budgets, goals, timescales, and teams. However, experienced project managers might reveal more as they explore and utilize agile. Sure, the idea of reaching the desti-nation is the same. The difference is that by using agile, the *how* becomes important because now, you are able to achieve your goals with a lot more satisfying results and fewer dents in your wallet. In other words, you save a lot more capital.

Here is a misconception: people think that before agile, projects were late and unsuccessful. That is not the case. Projects were delivered well and with varying degrees of success even before the introduction of agile. To think other-wise is hubris. However, the need for agile arose because there were far too many projects that would cross the budget, produce unacceptable results, and be delivered later than the projected time. And as we know, all of the aforementioned problems only lead to increased expenses and dissatisfied clients.

During the 1990s, software developers and personal computing (PC) manufacturers faced a crisis. Industry experts had named it "the application development crisis." According to them, the time it takes to translate a business need to production application was three years. This meant that when a business decided that it needed to include some new changes in processes, technologies, and teams related to the process of production, it would take nearly three years to implement them entirely. So why was that a problem?

The problem was that businesses were moving faster. You might notice this in today's world, where changes are almost instantaneous in organizations. Innovations, expansions, and growth are occurring almost every month. But even back then, changes were occurring rather quickly, and business systems, requirements, and teams were changing rapidly. In fact, in three years, entire businesses were likely to change. Because of growing technology, businesses would even change their business models. In some cases, not changing business models meant that the business could suffer in the long-term. Take the case of Kodak for example. The company was a leader in film-based cameras. When the digital camera revolution took place, they failed to adapt and lost their leadership position.

In other industries, the delays were far longer. The aerospace and defense industries could suffer a lag of 20 years before a complex system could actually be put to use. One such example was the Space Shuttle Program. Even though it was launched in 1982, it was using technologies from the 1960s.

The Growing Frustration

It was during the 1990s that Jon Kern, an aerospace engineer, became increasingly frustrated with the lead times taken by the organization. A lead time is the period between the initiation of a business process and its execution. In other words, it tells us how long it takes for a business or organization to form a need and then transform that need into the right process or technology. His focus was on the software industry, and he wanted to develop software without using the techniques of the time, as they were slowing down the development changes. It was not unusual at that time for IT companies to develop something and as the project was reaching its peak status, abandon it entirely with little or no tangible result delivered. This would cost the companies millions of dollars, but they would not think twice about the losses because what they would eventually develop would cover their costs. It was in the year 2001 that things began to crank up. Technology was moving at a faster pace. Software companies had to constantly innovate. This time, they could not afford to incur losses because they were usually handling multiple projects with increasing complexities. If they lose, they would not be able to recover from the loss. In fact, they would not even have the required capital to move forward to the production phase.

Because of this, 17 independent software thought leaders, including Jon Kern, came together at the Snowbird resort in Utah to focus on software development methods. Their conclusions were published in the *Manifesto for Agile Software Development*.

At that time, agile was mainly introduced to software industries and in some cases, automotive industries, since they had to develop their own software to improve the manufacturing of vehicles. Pretty soon, this software would become even more useful since cars began to come with numerous software components.

When it was first introduced, it worked well with software development. Eventually, people began to ask an important question: if it can improve processes in the software industry, can it also bring the same improvements to other businesses? Can it be used widely?

The short answer is yes. But to understand everything, we might have to travel back in time to the 1970s.

The Waterfall Model

It might seem rather unorthodox, talking about project management in the 1990s and suddenly shifting our focus to the 70s, but there is a reason for that.

Dr. Winston Royce introduced the Waterfall Model in 1970. It was the first Process Model created, and its advantage is in its simplicity. In the model, a project is divided into a set of phases. Each phase follows a sequence, which means that one cannot move on to the next phase without completing the previous one. This ensures that there is no overlapping of phases.

The Waterfall Model was also a type of software development process. When one completes a phase, the end result becomes the input for the next phase. This ensures that each phase is dependent on the previous one, save for the first phase of the process. Since the model has a linear sequence to follow, it is often known as the Linear-Sequential Life Cycle Model. The sequence it follows is given below:

Requirements
↓
System Design
↓
Implementation
↓

Integration and Testing
↓
Deployment of System
↓
Maintenance

Let us examine each of the phases in the above sequence.

Requirements

In the first phase, you understand the design of the software and the function, purpose, features, and other important components of that design. You are trying to put yourself into the shoes of the user and answer the question, "Why would someone require this software?"

In this phase, you study the features and specifications in detail. You try to visualize how the final product looks and works. At the same time, you also look into all the resources that you will need for this phase.

System Design

Once the requirements have been established, you study them along with the specifications to create the system design.

A system design is useful to prepare the hardware and software components that will be useful for the final product. You can also map out the overall system architecture in this phase. This phase can be used to create the software code, but you won't write the code until the next phase.

Implementation

In this phase, you create the system in small programs called units. All of the units that you develop here are tested to ensure that they can complement the overall structure of the system. This testing process is also known as Unit Testing.

The units won't be integrated together until the next phase. Which is why it is important to look into each unit, test for any problems or issues, and correct them immediately.

Since you will be developing the system in units, you can sometimes ensure that if one unit fails, then it won't impact the other units unless they are both interrelated to a high degree.

Integration and Testing

Once all the required units are created, they are then integrated into the system. The units are also tested once again to ensure their functionality is smooth before the integration process. After integrating the units, they once again go through another phase of testing in order to make sure that the units function well together.

To understand the above point, let's try and take an example of your favorite Operating System (OS), such as the ones for Windows or Mac. Now imagine that you are part of the OS development team and together, you have created various components of a new version of the OS. Everything seems to be going well. Let us filter through all those units and pick one for the sake of this example. We are going to start looking at a Word processing software that has been improved for the OS. As an individual component, there do not seem to be any problems with the Word processor. But as soon as you integrate it with the OS, you realize that the processor starts behaving erratically. Sometimes, you are unable to open the software itself. This error might not appear during your first integrated trial, but might occur in consecutive trials, making you believe that the software actually functions well when opened initially, but then encounters a bug in consecutive launches.

In such ways, you try and eliminate any errors that might creep into the final product.

Deployment of System

You have performed the functional – as well as the non-functional – tests. The time has come for you to release the product in the consumer environment or in a particular market.

Maintenance

This step takes place after deploying the product and involves making changes to the entire system or to an individual component. These modifications occur due to changes requested by the user, updates that you would like to add to the system to add more benefits, or because the system has encountered errors that you would like to fix. Usually, the owner of the software provides regular maintenance. You might have noticed this in the form of "software updates" on your mobile device, computer, or other electronic devices that use software.

So why exactly is the entire process called the "Waterfall Model"?

Since each phase has to be completed before moving on to the next, and the fact that the end of a phase is the beginning of the next means that one phase cascades onto the next. This cascading effect creates the idea of a steady flow of actions from one phase to the other. As depicted by the flowchart created earlier, the actions flow down the process, creating a waterfall-like scenario.

The method was easy to manage because each phase comes with its own set of deliverables. You can also create a special review section at the end of the phase to ensure that you have covered all the necessary steps in the creation of your software. Additionally, the Waterfall Method also gives you the power of departmentalization, which is the process of grouping tasks, activities, and objectives into various departments. You can set up a schedule and impose deadlines to make sure that everything is completed as per your preferences before a certain time. Because you avoid overlapping processes, you can make sure that complete focus is paid to a process without being distracted by other requirements.

On the flipside, the method makes it difficult to estimate the cost and time for each phase. Additionally, because of the focus on individual phases, it becomes difficult to backtrack the work to an earlier phase. This means that if you have brought the application to the testing phase and you come up with another idea that might have to go through the requirements phase, then you are not able to revert the process back to an earlier stage to accommodate the new idea without overspending on time, resources, and effort. Your only options are to either risk the costs to try out the new idea, which may or may not fit your software since it hasn't properly gone through the System Design phase, or to completely scrap the project and start over again. This is why this method is not suitable for projects that are constantly changing.

While the Waterfall Method spawned the inspiration for other methods that focused on incremental developments in processes, it did not directly inspire the agile system. It is for this reason that often, when you look through the history of agile, you find that it starts with Jon Kern and his software thought leaders.

In fact, it is a common belief that agile is a counter to the Waterfall Method. This is because agile is not as rigid as Waterfall, where one has to gather the requirements before the actual work begins or to deliver the project as a whole when all the phases are completed. Agile brings in more flexibility to the project, which we shall see as we understand agile further and dive into its workings.

Agile Manifesto, Values, and Principles

Time to head back to agile and look at an important component of its development: the Agile Manifesto.

When you look through the initial manifesto, then you will easily notice that the principles the creators laid down were specifically meant for the software industry.

Their first principle mentions that the method's highest priority is to ensure the satisfaction of the customers through the constant deployment of valuable software. The principle itself includes the phrase "valuable software." Yet try and apply that to a production process from another industry. Let's take an automotive industry for example. Isn't the aim of an automotive industry to make sure that the customer's satisfaction is a valuable component of the production process? Sure, they don't deploy software, but try replacing the word 'software' with 'car' and the principle still makes sense. Sure, you may not have to include the word valuable since the term is relative to a person's taste and preferences. However, if you look at the meaning of the principle, then you might find out that it actually applies to any industry.

To better understand why it is applicable anywhere, let us also look at some of the other principles.

Principle #2: You have to be open to the idea that requirements might change, even later during the development stages. Agile processes take advantage of changes, instead of shunning them, in order to create a competitive edge.

Principle #3: Make sure that you deliver software frequently.

How frequent you would like it to be depends on you. You could release software every few weeks to every few months. But you should ideally be looking at the shorter timeframe.

Principle #4: Developers and business people should work together during the project.

As you look at the principles above, remove their software-centric approach and try to understand their underlying philosophy. If you do that, you might realize that they apply to practically any industry. Let's see if we can figure them out together.

If you take Principle #2, then you know that changes are inevitable. As you are developing a product, you might often become aware of a new technology that could give you an advantage. But since you are already in the middle of product development, what do you do? The answer? You adapt. You try to figure out how you can incorporate the new technology into your product so that it can be used by your consumers. As you are developing your product, you might often realize that there is a way you can innovate it even further. You should ideally try to look for ways to incorporate that innovation, rather than keep it for a future product when it might be too late.

Principle #3 holds a lot of truth in today's world. Why do you think car manufacturers are shelling out new models of cars frequently? Why are clothing brands always bringing out new designs? Mobile phone manufacturers are practically creating a new model every 6 months. Brands and businesses are constantly creating new products. They know that if they stop bringing out something new, then they are going to be easily overtaken by the competition.

Principle #4 is fairly obvious. In any organization, the business part of the organization should work in a cohesive manner with the production part. That means that the marketing, sales, and manufacturing teams should act as cogs in a big machine. If even one part stops functioning, then the entire machine stops working.

In such ways, each of the principles applies to practically any organization. But what about the values?

Values of Agile

In order to compliment the Manifesto, a set of values were also released. These values were collectively called "Declaration of Interdependence" (and no, I am not making that up). The name of the values is rather creative, but it's the contents that are even more important.

There are a total of six values, and they are:

- Companies should focus on the continuous addition of value in order to increase their return on investment.
- The results delivered should be done by engaging with customers through frequent interactions.
- Uncertainties always arise. They should not be avoided. Rather, one should be prepared to go through the development process with the mindset that they are going to face unexpected challenges along the way.
- In order to unleash innovation and creativity, one should realize that it is the individuals who are the greatest source of value. Therefore, the organization or business should create an environment where individuals feel like they can contribute to the organization's growth and make a difference.
- One should boost performance by making certain that the entire group is accountable for results.

Responsibilities should also be shared in order to encourage effectiveness among the teams.

- It is important to improve reliability and effectiveness based on the situation. Each situation should have its own set of practices, processes, and strategies.

If I had not mentioned that the above values were for software-based industries, then you might have thought that they could be universally applicable for almost any industry. And there lies the adaptable nature of the principles and values established by agile. Just look at the above statements and you can distill them into the below points:

- Increase return on investment
- Improve reliability
- Expect uncertainty
- Release innovation and creativity
- Boost performance
- Enhance reliability and effectiveness

By breaking down the values, you now have a list that you can use for your business or organization, regardless of what industry you are part of. This is what made agile spread in popularity. People began to notice that they could incorporate its ideas into their businesses, even if they were not solely focused on developing software.

An Overview of Scrum

As agile grew in popularity, so did the idea of creating unique frameworks that can be used to adapt to a particular organization. While there are many options for agile frameworks, we are going to be focusing on two of the favorites among organizations, scrum and Kanban.

Let's first examine scrum.

We have to get this out of the way; scrum is like the darling of all the agile frameworks. If scrum was the rogue software Skynet from the Terminator series that takes over the entire world, then we would be in terrible danger. Thankfully, scrum does not have any malevolent principles or values.

So, what exactly is scrum?

As mentioned earlier, scrum is a framework. What it does is help businesses and organizations manage product development. The entire framework is empirical, meaning that you are using evidence-based methodologies to figure out what works, what doesn't, and what kind of innovations you should be looking for. One can also make use of the methodologies to make adjustments to existing projects. One of the best scenarios to make use of scrum is when an organization has a cross-functional team working on the development process.

What makes scrum ideal for a lot of organizations is the list of values that it encourages team members to follow. These values are:

Commitment

Team members have to personally commit to the achievement of goals and objectives.

Courage

Nobody shirks awake from a tough problem. If something seems intimidating, then they can make use of the assistance of other team members to solve the problem.

Focus

Concentrate on the work that has been identified for the entire team while achieving the best possible results in each individual endeavor. This value focuses on a strong relationship between individuality and synergy.

Openness

Team members are open about the tasks that they are doing, the challenges they are facing, and other important factors of the project.

Respect

Nobody gets to think that they are above anybody else. It is important that people respect each other and treat each other as equals.

What scrum does best is take the Waterfall idea and turn it on its head. When you are working with Waterfall, you are using a phase-based method for each and every project you undertake. Let's say that you have launched a product and you are thinking of an update in the near future. If you are using Waterfall, then you know that the entire process is going to be time consuming. However, scrum has a solution for that. On the other hand, scrum breaks down the features and delivers them in parts over a period of time. It takes large and complex work and breaks it down into simple pieces. It transforms large organizations into small teams and projects that are far-reaching and massive into short-timed milestones called sprints.

By allowing organizations to build their products and offerings incrementally, scrum allows them to bring out the products to the customers quickly. At the same time, they listen to customer feedback and incorporate it into the development cycles. This allows organizations to shape the results of their project based on real-world feedback and use, rather than focus on assumptions.

Self-organizing Teams

Scrum pays attention to the concept of self-organizing teams. This concept is based on two ideas:

- The teams are self-starting. It is not necessary to hold their hands and show them the way. They know what they have to do.
- They are self-governing. They get the job done and make sure that all of the members of the team are focused and driven. The team, as a whole, is also able to solve any problems or conflicts that might arise during the development stage.

There are three major roles in a scrum team – Product Owner, Scrum Master, and Development Team. Each of the three roles is created in order to ensure that team members are able to work cohesively and seamlessly without getting in each other's way. At the same time, the team is flexible and adaptable.

Benefits of Scrum

Scrum has been proven to provide a lot of benefits to organizations.

Better Quality

If you think about the main directive of a project, then you might realize that it is to achieve a specific goal. In most cases, people forget that doing things efficiently and achieving those goals does not matter if you have created a product that is subpar in quality. This is where Scrum comes in. Its framework allows for constant feedback and real-world exposure to dictate the changes that a project needs to make. This removes the idea of guesswork from the process and helps organizations achieve high-quality results.

Decreased Time to Market

Because scrum focuses on developing products incrementally, it helps the team deliver value to the user up to 40 percent faster than traditional methods. This means that teams are not only able to deliver good-quality products, but they are able to do it faster.

High Return on Investment

A happy customer is a happy organization. With the value that scrum offers and the speed at which it delivers, organizations are able to capitalize on their results and increase their return on investments.

High Team Morale

Team members who are happy with their work are highly productive. Most organizations search for many ways to bring about a sense of happiness among their employees. Scrum delivers that happiness. This is because scrum takes the decision-making power from the manager and places it into the hands of the team members. This gives the team members a greater degree of flexibility, and they are not bogged down by lengthy managerial processes. Teams also feel more in control and enjoy more freedom in their work. All of this boosts member morale, which eventually results in a happier and more satisfied workforce.

Agile Planning and Requirements

One of the biggest differences between agile and other traditional forms of project management methods takes place in the planning phase. There is a widespread opinion that agile does not require any planning. That is a misconception. Agile does require planning. The reason for thinking otherwise is because planning is done quite differently in agile. A technique known as rolling-wave planning is utilized.

What is Rolling-wave Planning?

In a traditional form of project management, team members and participants approach the planning phase prior to the commencement of the project. For agile, we disperse with traditional approaches. We defer the planning phase to what people in the professional world call "the last responsible moment." This moment refers to the latest time that a plan or a decision can be made without affecting the results of the entire project.

How does one work with the rolling-wave plan?

- You start the project with a high-level decision or plan that will at least establish the scope, objectives, and vision of the project. The level of detail required is enough to ensure the estimation and planning at that point in the project.
- Any further details of the plan are highlighted as progress is made in the project.

But you might wonder, isn't it better to get the planning and strategizing processes out of the way well before the beginning of the project? The problem with that scenario is that it involves a lot of speculation and guesswork. Quite often, teams end up speculating incorrectly, which results in efforts being wasted and copious amounts of time spent on re-planning in order to adjust to the changes. Additionally, it might also require teams to waste time and effort on changing various aspects of the work itself because of new planning decisions. When one defers the planning phase for as long as necessary, then they will be in possession of more information, which will help them make more effective decisions. At such points in time, there will be a drop in reliance on speculation.

The surprising part about all this is that rolling-wave planning has been in existence since prior to the introduction of agile. However, it was not widely used due to the popularity of Waterfall-based methods.

Managing Uncertainties

The reason for planning is that it mitigates uncertainties that might crop up in projects. When organizations or teams plan, they try to clearly define the requirements and goals of the project so that members are able to have a direction to follow in uncertain times.

If you think about it, then you might be inclined to adopt the Waterfall Method for your projects. After all, isn't it better to simply get the planning out of the way so that you are better prepared for the future? That is a reasonable way of thinking, but sadly, it does not apply to all projects.

When you have a project with high levels of uncertainty, then planning in advance is going to be folly. This is because you end up making a huge number of assumptions about the project which are, at best, questionable. You do not have enough information and your decisions from the planning phase might guide the team in the wrong direction or cause undue harm to the project. A considerable amount of time and effort might be spent on correcting or backtracking actions. In many cases, you might end up making decisions that lock you into a particular course, where the only alternative available is for you to scrap the project and start all over again.

So how does one use the rolling-wave process? Here is how it is done.

You first focus on the project-level. Here, you forego any attention to the minute details of the project. If you think about them, then you might end up making guesswork. You try to create a plan that helps you understand the overall scope of the project and the direction you would like it to take. You simply need a high-level understanding of the objectives and requirements of the project.

Once the project is underway, you enter into the "release-level." At this level, you are taking care of all the little details that are important for the completion of the project. You need to be a little more accurate in your decision-making at this point. But rather than make plans immediately, you should try to delay the planning process for as long as possible so that you have a lot of information. When you have enough information, you reduce the degree of guess-work you have to make.

Finally, you reach the sprint level. As we learned earlier, sprints are individual components of a large project. You deliver the project in parts, with improvements being released in successive parts based on customer feedback and your own research into the product. At the sprint level, you need to be concerned about two factors:

- The team needs to be informed about the estimated level of time and effort for a particular set of requirements so that they can conclude if the requirements can fit into the sprint. Based on the information received, they can modify the requirements as and when necessary.
- The team should ensure that they do not take any requirements into a sprint if those requirements have high degrees of uncertainty or too many issues. These uncertainties or issues could block or hinder the development process.

Even at the sprint level, you don't have to focus on making plans beforehand. Many of the details that you need in order to implement the requirements can be worked out as you or the team work on the sprint. This won't cause any significant impact on the estimates established for the particular sprint.

Agile Requirements

From planning, we move on to the requirements of agile. In numerous projects, organizations often involve a business analyst. This is because an analyst plays an important role in coordinating with the customers and users while also working on any essential documentation required before you or your team enter the development phase. However, one should note that agile encourages face-to-face or direct communication between the project team and the users or customers. It allows teams to understand what is required of them and their projects. In which case, it is not always necessary for you to actually have a business analyst, but you can, should you choose to provide extra help to the teams or in certain circumstances. What are these circumstances? Let's find out.

Ideally, you won't require a business analyst, but things don't always turn out the way we want them to. Sometimes, an extra pair (or more) of hands greatly helps quicken the project. Usually, the product owner is directly responsible for communication and defining requirements to teams in the form of user experience and stories. In some cases, such as the ones mentioned below, that may not be a viable option.

- In certain large projects, the workload and responsibilities of the product owner could be numerous. In such cases, he or she might not be able to handle all the tasks provided to him. When that happens, productivity might decrease. Your best course of action would be to bring in a business analyst.

- Not all projects are easy. In fact, it is safe to assume that most projects are complex in nature. It would be prudent to gauge the complexity of your project and then decide whether you would like to bring in a business analyst. Try to examine your budget and overheads so that you can make an informed decision. After all, adding more people results in an increase in expenditure.

When choosing a business analyst, make sure that you are aware of the points below:

- Do not allow the business analyst to take over all the responsibilities of an intermediary all the time. This might isolate the product owner from the business team and the team from the end-users or customers. You need to encourage direct communication between the product owner, team members, and users.
- The business analyst should be effective in improving communication and should not impede proper communication between various entities.
- Analyze areas that are broadly defined and then help the product owner define high-level communications and objectives. This will help the entire project team form a value-driven and well-organized framework to ensure that the required level of value is inserted into the project.
- Write down individual user feedback in a way that is easy to understand by the project team. They can then use the feedback to implement and understand project goals.
- Work with the product owner to integrate various requirements that might come from the stakeholders. This allows the project team to produce a solution

that not only caters to the needs of the users but also the requirements of the stakeholders.

Wants and Needs

One of the things that you can do while creating the requirements for an agile project is to clearly differentiate the wants from the needs. Often, people seem to substitute one word with the other, but each has its purpose.

- Wants are connected to the feature or specification that the user or client expects from the product.
- Needs are solutions to a particular problem.

Let's try and explain the above with the help of a problem. You have a customer who walks into an electronics store. He is looking to purchase a new mobile phone which has a high storage space, excellent speed, and an incredible camera. In this scenario, the desire to purchase the mobile phone is the need since it is going to solve a problem that the customer has. On the other hand, the storage space, speed, and camera features are wants that the customer looks for in the product. How can you be certain what is the want and what is categorized as a need? Break down all the components and see which one the customer is mainly choosing to buy. For example, in the mobile phone example that I just presented to you, you can split the storage space, speed, camera, and phone into four individual products. If you offer only the storage space, the customer would not be interested in making a purchase. Since if that were the case, he would be looking for a hard drive or memory storage device. Similarly, he is definitely not looking for hardware speed or camera. His main intention is to get a mobile phone. The others are features that he would like the mobile phone to have. However, that does not mean that wants are not important.

After all, if the customer does not find his wants in a particular product, then he might pick a competitor's product.

Five Whys

But what if there is a problem with the project? What if you would like to find out more information about the problem or problems? One process that you can consider when you are creating your project requirements is what is known as the "five whys." In this process, you have to answer the below questions, and based on the answers, you can develop your requirements much more effectively. The main purpose of the five whys is to discover if there are any problems that might have arisen from the project and use that as the basis to create requirements for the next project.

- Question #1: Why is our client unhappy?
- Question #2: Why were we unable to achieve the goals at the agreed schedule or timeline?
- Question #3: Why did it take longer to reach our goals?
- Question #4: Did we underestimate the complexity of the project? If so, why?
- Question #5: Could we have done something better? If yes, why did we not do it?

MoSCoW

What about priorities? Is there a technique to make sure that the things that are prioritized are arranged in the order of their priority? There is. We use the MoSCoW technique, and it includes the components below:

- The Must Have: Any requirements that you would label as a "must" should be included in the current sprint or timeframe in order for them to be a success.

This is because these requirements are of an urgent nature and cannot be delayed without repercussions.

- The Should Have: Those requirements that you would label as "should" are critical for the completion of the project. But you don't have to place them into the current timeframe unless you have allotted the time for the "must" requirements and you still have slots to add even more tasks.
- The Could Have: Those requirements that you think the project could have are not important. They are like nice additions that the product can have, but they are not necessary for it to function. You can focus on "The Could Have" requirements once you have worked with "The Must Have" and "The Should Have" requirements.
- The Won't Have: Finally, we reach the category that features those features that have the least benefit to the product or might not be required at the time you are working on the project.

Diving into Agile

Now that we have delved deeper into agile and scrum, it is time to start working on agile management.

2

AGILE PROJECT MANAGEMENT

The approaches used by agile project management are heavily based on a dynamic model of work and on trying to optimize the flow of work. This ensures that the project maximizes the efficiency and improves the productivity of the team rather than focusing on the project tasks and their structure. What this means is that the teams are given priority over how the tasks should be structured.

But that does not explain a lot. Not unless we use it in the context of flow.

Flow is one of the most important lean principles. It allows for the team to improve the efficiency of the work and its many processes. The meaning of flow is in the word itself: it talks about how smoothly work gets done. It does not have to be only related to work during the production process. Flow can be used to determine the efficiency of any work in the organization.

For example, if you have a sales team, then you might examine the team to find out how prospects are being sought out and if the team is reaching out to potential clients in an effective manner. If you have a salesperson who is researching prospects and then jumping on a call immediately as soon as she finds someone who seems like a potential customer or client, then she does not have the right flow in her work. Instead, the best way to maximize productivity is to spend some time researching prospects. Once the research has been completed, allot a period to reach out to each of them. During this period, the only goal is to make sure that a target number of calls have been placed. When the salesperson arranges the process in such a manner, they are much more successful and efficient.

The best way to understand it is to look into its many factors. These factors are:

Small Batches

Try to imagine a pipe. You have with you a certain number of balls, all having the same radius and size. You try to place one ball after another into the pipe, and each one runs through the pipe smoothly. You then try to roll in two balls at the same time and realize that they just made it. You then try to roll three balls at the same time, but they do not fit, and you end up applying a degree of pressure on one of the balls to force it to squeeze through, giving space for the other two balls.

The same scenario applies to your project. If you try and squeeze too much work into the process at one time, then your team might find themselves stretched too thin and their time occupied by too many tasks. Whether they complete all the tasks depends on their ability to handle the increased stress and tight deadlines. When you put your team through such a stressful scenario, then you are creating a recipe for disaster. In fact, if any one of your team members commits an error, then you won't have anyone to provide assistance.

You might be forced to stop the process until a solution has been discovered.

Just-in-Time

When you want to improve the efficiency of a particular work or process, then it means that you need to have the right materials, in the right amounts, and at the right time. Let's take a really simple example to explain this point. If you have a team of three graphic designers, but you only have two computers that do not have the latest software to make the work smoother, then you are not making sure that your team has the resources to complete the project or work. When you take the example of a manufacturing unit, then having excess amounts of raw materials is practically useless since you are going to lose incredible amounts of money on wastage. At the same time, having a shortage of raw materials is harmful to the production process as well. In the concept of flow, having all the right resources in the right amounts and when they are required is defined as "just-in-time." The idea is that you are just in time to start the production process.

Concurrent Processing

Flow encourages you to understand that if you have processes running simultaneously, then you have better chances of preventing delays and troubleshooting problems. If you start running work in a sequential manner, then you might find it difficult to keep a steady flow of work when you encounter a bottleneck. For example, let's say that you have focused your efforts on the development phase and then moved on to the testing phase. You realize that you have a limited number of QA testers and this, in turn, begins to affect the flow of work. But imagine if you have a process that allows you to complete both the development and testing phase concurrently, then you can use a collaborative method to immediately start testing as soon as a batch of systems or products is developed. This way, you don't have to wait for all the products to finish the development phase, only to realize you don't have enough testers.

Having understood the concept of flow, we now turn our gaze to two approaches and concepts related to flow: time-boxing and theory of constraints.

Time-boxing and Theory of Constraints

Time-boxing

In traditional project management methods, an approach known as scope-boxing or approach-boxing was used. In this approach, the schedule would be expanded to fit the task that is being performed. It is an effective approach if you are able to accurately and easily work out the scope or size of the requirements, because only when you are able to do that can you fix a proper schedule. Else, you might allot too much time for a task that could be finished early or too little time for a task that might require a longer period for completion.

The solution is to use the concept of agile and break up the work into smaller chunks, which we know are called sprints. You then allot a time-box to each sprint based on the activity. When you break the work down into smaller bits, then you are able to easily allot time constraints for the bits. For example, if someone asks you how long it would take you to manufacture 100 cars, then you might, at best, give a rough estimate. But if the same person asked you how long it would take to manufacturer 100 windshields for the cars, then you would have more accurate knowledge about the timeframe required to complete the task.

The question that arises when you are working with time-boxing is this: "How many of these small and incremental bits of work can the team complete within a sprint that has a fixed timeframe?"

Of course, in order to make this method successful, you need to be able to break down the work into smaller bits. But when you can, you discover that there are advantages to the time-boxing method.

Advantages of Time-boxing

Focus

One of the biggest advantages of the time-boxing method is that you have your team focused on a specific task for a duration of time. This allows them to avoid multitasking and bring all their creativity, problem-solving skills, and attention to the improvement of a single task. Any problems are easily recognized and dealt with. Innovations can be brought about easily because in some cases, you have multiple people dealing with the same task.

Productivity

When you have a timer and you are focused on a specific task, you have a greater degree of productivity. You are not bogged down by numerous interruptions that try and turn your attention towards another work or project. At the same time, you are able to measure your progress. After all, you have an understanding of the target you should reach within the time period. You are more likely to reach it since the result you have to achieve within that time period is not arbitrary.

Realization

When you break down work into timeframes, then you are more aware of how much time you have spent to get the job done. This allows you to see if you have been wasting time, if there are ways to save time, or if the timeframes you have allotted for yourself are too short.

Availability

What about the time required for the entire project? Time-boxing makes you aware of the available time for a particular project. Let's say that you have been working on various sprints. You can easily take the average time you spend on each sprint and make a rough guess about the time it might take you to complete the entire project. This becomes useful because you become consciously aware of how much time you use versus the time you had decided for the entire project.

Theory of Constraints

In some cases, you might find yourself dealing with bottle-necks. While they do not pose as much of a threat as they would if you were using a sequential form of project management, they are still a hassle to deal with. In such cases, you have the Theory of Constraints to help you smooth out the flow of work. The theory has five steps that are repeated over and over again until you are able to solve the issue. Here are the five steps:

Identify

In your first step, you identify the part or stage of the process of work where you spot the most critical bottleneck or constraint. For example, let us say that you have a marketing team comprised of three incredible and talented copywriters. Each copywriter is capable of handling five projects at the same time. If you push them to take on more work, they are able to oversee seven projects. But if they take on any more, they are going to end up lowering the quality of their work and increasing their stress levels. Suddenly, you receive forty new projects to handle. You realize that you don't have enough copywriters to handle all the work. This creates a bottleneck scenario, where everything is squeezed between three team members who now have to handle at least twelve projects each.

Exploit

In your second step, you optimize or exploit that part or stage in the project's process to try to improve its efficiency. For example, in the copywriters example that we just saw earlier, you can allow the team to work on the projects in increments. Each handles six projects, but they finish a part of it and send it for review to the clients. While the clients are reviewing the content, they can set to work on the next batch of projects. Rinse and repeat.

Subordinate

Once you have used whatever steps are necessary to optimize or exploit the process, you then have to subordinate things so that they work within the established limitation that you have created. Once again, we go back to the copywriters example. If the technique that you have established seems to work and working in increments is the right way to go about it, then you have to continue to implement the process for the next batch of projects. There is no point in hiring more copywriters because you think that having more people will smooth out the workflow. What if you don't have to deal with forty projects again for a long time? You are only going to have idle team members with no work, while you continue to incur expenses for each hour they don't spend being productive. If something works, then continue to use it.

Elevate

However, let us assume that you are going to be constantly getting more projects. This might be because you are expanding or you have increased your sales team. For whatever reason, your current team of three are going to find themselves constantly dealing with more projects than they can handle. In such cases, you can think of elevating your team and adding more team members. You should ideally think of adding enough members to reduce the bottleneck.

Check

Once you have solved one constraint, you might find yourself dealing with another. For example, now that you have solved the bottleneck that the copywriters were facing, you might find out that the graphic designers have their hands full now. When you notice that the bottleneck has moved from one part to the other, you repeat the steps mentioned above. Find out how you can remove the bottleneck and then apply your solution as a long-term process.

10 Smart Agile Objectives

Working with agile means that you have opportunities to create unique objectives for your organization. In fact, when you start using agile, some of these objectives might automatically be implemented in your organization. But did you know that there are certain smart objectives that can work for your organization? Let's look at some of them.

Focus on Fit-for-purpose

In this objective, you have to focus on your most valuable product. You then start building it incrementally. This allows customers to see your product as it develops and gives you the power to tweak it wherever necessary. Eventually, you are going to converge on the best outcome and create a product that truly works for your business. Think of the Apple iPhones as an example. They release newer models on a regular basis, sometimes even alternative versions of the same models. Rather than bring out another product in a year's time, they keep developing new products, look at the feedback that customers are giving on their current product, and then improve upon it to create a newer and better model.

Market Time

Sometimes, customers end up having a product that is close to its sell-by date by the time it arrives in the market. This happens when technology keeps improving at a fast pace, as usually happens in today's world. If you use a sequential method to release your product, then by the time your product reaches the customer, your competitor might have released a better version with improved features and technology. What you can do is simply get a product out the door quickly and then focus on bringing out updates and add-ons quickly.

Early ROI

Your return on investment can also become an objective that you can influence with agile. When the product is quickly launched into the market, then you can take advantage of the benefits of early exposure. Your returns start coming in sooner and you can build upon them from there. You are able to receive a much quicker ROI because of this.

Flexibility

When your production process is heavily influenced by change, then you can create objectives to take change into consideration. Agile allows you to react to changes quickly. As you work with sprints, you can easily add a new piece of technology after the completion of a specific sprint, rather than waiting for the completion of the entire project.

Reduce Risk

If you are aiming to reduce risk, then agile can help you with that objective. When you build your product or offering in increments, then you avoid failing outright or enormously. In a sequential method, you launch the entire product into the market and then suffer the consequences if it fails. Essentially, you are facing a huge risk by launching the product into the market. Agile allows you to face risks in small portions that can be easily managed and contained.

High Visibility

If your stakeholders are looking to have more visibility in the project, then you can accomplish that objective easily. As they are looking at the product in various stages of its development, they can inform you of any errors or design flaws that you need to take into account. This also gives them the confidence to trust in your project and to support you in your endeavors to see it reach its completed form.

Efficiency

Constant improvement is something many project managers dream about but are rarely able to achieve effectively. But in agile, project managers are able to gauge the efficiency of their decisions and plans, correct them wherever necessary, and work with teams to do things in a better way. Better, faster, and cheaper is every organization's goal, but usually, they have to sacrifice quality for it. Agile makes certain that quality is retained as much as possible.

Predictability

Project managers would love to have a greater degree of predictability when it comes to the projects they are handling. This can often be a challenge. With agile, project managers are able to keep getting positive results in the short-term. These results create a winning attitude among the team members. They are able to use that attitude to create even more positive results. Before the project managers know it, they have positive results at the end of the project.

Customer Satisfaction

By using agile, you can make tangible changes and improvements in your project. These improvements are reflected in the overall product. If you end up getting glowing feedback on your product, it shouldn't come as a surprise. In fact, you should be expecting it.

Morale

When you have a happy workforce, you have a lot of positive emotions floating around the workplace. Everyone is happy to face problems and deal with challenges. You might have highly motivated employees willing to show you who's best! This improves morale and keeps your team focused on the next project.

Agile Estimation

Before we delve deeper into agile estimation, it is perhaps best to examine the environment of an agile project, which affects the way that you perform estimations.

In a traditional project environment that uses, more or less, the techniques established by Waterfall or other sequential methods, there exists a form of contractual relationship between the business analyst or project lead and the team members. The analyst or lead agree on a set of goals and discuss it with the rest of the team. Once the team then provide a cost and commit to a delivery schedule in order to accomplish the goals, the analyst or lead provides a sign off on the agreed requirements to complete the project. All of this happens prior to the start of the project. After all, once the project has begun then the team has to either take it to its destination or stop everything to start all over from the beginning.

On the other hand, agile functions a bit differently.

- The first thing to note is that requirements are not accurately defined or laid down in detail. This is because agile considers changes as the norm rather than thinking of them as the exception. Any estimates that you make are as good as the requirements that you have established and if any requirements go through changes, then they automatically void the initial estimates. That is why estimates made in agile account for a degree of change. Some people think that it is quite futile to even consider making estimates. But that shouldn't be the practice that you follow. You should make estimates and be prepared to change those estimates after you gain more information about the project that you are handling.
- As you work with agile, you have a greater degree of transparency. This allows you and the stakeholders to have a better understanding of the risks and uncertainties involved. Of course, in the initial phases, your assumptions of the risks might be slightly higher since you have a deficit of information. As you complete numerous milestones in the project, a clearer picture is drawn for you.

Now that you understand how agile works, it is important for you to understand the problems with estimation.

Two Problems with Estimation

Problem #1: Analysis Paralysis

When people begin to analyze something in order to draw

estimates, they have to realize that they are not going to get proper results. This is because of the many uncertainties involved. However, they often end up spending too much time trying to create estimates as accurately as possible, based entirely on unreliable and uncertain information. Eventually, they end up making decisions that have low levels of certainty and might cause more errors.

You should make sure that you do not put yourself in the same position. Understand that you cannot make an accurate assessment of a situation or criteria without having the proper information. Before the start of the project, there is no way you are going to have all the relevant information. So do not become stressed out trying to look for accuracy.

Problem #2: Cavalier

On the flipside, some people dive headlong into a project without worrying about any uncertainties or risks. This move is the height of folly. It will keep them unprepared and they might end up facing risks and challenges without having a clue about what steps to take next.

When it comes to your project, you should aim to have a certain level of planning and estimation so that you are prepared when the worst comes to pass.

The Right Approach

The right approach is to stay between Problem #1 and Problem #2. Do not become overly engrossed in figuring out the most accurate estimations possible, but don't neglect making estimations entirely either.

Management of Uncertainty

When you are making estimations, then you often face uncertainties. How do you deal with such uncertainties? You use the approach described below.

You have to start by first analyzing the situation. This can be done by answering the questions below:

What information do you know for certain?

Bring together all the facts and information you have about a particular uncertainty. Even if the amount of information that you have is small, it does not matter. What matters is that you have something to use. When you have collected all the information, make a list of it. For example, if you are part of a laptop manufacturer, then the information you have might look something like this:

- I am able to use powerful operating systems in the laptops.
- These operating systems are the latest versions, and there won't be another version for at least two years according to the OS developer.
- I can complete the production of the first batch of laptops and get them ready for shipment in three weeks.

Keep listing all the information that you have. Do not worry if it sounds unimportant or obvious. At this point, you are not judging the efficiency or quality of the information. You are merely listing as many facts as possible.

What information is unknown?

Here, you have to list all the things that you are not certain of. You could have questions or uncertainties such as these:

- What operating system is my competitor going to use?
- How fast will my competitor be able to launch their new range of laptops?
- I am not sure if the hardware within the laptops we

are manufacturing is durable and whether it will generate too much heat. I need to find out more.

Remember that every question that you write down is an opportunity for you to explore more. Don't hesitate to list all your doubts.

What reasonable assumptions can I make?

You are trying to work with estimations and probabilities at this stage. You have to make sure that you think about various scenarios in order to get a clear picture of where you stand. For example, you could think of the points below:

- There is a strong possibility that the competitor might launch their laptops with faster hardware.
- If that is indeed true, then I have to bring more focus onto the laptop's hardware.
- We might not be able to manufacture all the parts, but I am aware of a supplier that I trust who can get the required parts for us.
- I need to make sure that my team is on standby to check all the parts that we receive from the supplier.

By listing down all the assumptions you are able to make, you slowly start gaining a clearer picture of the scenario. You will be able to make better decisions. You might have better solutions not only for the uncertainties you are facing but for any uncertainties that might arise in the future.

Agile Communications

We have already looked at how agile promotes transparency and openness. This was not the case with traditional project management systems. In those systems, the spread of information was severely limited. Information was controlled to such an extent that any negative news or failures were hidden. In some cases, such information was altered in order to present more positive news. In fact, one of the important roles of a project manager using traditional project management systems is to staunch the flow of information.

However, when you are working with agile, you will have to keep your information accurate and transparent. Which is why modern project managers do not have to concern themselves with information control. They should keep their entire focus on the project itself.

But transparency is not the only thing that should be kept in mind when establishing communications in an agile project environment.

- Information in a project keeps on changing. These changes occur dynamically and rapidly, and hence, they have to be communicated to the team efficiently. Without the necessary information, teams are going to commit more errors.
- If you would like to see better collaboration between team members, then you have to establish proper communications. Through proper communication, you can improve collaborations among the people who are directly part of the project team and those who are in the periphery of the project team.
- When you communicate openly, you are able to get the stakeholders on your side. The stakeholders are taking on a degree of risk in your project. When they are given the right information, they can provide assistance when required. Else the only thing you might accomplish by keeping the information from them is to keep them in the dark until the moment when the project starts showing so many problems that you are forced to reveal the situation to them. By then, it might be too late for anyone to do anything.

Measuring Success

One of the problems with metrics is that not many people like them. It is that moment of truth when people check the numbers to see just how far they have reached. Sometimes they receive good news and they expel a long-held breath. Other times, they check the numbers and wonder why it is that they have made only a little progress when they have been working non-stop on their project. After all, if one hour can produce 1 piece of your product, then putting in 10 hours means that you have 10 products. But the reality is not so simple. When you look at the numbers, you notice a different story. Some management teams use such metrics to make their teams and workers put in even more time into the project, even though their teams have been working hard already. And the uncertainty of having to find out how things went wrong is what most people dread. However, the reality of the situation is this: if you cannot measure something, then you cannot improve it.

Agile has a new way of looking at metrics. Rather than hand over the metrics to one individual, it gave ownership of the metrics to the team. Because of this, teams have now embraced metrics and use them to make effective decisions. Without proper measurements, agile tools such as scrum and Kanban cannot be used properly. It is also true that the metrics used in agile are relevant to the entire organization. However, they cannot be used to squeeze more out of teams or workers.

Since the teams are managing the metrics, the results that those metrics generate are more accurate. You might notice this when teams measure 'velocity,' which refers to the speed at which the team can deliver a certain objective or requirement. If metrics were handled by someone outside the team, which is the case in traditional project management systems, then the person would make estimations based on his or her understanding of the results. However, since agile gives the power of the metrics to the teams, then they can accurately provide estimations based on the work that they have been doing. The forecasts that the teams form are based on past performance and experience rather than arbitrary scales established by one person.

When you have a system focused on the teams, then you can make accurate predictions about the work. For example, you can say that Team 1 will finish features X, Y, and Z in about N number of weeks while Team 2 might require M number of weeks. When you are able to make such predictions, then you know the cost that you might incur for that period.

So how do you use velocity? Let's look at the guide below:

- Use a scale that ranges from 1 to 5 to describe the size of the work handled by the team. The range is used in ascending order, meaning that 1 denotes the smallest size of work and 5 indicates the largest. What you consider small or large depends on your industry and just how much work you are capable of doing in a particular period.
- You then have to use a timescale to measure the work done by the team. You can use any timescale but once you select one, you have to make sure that it is used for all the work done by your team. For example, if you use a two-week period as the timescale, then you have to make sure that you are using the two-week timescale for measuring all work.
- Using the timescale you have established, calculate the number of units produced. For example, you can say that your team has created 10 units within 2 days. That becomes your team's velocity.
- Once you have a velocity, use the result you

discovered to give a maximum and minimum number of units that can be made during the period. For example, you can say that the maximum number of units that can be produced within 2 days is 13 and the minimum is 8. This gives you a range to work with. If certain issues occur, then you know how many units you can expect from the team and if things are going well, you have an idea of how many extra units you are going to have.

- Take away the maximum and minimum number – as that gives the team a range to work with – and then calculate the total units that have been delivered so far. Divide that number by the number of periods. In the example above, you have used days as your periods. So, if your team has produced 30 units at the end of 6 days, then they are capable of producing an average of 5 units per day, or 10 units in 2 days (which was the timescale that you had used before). Let's look at another example. If your team has produced 24 units in 6 days, then on average, your team is capable of producing 4 units per day, or 8 units in the timescale that you have established.

- When you have determined your average velocity, then you can plan out your future work based on the result.

Dual Purpose Reporting

When you have poor communication, it often causes projects to run off track. Project managers who use traditional project management methods have a habit of being overly positive about the results that the team might achieve even before the start of the venture. As the project continues into its later stages, the project managers find themselves trying to downplay the poor results that the project has been generating.

But why the tendency to be over-optimistic? The reason has to do with the fact that once projects began, they would continue on sequentially until the project ended. Project managers had to provide an estimation and if their estimations fell short, they would have to face endless questions on why things couldn't be improved or why the production rate was so poor. This could also mean that said project manager's job was on the line. Even those asking the questions could not look at a project and make proper estimates. Which is why their expectations were usually high in order to meet a certain profit margin. As you might have guessed, the situation caused a whole lot of problems for everyone involved.

In an agile environment, the business does not have to spend too much time requesting progress because they are completely involved and engaged. The environment provides regular updates and news that can be expected at the end of a certain fixed period. Typically, project managers choose a two-week period to provide updates because two weeks is enough time to see progress and not too long to make the board members, stakeholders, and members of upper management impatient.

Additionally, the organization can focus on running a business that is based on true and honest facts. The project manager is able to receive vital advice and assistance from the upper management team. He or she won't have to cover-up the information because of false estimations or expectations.

At this point, it is important for you to know an important component of agile: user stories. So, what exactly is a user story?

The User Story

Essentially, it is a simple description of a product feature from the perspective of the person who desires such a feature, who is usually the customer or user of the product or system. User stories are usually written in a certain template. The template is as below:

As a < customer, user, or other individual of concern >, I want < enter goal > so that < enter reason >.

The advantage of using stories is that you can create them in varying degrees of complexity. For example, you can create a user story such as the one below:

As a customer, I would like to store more items on the hard drive.

Simple, isn't it? Now, what if you would like to add more details to the story? You definitely can. Your user story might look something like this:

As a customer, I would like to have 128 GB of memory space so that I can store more images and videos on the hard drive along with the ability to create folders and sort the items as I see fit.

In some cases, the simpler a user story, the more epic in scale it becomes. That is why such a user story is often known as an epic. And they might be easy for the team to translate into proper actions or milestones.

For example, let's take the above example:

As a customer, I would like to store more items on the hard drive.

When your team has to work with a user story like that, then they cannot provide you an accurate estimation. That is because there are so many components that go into building a hard drive. At the same time, the task is too large for the team to complete in just one sprint. But let's try and break down the epic into smaller components.

As a customer, I would like to have at least 128 GB of space to store my images and videos.

As a user, I would like to create folders on the hard drive.

As a user, I would like to arrange the items into separate folders and organize them.

You took one epic and chunked it into smaller user stories. Now your team is able to work with what you have given them. This is also the way you can add more details to the epic. When you start breaking down the epic into smaller components, you not only create simpler components, but you give clarity to the overall epic.

When talking about user stories, people often ask the question of just who is responsible for writing down the stories. The answer is that there is no designated person who manages the user stories. Anyone can create user stories. However, it is the responsibility of the product manager to manage the backlog of user stories so that the team remains focused on what they are supposed to achieve. Over the course of an agile project, you can always expect to have a large number of user stories written by each of the team members. When something seems viable, it is used, and if something does not fit the overall goals and requirements of the project, it is tossed aside.

Remember that it does not matter who creates the user stories. But it does matter who is involved in discussing the stories in detail. This is important because valuable inputs can come from any person and if you are excluding someone from the discussion, then there should be a logical and rational reason for doing so.

You might find that user stories are created throughout the project management phase. However, in many cases, there is a special story writing session before the commencement of the agile project. The purpose of this session is to get everyone on the same page when it comes to the goals and requirements the team should be achieving. Additionally, it also allows everyone to create a backlog of stories that fully explain the features and functionalities of the product that they are working on. With the backlog, the team is able to chart the course of the project over a specific period of time. Let's take a very simple example to see how this happens. Let's say that your team comes up with the stories below:

As a customer, I would like to have at least 128 GB of space to store my images and videos.

As a user, I would like to create folders on the hard drive.

As a user, I would like to arrange the items into separate folders and organize them.

Once the above stories are written down, then the team might start fixing a time for their completion. For example, they might give the timeline below.

As a customer, I would like to have at least 128 GB of space to store my images and videos. - Week 3

As a user, I would like to create folders on the hard drive. - Week 7

As a user, I would like to arrange the items into separate folders and organize them. - Week 10

The above timelines are going to be prepared as part of the pre-start story writing. Once the stories have been written, the team will then begin working on them. During the course of their project, they might come across more stories that they will choose to add to the backlog. This will allow them to then plan out a course to incorporate the new stories created.

Stories in Dual Purpose Reporting

And now we come back to dual purpose reporting and the concept of transparency. When you have story points charted out for the project, it gives a rough estimation of how long it might take to complete the project. People are aware that if more points are added, then the project time frame will expand from its initial estimate. This allows everyone to manage their expectations and plan out other business processes necessary for the launch of the product accordingly.

An important thing to remember here is that agile does not provide complete protection against the problems that projects face. However, what it does is try to minimize the occurrence of those problems. Regardless, do not start your project under the expectation that you are now completely immune to the tripwires of projects. Know that even though uncertainties are reduced, they could happen. You need to operate under such presumptions and ensure that you are taking precautionary steps or have alternative solutions when such tripwires occur.

Having understood agile, it is time to look at how you can adopt it in your business.

3

ADAPTING AGILE TO BUSINESS

One of the biggest mistakes that companies seem to make is failing to understand just how well agile can fit into their overall business strategy. To them, they think that agile is simply a small process that needs to be isolated from the rest of the business processes and that higher management does not need to be a part of its functions.

If you look through many different books on agile, then you might notice that they are focused on the aspects of teams and how to optimize agile at a team level. Not much importance has been given to adopting an agile process into the organization's overall business strategy. In some cases, people think that the business will automatically adjust itself to the agile process. One does not need to modify the agile process based on the organization. This is where most people are wrong about agile. Which is why it is important to focus a little on agile and the different business environments that it can fit.

Product-oriented

Those businesses that focus on developing products for the purpose of selling might be able to easily adapt to the agile processes. But just what kind of products are we talking about here? These products could be:

- Software products. For example, companies such as Intuit, Microsoft, and Oracle.
- Companies that provide services using a software. For example, companies such as Twitter, Facebook, Instagram, and Google.
- Hardware manufacturing companies that utilize a substantial amount of software. For example, companies such as Garmin, Circo, HP, and Apple.

When you take into consideration such product-oriented companies, then you might find that there is a natural connection between the company's business strategies and goals and the practices and principles of agile.

What exactly is the reason for this strong connection?

It is because such product-oriented companies base their success on the development of cutting-edge and technologically advanced products that aim to dominate the market. These companies know that they have to get their products into the market as soon as possible in order to maintain their competitive edge. At the same time, they have to ensure that their products reach the customer in the best quality that they can produce. The aims of companies to develop technologically advanced products on time and in the best quality are consistent with the goals of the agile process.

Such product-oriented companies will succeed if they take on a pure agile approach. The reason for this is that these companies tie in their product development process directly to their business objectives and goals. They have to respond to the rapidly growing consumer market if they hope to have a chance of reaching the profits they want to achieve. In some cases, the companies have to adapt their products to market needs while the product is still in the development process.

As you can see, all of the above company goals can be achieved by completely integrating agile into their business environment. Furthermore, agile also allows the companies to focus on the factors below:

- Companies don't have to create a single project to achieve their goals. Rather, they focus on creating a team and fixing a budget that focuses on the constant evolution and development of a product.
- There is a constant need to modify the product based on competition and market needs.

In some other scenarios, schedules and costs are not as much of a concern. For one, the cost of maintaining the team is fixed, as is the cost for most things in the development process, unless there are some radical changes that need to be added to the product. In those scenarios, the ability to develop a competitive edge to the product and launch it as soon as possible is a greater priority. In such cases, agile works well with the companies since the companies can focus on the below:

- They can create a budget that will allow for the ongoing development of the product. It will also provide the development team a little room to maneuver around, in case they need to spend a little extra for an important process.
- Companies can shift their focus to create a pure agile environment where the primary concern is to

allocate their resources to provide constant support to the development team.

- In some cases, costs might not be a problem, not because they are fixed, but because the priority is on the product itself. Even if the organization had to spend more on the development process, they would not mind doing so since they are willing to risk it so they can get the product into the market. They bet on the fact that the advance launch will allow them to cover their expenses and also improve their ROI.

As you can see, there are many ways for a product-oriented company to utilize agile. The trick is not to think of agile as a small component, such as one would think of a task or an objective. Rather, it is a vital part of the business's decision-making process. After all, by using agile, you are changing the very methods you use for the production process. The product launch, its quality, and eventually, your profit margin depend extensively on how well you run agile in your organization.

Another thing to note at this point is that agile gives you the flexibility to prioritize the features and specifications that you would like your product to have. If you allow yourself to brainstorm for a bit, then you might come up with numerous product feature ideas. But that does not mean that you can implement all of them. Sometimes, adding too much to your product will just cause your product to provide unnecessary features. For example, let us say that you have developed a brand new smartphone with all the latest technology. The phone comes loaded with software to make things easier for the user. But you have to think about something: is it really important to load all that software into the phone?

Let's say that you have added a news application by default on the phone. The application's file size is not small, so it occupies a fair bit of space on the phone. Wouldn't you rather allow the user to decide if they would like to add the news application on their phone rather than forcing it into the device? Perhaps the users would like to use the space occupied by the application for something else. They would prefer to add more personal data on the phone instead of reading the news. Of course, during brainstorming sessions, the thought of adding a news application might sound tempting. No one else is doing it so why not us? By using agile, you will be able to prioritize the features that should be added to the phone. The news application might receive a lower priority. Think about the MoSCoW technique that we discussed earlier. By using it, you are giving features priority. When you run through the ones that your product must and should have, you are left with nothing but optional additions that will not influence the final sales one bit.

After all, you are not going to release your new phone with the best hardware, speed, camera, and internet capabilities with the tagline, "The all-new Phone X. Read news like a pro."

Technology-oriented

Another group of companies that work well with agile are those that do not deal with developing products directly but have technologies that play an important role in the progress and business success of the company. We are talking about companies like Expedia, eBay, and Amazon, where the focus is not on creating new products, but on having the best technology for the customers to make use of. These companies provide online services, where the platform that they oversee is more important than the products that they offer.

Think about it this way. Would Amazon or eBay really exist if superior internet capabilities and technology was not available to them? This is why, where product-oriented companies use their products as the basis of the distinction between their competition and themselves, technology-oriented companies use their core technology as the basis of comparison. Their technology itself gives them their competitive edge.

But how can agile be used in a technology-oriented environment? It is quite easy to envision one using agile project management in a product-based company. When technology is involved, we become confused because we are not dealing with any tangible products anymore. The situation becomes even more complicated when we try to imagine just how agile can lead to technology development.

Let's see if we can figure things out together.

In fact, let us take the example of Amazon and their special books section. If you think about the book section, then you can imagine it as a product. After all, it is a unique offering by Amazon and has its own set of features and benefits. When working with agile, Amazon would have to first set up their story writing session before the project. The project team would come together and then discuss the various stories that they would like to implement in the books section. They would then chunk a large task into smaller sprints because even when you develop technology, there are numerous parts that one has to take into consideration. In the case of Amazon, the project team would have come up with an epic like the one below:

As a user, I would like to have a separate section for books.

After defining the epic, the team would then break it down into stories. They might look like the ones below:

As a user, I would like access to millions of books.

As a user, I would like to browse through books based on genres.

As a user, I would like to see reviews of the books so that I can make up my mind about the purchase.

As a user, I would like to know all the details of the book so that I am aware of what edition or version I am getting for myself.

The above stories are just some that I could think of off the top of my head. I am sure if the task were to be given to the Amazon team, they would come up with numerous possibilities. After all, whatever they create should have a competitive edge. It should be something that people will consider over any other online book platform.

Once the stories are set, the team will then translate them into objectives or goals. They will then set up numerous sprints to achieve those objectives. For example, let us take the first user story: *As a user, I would like access to millions of books.*

One has to come up with a solution for how they can give access to millions of books. After all, not all books come in just a single version. Books have multiple editions and versions that must be taken into account when developing the platform. Hence, the first job of the team would be to decide how the book layout page will appear. They need to find out just how the information about the book will be displayed to the users. Their decisions will go a long way in creating a comfortable user experience.

In similar ways, the team will start chunking the various parts of an objective into manageable sprints and then focus on completing them. Eventually, what you have is the agile system used effectively to create the desired result: a book section on Amazon.

At the highest levels, the company should focus on allotting a certain amount of investment for the development of the technology. Once again, the project will display a high degree of transparency so that upper management can make important decisions concerning the core technology. Think of it this way, Jeff Bezos might not have the time to look at each and every action carried out by his team. But with the proper level of transparency, he might be able to see if the technology is being developed the way he envisions it. This allows him to give quick recommendations and perform small changes wherever necessary.

Now try and apply agile to other technological products or platforms that you know about. Chances are that you might just find out how adaptive agile can really be.

Project-oriented

The area in which it becomes difficult to fully utilize the capabilities of agile is within project-based companies. The reason for this difficulty is the fact that these companies do not strictly follow a product development process. Product development does not comprise the main component of their business model or define their success. They might require a certain amount of software applications in their business, but this does not exactly define what they do. They don't have to constantly focus on improving their software capabilities in order to run their business.

What kind of companies are we talking about here?

We are referring to companies that provide products or services that use technology indirectly. The technology that they use is only to ensure that they can smooth out or improve their operational efficiency. Let's take an example right here. Think about non-profit organizations that take care of certain services for some other entity. Alternatively, you can also take the example of event management companies. These companies don't exactly deal with technology themselves but make use of external resources in order to set up an event. The end result, which is the event itself, is not something that belongs to them. It is a product that is used by another entity.

That might seem rather confusing. Let's see if we can understand it more clearly.

Let's say that Google wanted to host an event. They accepted the help of ABC Event Management to make sure that everything is set up properly. ABC Event then uses some incredible laser technology for laser shows and works with some of the top restaurants in the city for food catering. In the end, laser technology and food catering are products that ABC Event does not own personally. They are simply making use of external resources. Additionally, once the product – which is the event in this case – has been completed, it does not belong to ABC Event. Instead, it belongs to Google since it is their event. What you have seen here is an example of a company that takes care of projects for external clients.

When you think about it, it is quite difficult to use agile project management in a project-based business, which seems rather ironic. You could perhaps use certain aspects of project management. Let's look at the example of the event management company. You might be able to apply the principles of breaking down a large task into smaller chunks. But you cannot give specific timelines for the completion of that particular chunk or sprint. The reason being that you are not in charge of every single aspect of the work. If you are using food catering from another source, then your timeframe is dependent on their timeframe. You could try and fix a particular time frame, but that will still be based on your best estimates rather than a confirmed fact or information. Additionally, since you are managing the project on behalf of someone else, their time frames might clash with your estimates. ABC Event has to rely on Google for many of the tasks that they have to complete. If Google does not respond or provide assistance on time, then ABC Event cannot make proper estimations for their sprints. Additionally, the project team of ABC Event does not control the team from Google, so they cannot improve their estimates even if they would like to.

As you can see, technology and software are not directly connected to their business objectives. In fact, ABC Event can choose a venue that already comes with all the technological requirements that they need. That way, they won't have to think about getting a certain technology or software for their final product.

For such project-oriented companies, the main focus is the management of schedules and costs. They do have a budget allocated for software and technology. But that budget is not for a specific product. In many cases, there is a considerable requirement to minimize expenses as much as possible since most of the expenses are not going to add any value to the company's offerings. Minimal costs and expenditure ensure that the business can increase its profit margins.

When you examine such project-oriented businesses, then you might notice the aspects seen below:

- The business proposes projects to cater to certain operational needs. What this means is that the business has to conduct a certain number of operations – which are the projects that it undertakes – within a certain period of time to ensure that they have continuity and profits. Most projects that these companies undertake have a beginning and an end with certain well-defined objectives to accomplish.
- The company uses a certain portfolio management

form of approach to prioritize the projects that it handles. That, in turn, decides how large of a budget the company is going to allot in order to accomplish its own goals. For this purpose, the company looks at the projects it is going to manage and then creates a rough estimation of the schedules and costs for each project. In many cases, there is no need to break down the project into smaller components since the schedule and cost cannot be simplified further. The main reason is that project-based companies have more flexibility when it comes to allocating their budget. They face even more uncertainties because of the fact that they have to deal with constant changes and modifications.

- Project-based companies are not looking to beat the competition when they are working on a project. They don't have to look at any unique features or specifications. They don't necessarily have to research new technology while they are managing their projects.

- The key focus is not about whether the business is building a product that will be able to provide quality, be released on time, and have a competitive edge. While providing quality service on time is definitely an important factor, the main concern for the company is choosing their projects and deciding if they are making wise investments of their time, effort, and money. By understanding their investments, they are able to gauge if their return on investments will meet their expectations or not.

Based on the above points, many might come to the conclusion that project-oriented companies or entities will not be able to make full use of agile management processes. But that is not entirely true, as you will see under the section "adopting an agile into a business."

It does not matter what kind of business environment you have. You can always use agile. However, the degree of usability might vary depending on the business. For example, a project-oriented business can still use agile, but it won't be as extensive as a product-based business.

In the case of a project-oriented business, you have to remember the points below:

- You might require some level of advanced financial analysis and planning in order to support the portfolio management of projects. This is done in order to determine which projects are going to provide optimal returns to the company.
- Once you have determined the projects you wish to undertake, you need to have a degree of tracking to make sure that the projects are actually providing the returns that you expected them to.

Once you have performed the above tasks, you can adopt agile into the projects. Do note that you might not have the ability to use a pure agile approach. As we have seen, you might not be able to use sprints in as much depth as you would in a product-oriented company.

Hybrids

Hybrid companies have a rather unique model of work. They don't develop certain products or offerings that are used for external sales. Rather, these products are created in order to leverage other products or services that generate profit or revenue for the company. One of the best examples of a hybrid company is a bank. You might have noticed that these days, banks provide you with greater accessibility in the form of mobile applications. You can use these applications to perform certain bank and financial transactions. The mobile applications are a form of product. But they don't directly make any money for the bank. However, they complement the other banking processes – which you make use of through the application – by providing you more convenience and allowing you to make transactions more quickly. Faster transactions means faster returns. Here are some characteristics of hybrid companies:

Most of the additional products that these companies develop are offered to the public at no extra charge. The companies usually have to spend a little extra in order to keep the products running smoothly. However, the cost of maintaining the products is negligible compared to the returns that these companies gain.

- Despite the fact that these software or applications are not sold to the public, and therefore generate no direct income for the companies, the performance of the software might impact the ability of the companies to leverage their primary services or products. For this reason, there is a constant development phase to ensure that the product is performing in peak condition and provides better features than the competition's product. For example, some banks allow you to pay your bills using the application, which adds a layer of convenience. Other banks that do not have that feature will miss out on capitalizing on it. They might even lose future potential customers to the competition.
- They do not invest in a product unless it has the potential to generate revenue for their business. When they are handling projects, they have a

portfolio approach to gauge their clients and make decisions on whether to do business with the client or not. The companies choose the best combination of projects to align with their business goals and give them the best return on their investment. Because of their portfolio-based approach to work, any investment made into a product is well thought out and planned. Unlike project-based companies, where the idea of including products in the business is truly optional, hybrid companies do not invest in products if they think that they are only going to be optional offerings.

If you want to adopt agile into a hybrid business, then you have to first focus on a particular product being developed. Once you have chosen the product, you can essentially use the techniques mentioned under product- or technology-oriented business.

This is because the software or application released by the company is akin to a product. It follows the same pattern of creation, except that this time, the company won't be able to use it to directly to generate revenue.

Now that we have understood everything we need to know about how agile can be adopted by various industries, it is time to look deeper into Kanban.

4

USING KANBAN

When Kanban was first introduced, it was used as a scheduling system in automotive industries. Its main purpose was to work with the assembly lines and maintain a high level of production. The renowned car manufacturer Toyota was the first to develop Kanban with the aim of providing their workflow with self-improvement and fine-tuning capabilities. Over time, Kanban began to develop into something else. It transformed into a pipeline process and began to be used by various industries and business sectors.

Kanban has a simple philosophy: it is all about getting from point A to point B in the most effective way possible. Even though Kanban has transformed, the core philosophy still remains the same. The simplicity that was part of the process when it was first created is what attracts many businesses and organizations toward it.

Let's dive deeper into the process.

Kanban Fundamentals

One of the things to remember about Kanban is that the

process focuses on an evolution, not a revolution. What does that mean? Kanban encourages teams to start working in their current positions and then start building themselves from that point using the people directly involved with the Kanban process. Some organizations who are not well-versed in the philosophy of Kanban might think that the process encourages people to take over the positions of the people above them. But that is not true. Kanban is not persuading people to challenge authorities or the position of the people above them. It is giving them the opportunity to work with their superiors so that they can show how valuable they are to the organization and improve their position.

Kanban has three guiding principles:

- You begin your work with what you know or are good at.
- You should agree to work on your evolution, where you see incremental changes in your work and responsibilities.
- Make sure that you respect and accept your current responsibilities, roles, processes, and title.

At the most fundamental level, there are five key steps one should follow in order to successfully implement Kanban. Here are the five steps:

Visualize Workflow

The first thing that you need to do is start off with a visual representation of your work from beginning to end. Tasks at the beginning are typically labeled as "to-do" and those at the end are labeled "done." The way tasks move from one step to the other depends on the organization and the nature of the tasks or project. For example, some organizations prefer to use a three-step method for the direction of workflow: To-do, In Progress, and finally Done. Other projects might require a more detailed division of the work. In such cases, the workflow gets divided into numerous stages such as to-do, plan, design, draft, build, test, deploy, and done. The number of stages you have depends on the work you are planning on doing. Let us look at an example. Assume that you are part of a marketing company. You receive the project from the clients, hand over the project to your team of copy-writers and graphic designers, and then transfer the results back to the client for approval. You might have stages listed like below:

- To-do
- Brainstorm
- In Progress
- Evaluate
- Send for Approval
- Done

Or you could even have something as simple as:

- Start
- Brainstorm
- Work
- Send Complete Versions

Look at the project you are handling and think about how many stages might fit your work. Think about whether the stages you have set work conveniently with your project.

Reduce Work-in-Progress

If you are trying to handle too many tasks at the same time, then the results might just be disastrous, and those results might apply to both teams and individuals. It is important to note that multitasking is not a preferable method of working. It causes too many distractions and increases stress levels. Even if someone is capable of handling multiple tasks at once, you need to make sure that the person's focus is on specific tasks. This ensures that the quality of the work is preserved and that you maintain productivity. Kanban places a limit on the number of items that you can add to the Work-in-Progress list, also commonly known as the WiP list. This allows people to put on display maximum efficiency in the work that they do. Initially, you can make use of your own understanding of the work to reduce the number of WiP tasks. As you gain more experience in the project, you will be able to fine-tune the tasks during future repetitions of the project.

Manage Workflow

Your mission, should you choose to accept it (and you ideally should), is to make sure that there is a fluid movement of work from start to finish. When you are able to smooth out the workflow, your project will be functioning at maximum efficiency which ensures that your business receives maximum value in the least amount of time, something that all businesses aim for. At the same time, when you have smoothed out your workflow, you should be able to repeat it again and future iterations should maintain the consistency of previous workflows.

Process Should Be Explicit

Never make ambiguous statements about how you should perform the work. For example, if your copywriting team is working on a set of projects, don't simply give a statement that says, "Make creative copies." That could mean just about anything. Besides, creativity is subjective. You could find something creative, but another person might not. Try and add a bit more information for copywriters to follow. You could say, "Make creative copies. Focus on highlighting the aesthetics of the product. You could talk about the color options."

When you give specific instructions, you are able to avoid any scenarios where the results achieved by the team are far different from what you envisioned or what the client or customer expected. Additionally, if you have set clear objectives, then you have a common understanding with team members. This allows you to resolve any issues easily and impartially. Make sure that that there are clear rules for moving from one step to another. This could prevent any confusion that might arise when the team starts the next task.

Improve Collaborations

Once the work is underway and the attention turns to the workflow, you will most likely notice a great influx of ideas from various sources on how to improve it. When you start placing a WiP limit, then you force teams to work with the tasks that they have. This allows for interesting techniques and ideas to develop that could help the team approach the project from a unique perspective. You should encourage such collaborations between team members, where they are able to help others resolve issues, as much as possible. Try to limit the number of tasks per person to two. This will help them discover problems that might impede the process of the workflow and resolve those issues.

Kanban Board

When you use Kanban, you are going to come across a simple tool: the Kanban board. If you have been working on collaborative tools such as Trello, then you should realize that those tools are based on the Kanban board concept.

People usually think of these boards as a visual representation of the to-do list. But to follow the same thought process would be over-simplifying the Kanban board. But that is a good place to start because the board does look like a visual representation of the work that needs to be done and the work that has been completed. Here is a truly simple form of the Kanban board:

Not Started

In progress

Done
Bring in the raw materials

Introduce the new project to the team
Artwork for Client #1

Preparation of flyers
Sent across final versions of brochures to Client #1

Purchase new equipment

Create job listings

For some tasks, a simple Kanban board will work. For

others, you might need more complexity in the board in order to account for the level of detail and the number of steps that go into completing the work. In some cases, you might start out with a simplified version of the board because you are not used to working with it. Once you become acclimated to the way the board works, you might start adding more sections to it. For example, you might break down the WiP section into many parts, especially if you have numerous people working on one task. At the same time, remember to avoid creating too many sections or things might get complicated.

Here is an idea that you can use initially. I like to call this the four split, and it features four sections:

Ideas

Your team is allowed to brainstorm new ideas and then place them in this section. At the same time, you can use this section to decide whether a particular suggestion or idea is a maybe or maybe not.

Try not to apply any restrictions to this step. Allow the thoughts to be more free-flowing. It does not matter how outlandish the idea might seem. Let the team provide you with recommendations. You can then decide whether you want to keep them or not once the idea generation session is over.

To-do

The ideas have been considered properly and only those that have passed the review process make it into this section. When the ideas reach this section, your only concern should be about who is going to do what task and when they should start.

In Progress

The work has been assigned to the concerned person or group. The work should be underway at this point.

Done

When you reach this section, then the work has been done. All you have to do is bask in the glory that you have done it and reap the rewards that follow.

Once you get used to using the above sections for your Kanban board, you can start modifying them or create one of your own to properly fit the work that you are doing.

When is Done Considered Done?

It is always a challenge in any project management scenario to accurately pin down the task as done. Let's take an example right here. Let us say that you have completed a campaign for a client. The work is actually done, but since it is sent for client review, it might come back with changes. But since you have technically completed the work, shouldn't you mark it as done? If there are changes, shouldn't that be considered a second task instead of becoming part of the first task?

So, when should you consider something as truly done?

The trick is to set down the criteria that define what is considered 'done.' You should do this for each task so that you can avoid any conflicts in the future. Why should you define 'done' for each task? The reason is that they all function differently. What could be considered as completed for one task might still be thought of as incomplete for another.

One of the best ways to understand what constitutes a completed task is by using the agile principle of engaging with the customer. When you interact with the business or customer, you understand how much work you should put into a task before you can define it as 'done' or 'completed.'

For example, let's suppose that you manage an electronics manufacturer and someone orders a washing machine. When do you consider the job as done? Is the job completed when the customer pays for the washing machine or do you truly consider it done only when you have delivered the product to the customer's home? Is installation included in the package? Are you going to provide an additional warranty? All of these questions can be understood by trying to get feedback from the customer. In some cases, certain services might not be viable for your business model. But you should find that out by actually interacting with the customer and not by relying on guesswork.

When you start breaking down the work into smaller components, you realize that there are so many ways to complete a single project. Everything depends on various factors including your business objectives, resources available, and the time allotted for the tasks.

Another technique you can follow is to sit down with your team and have a discussion about what you think 'done' should be. Don't wing it. Don't try and assume anything. You are going to put yourself in a tough spot if you do.

Deciding on a Board

Once you have decided on the overall format of the Kanban board, you should then decide on whether you would like to have a physical board or a digital one. Both have their advantages and disadvantages. The accessibility provided by a digital board is fantastic. You can take it around with you, as most virtual Kanban boards provide you with a mobile application. This allows you to work on tasks from anywhere. However, physical boards provide you with a greater degree of visibility than virtual ones.

A physical board is like a beacon. It becomes a fixed object that draws people's attention. And that is precisely what you should be aiming for when getting a board: to get your team members to look at is and understand what their next task is. Additionally, having a physical board creates a good impression on upper management. It shows them your work process. It allows them to see how organized you and your team can be, how creative your ideas are, and the fact that you have covered practically every important aspect of the work.

You don't need a lot of materials to get started on your very own Kanban board. You might need a plain whiteboard, a few markers, and maybe post-it notes to allow you to make quick notes about the tasks without changing the board itself. As we have seen, you can start off with four columns that can easily fit on the whiteboard. However, if you feel that you are going to need a lot of columns that won't easily fit on a standard whiteboard, then you are free to make use of a virtual board. I would recommend trying to simplify the process so that you have fewer columns to work with.

Once you have the board with you, keep it in a location where it is clearly visible, and the team is able to see it on their way to work. Do not keep it in a place that your team is least likely to visit or that they don't pass by too often. You need your board to be visible.

But what if you do not have any whiteboards? How can you create a Kanban board then? There is a solution for that.

- Get some masking tape. If you can get tape of different colors, then that would be even better. If you cannot find masking tape, then any tape will do.
- Now choose a wall that you are allowed to use for a Kanban board and the upper management won't think twice about when they find tape stuck on it.

- Cut out 4 x 3-meter strips of tape and stick it on the wall horizontally, one above the other. Cut off 4 more 3-meter strips of tape and stick them vertically, one next to the other. Your entire arrangement should resemble a 3 x 3 boxed grid.
- Once done, get sticky notes of two different colors. Use one color for headings. They go into the topmost grid and will let everyone know what that particular column represents. The sticky notes of the other color can be used to mention all the tasks that go into each grid.

This way, you have your very own Kanban board and you can effectively begin to assign tasks to your team.

When Technology Takes Over

Despite how impressive traditional forms of the Kanban board might be, it is sometimes more efficient to use a digital version. If you find yourself working from different places using an internet connection, if you are constantly on the move, or if you have your team members are spread over different locations, then you might want to use a digital Kanban board in order to keep everyone apprised of the situation to allow them to work more efficiently.

Remember that the digital version should only be used in extreme cases. Do not resort to it if you or your team members are on the move occasionally. Nothing can replace a physical Kanban board.

As I mentioned before, Trello is one of the most popular boards that you can take advantage of. It is free to try out, and you only have to pay if you would like to add more members to the team.

Building a Backlog

At the core of the Kanban board, you will find the 'to-do' items. These items are also known as a backlog in agile. When you are creating a backlog, one of the most important things to remember is that you have to create a list where every task is focused on delivery. These tasks should also deliver value to the business, either directly or indirectly. Do not include tasks that have no real value. The purpose of the Kanban board is to improve the productivity of your team while keeping them focused on the overall goals. If you find an item on the board that does not add any value to the business, then you can make a note of that task and communicate it using another method, such as an email or a face-to-face conversation.

Here are other things that you should remember about Kanban:

Try Creating Items of Similar Size

You can use user stories for your Kanban board. The only difference with a Kanban board is that you create a user story and then convert it into a task. Let's take an example. Assume that you have the user story below:

I am a user and I would like to have the ability to connect my USB memory stick to the printer.

You cannot place the user story directly on the Kanban board. You have to first convert it into a task. Your task might look like this:

Add a USB port on the printer.

You now have a task. Your next set of tasks should also be of the same size as your first task. For example, here is a list of tasks that you can work with.

Add USB port on the printer.

Ensure multiple ports are available

Add button to show contents of USB on the printer display

By adding similar sized tasks, you can ensure that there is continuous progress. Or you might find that you or your team might get stuck on a task that is slightly bigger than the others. What about those tasks that are actually bigger in size? In such cases, you simply take the large task and break it down into smaller – and more manageable – chunks. You should create it in such a way that all the tasks on your Kanban board can be finished in bursts of timeframes.

Use a Pull Strategy, Not a Push Strategy

A team working with Kanban is always looking to find out what is next rather than waiting for the right package of resources to be made available for the task. This is a pull strategy, where the team pulls the task into their schedules as soon as the resources to complete the task are available. In a push strategy, you might find yourself pushing things into other people's schedules, trying to make them do something. It is also important to remember that motivation is key at this point. Don't just expect your team to be motivated. In some cases, you need to make sure that you are boosting the morale of the workplace.

Shuffling Things Around

Now that you have dealt with the to-do section and have arranged the tasks in manageable and meaningful ways, it is now time to create a sequence of work. Simply dropping objectives and tasks for everyone to do does not help you reach your goals. Some items on the Kanban board might be interrelated. Some might be independent. You have to arrange the items in such a manner that they either help with other tasks or follow a logical sequence of events.

You would be surprised to know that a number of people actually wade through their tasks spontaneously and without a set goal in mind. They pick up any task that they find fancy or choose those tasks that they can complete, just to show everyone that they have been productive. It is true that we have arranged tasks in such a manner that they are all more or less of the same size. But even so, some tasks might be easier than others, depending on the skill of the team member, the resources available, or the objectives the team has to achieve. In fact, many organizations choose to work on a job for a 'simply because' reason rather than 'this is how it should be done' reason.

As we had seen before, one of the core concepts of all forms of agile variants, including Kanban, is that work should be done in order to create value for the organization. So how do you arrange work in Kanban? Here are some criteria you can use:

- Think of the work that provides the most value. Try to prioritize that above work that only provides marginal value. If you discover that two jobs have the same value, then pick the one that is easier to complete so that you can derive some value out of it while you focus on the other task.
- At the same time, do not get hung up on assigning business value to tasks. You have to regard work based on its importance, not a detailed analysis. If you find yourself in a position where you are unable to place value on the tasks properly, then think about the importance of the tasks. Which task should be completed first in order for other jobs to begin? Is there a job that needs to be completed on an urgent basis? Are there timc-sensitive tasks? When you start asking yourself logical questions, you realize that you

have a better idea of how to arrange the tasks on the Kanban board.

You can also use the method described below to prioritize work:

- Look at your backlog and arrange everything into work packages.
- You then assign a business value to them based on how much returns they are capable of bringing to the company. The values range from 1 to 10, where 1 denotes a task with the lowest value and 10 shows a task with the highest value.
- Next, you have to assign a cost delivery rating. The values range from 1 to 5, where 1 is the most expensive task to deliver and 5 is the least expensive.
- You then use this formula: business value x cost delivery. You are going to have a set of values. Once those values are set, you then simply have to arrange the tasks in descending order of values. The task with the highest score gets to be the most important one, and then you continue down the list until you reach the task with the lowest value.

Simple isn't it? This technique will allow you to decide how you would like to arrange the jobs. When you are able to make such arrangements, your team can move from one task to another in a fluid manner. There are also fewer chances of your team having to backtrack in order to complete a task that should have done earlier. Even if the upper management were to drop by and ask you the reasons behind your arrangement, you can give them the calculations you did and the logical steps you took to arrange the tasks. Doing so could bolster their confidence in your leadership and your ability to see things in a rational light.

At the same time, you can also shuffle the cards or tasks around easily. When you have given priorities to the tasks, you can sit down and discuss with your team in order to get their feedback on the priorities. They might have a different opinion on one or more of the tasks on the board. After the discussion, if you discover that you might need to rearrange some or many tasks on the board, you can do so easily.

This freedom to shuffle jobs is what allows you to create the best arrangement of jobs for your team.

Controlling Work in Progress

If you were living in an ideal world, then all you have to do is pick each task from the to-do list and you will be able to transfer it to the done or finished column without any problems or challenges. At the same time, you will be able to complete the tasks one at a time. Sadly, we do not live in an ideal world. No matter how hard you try, chances are that you are going to be handling multiple jobs at one time.

You might think that it is merely multitasking in action. But the reality is not that simple. What you are doing is not multitasking but switching from one task to another without giving the proper attention to any one task. Also, multitasking is a myth. That is not a conclusion I conjured in my head. That is something psychology has to say (Napier, 2014). You see, your brain is so adept at switching from one task to another that you don't necessarily notice the switch at a conscious level. You automatically assume that you are so good at managing multiple tasks simultaneously. The problem with multitasking is that it prevents you from keeping your focus on one job and taking it to its best conclusion. In an organizational setting, one cannot shirk away from handling multiple tasks all the time. You might inadvertently find yourself working with multiple jobs because it is important to reach your goals.

Thankfully, Kanban helps you to reduce the number of tasks you can assign to one person. The concept of Work-in-Progress limit or WiP limit can be applied to both individuals and teams. The limit is set forth after looking at your team's performance and their capabilities. In most organizations, the popular limit that they establish is three. Once an individual or a team is overseeing three tasks, they are not allowed to take on any more tasks until they have completed the ones they are working on.

It is important to note that imposing a WiP limit is non-negotiable when it comes to Kanban. Without the limit, anybody can modify the board to make it look like one convoluted and glorified to-do list without any rhyme or reason behind the jobs on the board. If you are aiming to reap results through the use of a Kanban board, then you have to make sure that you are keeping everything within the WiP limits. It is tempting to break the limit when you are faced with certain tasks. When the temptation arises, ask yourself the questions below:

Why do I feel the need to add more tasks and push beyond the limit?

If something has not been completed, then the problem is not that I haven't created a proper limit, it could be that the team has failed to complete the task on time. In which case, have I provided a really short duration for the completion of the task?

Were the team able to tap into enough resources? Did they face certain roadblocks along the way? Was I able to help them navigate around the roadblock?

What can I do to ensure that future tasks are completed on time?

When you begin to examine the tasks themselves and the

way they are completed, you might just find the problem. Solving such problems is critical because doing so will ensure that you have found a permanent solution. Simply increasing the limit in order to make space for another task is a stopgap solution.

One of the things that you might notice with Kanban is that the process of organizing work does not start smoothly in the beginning. But as you get better with the framework, you get better at managing tasks. Eventually, you will be running a smooth Kanban process that allows you to meet project goals quickly and efficiently.

Remember that it is okay to make mistakes in the beginning. It allows you to learn what you should not be doing and what needs improvement.

Final Words

One of the important aspects of Kanban is that when used effectively, it prevents you from disrupting tasks, even if you have to solve a problem with another task. You can make subtle, yet non-invasive changes to ensure that the entire project is running smoothly.

Of course, introducing Kanban into an organization that has been functioning without it is easier said than done. You might find some resistance against the technique. But without actually using it, one can never make informed decisions about it. Which is why the responsibility might fall on you to make sure that Kanban has been implemented well in the organization.

But that is where your greatest advantage lies: introducing Kanban into the organization.

To many people, agile can be a difficult nut to crack. Applying it throughout the organization might seem like a daunting task. While some are able to easily understand its complexities and start working on projects using its techniques, others are left scratching their heads when things do not go the way they want them to. Which is why Kanban is like an introduction to agile. When you implement Kanban, people are able to see just how effectively work is assigned to teams and individuals and just how well progress is made in projects. When they see the results it provides, they become more inclined to give agile a try. Kanban is like an incredible and engaging trailer while agile is the actual movie; with an interesting trailer, you can definitely get people to go for the movie.

In fact, Kanban is a simplified version of the agile project management framework. It allows people to understand all the key components of agile. While it is true that Kanban is a type of agile framework, it is a framework that is easy to utilize. It allows people to become used to one framework of agile before they decide if they would like to venture into the world of agile.

But while Kanban is easy to understand, remember that its effectiveness depends on how well you organize the tasks and the fact that you keep a strict WiP limit.

5

WORKING WITH SCRUM

S crum is a wonderful tool. But like all tools, you can reap greater and greater benefits from it the more you practice using it. Scrum is based on a cycle of repetition. It is designed to compel you to perform useful tasks again and again until they become second nature. And this is where many people end up committing errors while using Scrum.

You might find people who use Scrum performing detailed planning or Scrum. While the temptation to increase the accuracy is always there, remember that it is not necessary. The best way to use Scrum is not to plan everything beforehand. Rather, you should use the concept of "inspect and adapt," where you make incremental improvements as you are using Scrum.

In some cases, you might face a few big challenges. Some might complain about the location of the team while others might be anti-Scrum. But the trick is to know that the big issues will be resolved eventually. That is how Scrum works; you might not have a lot of support in the beginning and the framework might not convince you of its capabilities. Once you get used to it, you will wonder how you could ever work without it.

The Framework

Scrum is open to misuse and misunderstanding. That is why it is important to understand its framework.

Scrum cannot be thought of as a proper project management tool. Rather, you could think of it as a framework for delivery. You might think that a project management tool is used for delivery, but there is a subtle difference here that you should be aware of.

Scrum is present in order to support delivery, where the end goal is to deliver high-quality products.

The Scrum framework has three important roles that you should be aware of.

Product Owner

The product owner's main responsibility is to try to maximize the work of the development team and the value of the product. The manner in which this is done varies from one organization to the other.

The product owner is also the decision maker in the project, represents the interests of the business or stakeholders, prioritizes the jobs that need to be done, and also ensures that the team has a direction. Usually, it is only necessary to have one product owner when working with Scrum. But an exception can be made when working with large organizations since they have multiple stakeholders, projects, interests, and goals.

Scrum Master

Scrum Masters ensure that the team and other members of

the project understand Scrum and are able to enact it. They are the go-to people for anything related to Scrum practices, theories, and rules. They have to facilitate the team, but they do not have to give the level of direction to the team that a product owner provides. In fact, the team should aim to be self-organized, independent, and empowered. However, as we have discovered, through repetition, one can become better at Scrum. For this reason, a scrum master's role becomes essential in the initial stages of Scrum usage and implementation.

Team

Finally, you have the team that takes care of the project. Under Scrum, the team is expected to act independently without much guidance. The team members should work cohesively and should ensure that collaborations take place freely. A team may consist of people with similar expertise or with different specialties. The choice of team members depends on the project and the overall goals of the organization.

Understanding Backlog Refinement

When you have a fairly long backlog, then you might have to prioritize the tasks on the list based on their value to the organization and the cost of working with them. You might have noticed a similar approach when we were working with Kanban. However, when it comes to Scrum, we do not use the same formula that we had applied when using Kanban to determine the value of a task. Rather, the final arrangement depends on the judgment of the product owner. What's important to note is that you should not become engrossed in the act of arranging everything in a sequential order that makes sense. What you should be focusing on is the value of the task. If you feel that a task has a high value, then it should be placed on top of the list followed by the remainder of the tasks. What's important is that you give more importance to your user stories.

In some organizations, there are teams dedicated to checking the backlog every day just to make sure that everything is going well. Other organizations adopt a more laissez-faire approach, where they are not very strict on inspections. However, the best option would be to spend as much time as possible checking the sprints before the project starts, and once you have started working on the projects, focus only on the sprints. There should still be backlog inspections, but they don't have to be done rigorously, just enough inspections to make sure that everything is running smoothly and that there are no problems in the foreseeable future.

Acceptance Criteria

The fastest way for you to get the team to develop the wrong product is by not making them completely aware of the requirements. In many cases, such misunderstandings cause a huge problem in product development. Mostly, you will be able to weed out the misunderstandings at an early stage, but there might be small cases that you might not notice at all. These cases eventually turn out to be something much bigger, causing problems along the way.

So how do you get rid of these misunderstandings? Simple. You get your team together and work out the user stories. While creating your user stories, try and ask the statement below:

I know I will have got <whatever> when <something happens>

The "whatever" clause refers to any form of product feature or any tangible delivery that you can provide. The "something happens" refers to one or a set of experiences that lead to the activation of the product feature. By keeping this statement in mind, you will be able to refine your user stories and create them with the greatest degree of accuracy. There will be minimal room for misunderstandings. You can also use the techniques below to refine your stories:

- Create a simple description of the end result or outcome that you would like to see. Try not to add too many details.
- Make sure that you list the user stories in bullet points. This allows the team to realize that each bullet point could be a task on its own.
- Create "conditions of satisfaction." These are the elements that you want the product to have in order for it to be accepted. The conditions of satisfaction can also be based on the goals of the organization, the remarks and feedback from the stakeholders, any research conducted in the market, customer demands, and other important criteria.
- Use Gherkin language in your writing. The language consists of statements made using the Given, When, Then format. Let's look at an example of this format.
- *Given that a customer would like to access the Android app store through his television monitor. When he uses special buttons on the tv remote, then he will be able to access the app store.*

The format is simple, but in some cases, it requires a lot of thought. People are often put off by the Gherkin language due to the fact that they have to think intensely in order to simplify a user story or task. But think about it this way, if you cannot simplify the task, then how can you expect your team to achieve it with greater success? How can you prevent misunderstandings from happening? For all intents and purposes, the more complex a user story or task is, the more chances there are for your team to become confused by them.

The Art of Prioritization

When it comes to Scrum, don't think of the act of prioritizing as running a marathon, where the first three get to stand on a podium and the fourth one is left out. In the case of Scrum, the question that you should be answering is: in or out? What matters is whether the task is part of the project or if it has been excluded entirely.

Starting Sprints

When the sprint begins, then the first thing that you should be focusing on is sprint planning. Sprint planning is different from project planning. Team members should be able to look at a sprint and then give the product owner a rough estimate of the result that will be formed at the end of the sprint. This gives everyone a target to aim for. The objective is to take a sprint and then return it to the product owner in the form of a working product. For example, if the sprint focuses on creating a new type of software modification, then the idea is that at the end of the sprint, the product owner should be able to use the software modification.

The Mechanics of Preparations

If you have prepared the project well with the proper use of acceptance criteria, user stories, and sprints, then your planning session should not be a lengthy one. All your team might end up doing is confirm that they understand the project and then get started on it.

Here are a few factors to consider when discussing the project with the team:

Logistics

The Scrum Master must plan out the logistics of the meeting. He or she should make sure that everyone attends the meeting. Too often, you have one person missing from the meeting with the other attendees deciding that they will give all the details of the meeting to the missing person later. This does not work and only serves to alienate the missing member from the experience of the actual meeting. In the meeting, people can discuss in detail, allowing everyone to deeply understand the project they are working on. However, if someone were to be absent from the meeting, then all the person might end up receiving is a snippet of the entire conversation and planning process.

Duration

The planning process is essential, as we just understood in the previous section. But it is not realistic to keep it going for hours on end. For that reason, it is the Scrum Master's aim to keep the meeting focused and short. The Scrum Master must prepare all the talking points in advance, keep the meeting from straying away in random directions, and ensure that people are quickly coming up with productive ideas and plans. Ensure that each talking point has a fixed time for discussion. As a Scrum Master, if you find out that people tend to get distracted by unnecessary talking points, then deftly bring the conversation back to the topic at hand.

Outcome

There is no point in having a meeting if there is no valuable outcome from it. The Scrum Master should ensure that each and every meeting produces a plan of action. The best way to go about this is by asking and answering the questions below for every point that is made during the meeting.

- What is the focus of the discussion?
- Do we foresee any problems or issues?
- What are the potential solutions for ensuring that the sprint is successful?
- What happens if things don't turn out the way we

want them to? Do we have alternatives?

- What about damage control? How can we make sure that we recover from any potential damage?
- Are there any issues that the team needs to resolve before starting on the project?
- Are there any important points that you would like to discuss before moving on to the next sprint?

When the Scrum Master has focus, then he or she will be able to direct the meeting to the best possible conclusion.

Avoid Personal Issues

You might find out – over the course of the project – that some of the biggest problems you face come from people. In other words, we are referring to your team.

During the planning stage, you have to strengthen the inter-actions and relationships between team members. While doing so, there are plenty of things that could go wrong.

Disengagement

When you are planning, make sure that you are making the process engaging and allowing everyone to speak their minds. Generally, if the team finds the meeting boring, then there are usually two reasons for it:

They are not able to engage properly. This could happen either because there is not much room to contribute ideas or the team members feel like their voice does not matter. When people feel excluded, they quickly lose interest and, even worse, motivation.

The planning session is not relevant. Make sure that you have brought in people who are concerned with the topics of discussion you are going to focus on. If you invite too many people in the hopes that you are going to get something more out of the meeting, then all you might end up doing is causing too many distractions and looking at too many bored faces. You really don't want to conduct a meeting where you spot a face that looks like it wants to be anywhere but the meeting room. At the same time, keep the meeting productive. Do not be too critical about ideas. After all, it is the planning phase. No idea is a bad idea. You either have good ideas or inspiration for good ideas. Keep that in mind as you navigate the meeting.

Arguments

You cannot always prevent people from arguing. It is healthy to encourage debates and discussions, but arguments only serve to sap the energy out of the room and create lower morale. What's the solution? Inform the team that the person who is going to be making the decision is the product manager. While suggestions can be made by anyone, the final decision will be made by the product manager. This ensures that people are able to cooperate and avoid any unnecessary conflicts. If people come to think that they can make decisions, then they have personal motivations involved in the meeting. It is not healthy to make things too personal. The purpose of the planning stage is to come up with productive ideas to use, not create personal issues.

Frustration

Do not let people be ignored. It might lead to frustration. At the time, you should not be ignored in turn as well. Conduct the meeting in a professional manner. Make sure everyone knows that each and every member of the meeting is important for the overall success of the project. Their feedback matters. After all, it is based on their feedback that objectives can be properly established.

Self-organizing Teams

The essence of Scrum depends on the concept of self-organizing teams. What does it mean to be a self-organizing team?

Essentially it is the idea that teams are self-governing and self-starting, and they do whatever is necessary to get the job done. Here is how to create a proper self-organizing team using the pivotal components of your team, the product owner, Scrum Master, and the team itself.

The Product Owner

The product owner, or PO for short, is the final decision maker. He or she decides what the final version of the product delivers and what the project is all about. The PO has to blend the business side of things and customer demands.

The PO also manages the scale, scope, and direction of the project that the team is working on. If you think about it, the business owner is like a politician, who has to navigate a fine line in order to not only keep the project going, but also keep everyone happy. And by everyone, we are talking about the stakeholders and other concerned people on the business side, the customers, and the team as well. Because the PO is the one to make the final decisions, he or she has to take complete accountability of his or her actions. The PO should also be responsible for giving accurate reports to the investors. After all, they need to know where the money is going and whether it is being utilized productively. The PO should be able to answer any questions from the team or from the people managing the business. At the same time, complaints should be dealt with and team conflicts should be managed.

Just by reading the above, you can imagine just how challenging the job of the PO can be. It's a delicate situation to manage people and progress at the same time. But through effective Scrum management, the PO will be able to find success in his or her project management capabilities.

Scrum Master

You can think of the Scrum Master as the organizer of the project. He or she is the one who makes certain that everyone is on the same page. While the project manager takes a top-down approach to the project, a Scrum Master plays the role of an enabler, who ensures that the team remains self-managing.

The Scrum Master arranges all the events and meetings that are required. He or she makes sure that all the right people attend, that information is being distributed well, and that everyone is aware of the goals and tasks of the project.

The Team

Everyone else who is involved with the development of the project is part of the development team. Their main objective is to take all the prioritized tasks and then convert them into proper results. They make sure that all the decisions made by the product owner are translated into the product. We have mentioned the word self-organizing numerous times. And what that means is that development teams are trusted to work together with minimal conflicts and as sensible professionals to get the job done. They are ready to motivate each other and then provide assistance wherever necessary. They are not worried about petty rivalries or having an unfavorable opinion about someone else that gets in the way of progress.

In many cases, the product owner is not available to look into each and every job that the development team undertakes. This is why no one knows the details of the work better than the team themselves.

Key Scrum Events

We have already looked in detail at one of the key events of Scrum, planning. Now it is time to move on to the actual work. What happens during this phase depends on the nature of the project and the agreed-upon decisions that were made during the planning phase.

During this time, the Scrum Master's role becomes even more important for the following reasons:

Maintaining Momentum

Is everyone clear about their responsibilities? Does anyone require any additional information? Are the team members waiting for something in order to get the job done? All of these questions are important, and the Scrum Master makes certain that everyone knows what they need to know in order to complete their job. If there is a need to bring the product owner into the loop, then the Scrum Master makes sure that it can be done as well. At the same time, he or she is proactive in finding out the issues that the team has, discovering if they need any motivation, or if there is a need for another meeting to get everyone tuned to the same goal and objective frequencies.

Removing Hindrances

This is one of the most important roles of the Scrum Master. They have to constantly ask the question: are there any blockages or hindrances that they should get rid of? Scrum Masters should do everything in their power to keep things moving. They should be able to provide the necessary assistance to the team, from surprisingly small tasks such as making sure everyone has proper computers or equipment to major tasks such as assisting the product manager in preparing reports to send to the stakeholders.

Free Flow of Information

It is always important to keep a two-way communication, which should exist between the product manager and the team. The team will expect to contact the product manager for a lot of reasons. But it won't be possible to get the product owner into a meeting at all times since the PO will be engaged in other tasks as well. Scrum Masters should then figure out how to get the product owner and the team together without disrupting any tasks. It is imperative that the Scrum Master does not use favoritism to make decisions. They have to remain impartial and provide assistance to both the product owner and the team. It might be tempting to support the product owner since they have a higher authority. But the Scrum Master should act as a link. Not someone who plays office politics.

Preparing for the Next Sprint

Is the backlog being reviewed continuously? Are the user stories easy to understand and visible to everyone? Are logistics being taken care of? Are the teams and the product owners prepared? These are all important questions to answer. When you are able to create a proper planning phase, then you are able to avoid all the disagreements, delays, and issues that might crop up during the planning session.

The Most Important Tasks

So, let's review what we understand so far about the Scrum process.

- The first thing is to make sure that everyone knows their roles. You need to have a product owner, Scrum Master, and a team or multiple teams, depending on the project and tasks.

- Next, you need to set up the planning phase. Follow the tips provided earlier to make sure that the meeting is carried out efficiently, everyone gets to participate, and that real and achievable results are created at the end of the meeting. Ensure that people leave the meeting with action points.
- You need to prepare your backlog based on the decisions made during the meeting. Make sure that the backlog is well thought of.
- Start planning your sprints. Look at the tasks on the backlog and then choose the most important ones for the first sprint. Team members have to work on their tasks and make sure that they report back to the product owner on the progress of the tasks. You can create a daily meeting to bring everyone up to speed on the progress made. But remember something important: the meetings that you schedule to catch up with the team should be short. You should not spend more than 15 minutes a day on them. In fact, try and keep a certain pattern for the meetings where you ask a specific set of questions. You can use the one below or make your own, but once you have your own set of questions, repeat them in every meeting so that your team is prepared:
- What did you focus on yesterday?
- What will you be focusing on today?
- Is there anything acting as a blockage or hindrance to your work today and is there anything anyone can do to help you?
- Is there anything you would like to share that you think will help the rest of the team?
- By simply creating a template of questions and repeating them daily, your team will be ready for their tasks every day.
- At the end of the sprint, the team gets together to

review the work and then show what they have accomplished. If you need to make any changes or modifications, you have to do it at this point, before venturing forth into the new sprint.

Make sure that you also review the work process and see if you need to make any adjustments to it. You might find new ways of tackling the work in the next sprint. Perhaps you might identify a way to streamline a particular task or get more help to complete it. Get the team together so that everyone can provide recommendations on how to improve the sprints.

Once you have completed one sprint, repeat the above process with the remaining sprints. As you go from one sprint to another, make sure that you find ways to improve them. Here is where the essence of Scrum lies. It gives you the power to keep improving the processes until you are able to create something fluid.

Backlog Refinement

We have already taken a look at backlog refinement. But there are a few more things that you should be aware of during this process.

Backlog refinement is also known as Product Backlog Grooming. The main purpose of focusing on refinement is to ensure that the backlogs are kept neat and tidy. Product Backlog Grooming, or PBR, is a process that takes place at the end of a sprint. The teams get together and then discuss to see if the backlog is ready for the next sprint. They reorder things, if such rearrangements are necessary, and add new tasks, should the need arise. The purpose of the PBR is to make sure that the next sprint proceeds as smoothly as possible.

Once again, the meeting to discuss the backlog is set up by the Scrum Master. If you are the Scrum Master, then you can follow the steps that we discussed earlier for setting up a meeting. Once the meeting starts, the point of focus should be on resolving issues and creating new methods of work.

The product owner, as always, makes sure that the final decision is made by him or her.

A day or two before the end of the sprint is the time that the Scrum Master must be on high alert. He or she must make use of the time provided to prepare everything for the Scrum meeting at the end of the sprint. However, Scrum Masters can use the daily meetings to get rid of certain issues that don't require an entire meeting to discuss. Here is how to do it:

They should encourage everyone to present any issues that they are facing. Once the issues are laid down, then Scrum Masters can evaluate each problem to gauge its complexity.

They then offer the team members a chance to come up with a solution. If it takes too long for someone to form a solution, then the Scrum Master should move on to the next problem. The issue that was skipped over should be added to the list of issues that will be discussed during the sprint meeting.

If a solution can be discovered, then the Scrum Master should ensure that the solution is implemented immediately.

Through this simple process, any queries or problems that can be resolved immediately can be resolved during the quick meetings. Anything else can be reserved for the big meeting. Additionally, talking about any small problems immediately allows Scrum Masters to spot any festering issues and nip them in the bud. One cannot be certain of what could happen if the problems were allowed to persist for even a day longer. Some people might feel intimidated by the fact that they are going to face a big meeting at the end of the sprint. After all, it is almost like a job review process. But remember that the meetings are there to help the team, not alienate them if they make a mistake. Reinforce this idea in the small meetings. Scrum Masters should let the team know that the meetings are there to help everyone. No one is going to be judged or humiliated in front of others. Make sure that any personal problems are dealt with in a private setting. The meetings are only about work.

Getting the Mechanics Right

Finally, we need to focus on a few mechanics that are important for the overall success of agile. Let us start with the reporting process.

One of the most widely used reporting methods in sprint is the burn down chart. It uses a unique technique to track progress. It plots the work that is remaining in the sprint against a predetermined burn down rate. The method involves a graph that shows two lines. One line represents the "work outstanding" whereas the other line represents the "target burn down."

How does this work?

On the x-axis, you plot the days. On the y-axis, you plot the total work to be done, in units. If you don't have any units, then you can make use of percentages.

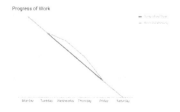

Once you have the points plotted, you start off on the first day. Let us assume that the first day is a Monday and the total number of units left to complete is 100. If you are using percentages, then you have 100% of the work left to be done. You are then going to make projections. You predict that on Tuesday, 80 units (or 80% of the work) will be left for completion. This goes on until Saturday, where 0 units are left for you to work on (or 0% of the work is left to be completed). At that point, you predict that there won't be anything left to do.

After you have made your projections, you then start marking the actual work that gets done using the "work outstanding" point. Let's suppose that on Monday, your team completes 20 units (or 20%). Which means that they have 80 units (or 80%) left. This is just as you predicted. Then on Tuesday, they only complete 10 more units (10%), bringing down the work that is outstanding to 70 units (or 70%). This falls short of your prediction. When that happens, you can bring up the progress in the next morning meeting, rather than waiting for the sprint meeting. By immediately addressing the problem, you are able to nip it in the bud, rather than allowing it to grow into something much worse. By applying such simple solutions, you can keep track of your project and ensure that you correct any errors before they veer out of control.

The charts also serve another purpose. You can use them to make comparisons, showing the progress made between two sprints. Using two charts, you can show the team whether they have improved or if the work has slowed down from the previous sprint. This will give the Scrum Master a way to find out reasons for the improvement or deterioration of work. Discussions can be held to find out what the team did right and replicate it. In the case of poor performance, the team can be guided toward better progress in the future.

You don't need to have any special software for creating a chart or graph. Simply use a whiteboard or a wall. I personally prefer a whiteboard and a wipe-clean marker as it helps keep things neat and tidy. You can even keep the whiteboard in a place where everyone can see what is happening. High visibility will let the team know what they have to focus on.

When the End is Bad

If you reach the end of the sprint and work remains unfinished, then it is not the end of the world. Think of it as an opportunity to improve and get better. In fact, it is another way to show you what you shouldn't be doing. Your next course of action is to find out exactly what your team has done that shouldn't be repeated again. Conduct your own investigation first. Once you have gleaned enough information, you can then ask the team to give their opinion during the sprint meeting. See if there is any information that tallies between your research and the team's feedback. Explore those commonalities. Once done or if you did not find any common feedback, try to see if you have found any points that are worth mentioning to the team. Then you should shift to the feedback given by your team.

During this process, remember the points below:

- Make sure that you are taking an objective stance when discussing the progress and issues of the team. Do not resort to "finger-pointing" tactics.
- If you feel that someone's performance has decreased considerably, then make sure that you discuss the situation with the person directly. Do not embarrass anyone in front of others.
- Ensure that the meeting is a productive one. You need to close the meeting with actionable results. The team has to leave with some valuable insights

and recommendations. Do not leave them wondering what the next steps are.

- If you feel that user stories are left incomplete, then find out ways to incorporate them into the next sprint. Make sure that you let the team know that you have no choice but to add the user stories to the next sprint. You are not doing it out of spite or prejudice. You are merely taking the next logical step in order to get the work done.
- The end of the sprint situation shows the overall progress made in the project. This lets you make predictions about the time it would take to complete the project. Always keep a worst-case scenario. Remember this motto: work for the best and expect the worst. Your job is not to always think about an optimistic approach. Your job is to deal with the situation, whether it is positive or negative, and the best way to do that is to be prepared for both scenarios.
- If you feel that there are important points that the team needs to know about, then make sure that you encourage the team to take notes. Make it mandatory for everyone to bring a pen and paper (for best results) or any other form of note-taking system. When you make this a habit, then any essential feedback or remarks are noted down for longevity. After all, memory is not the most reliable place to store information, especially since people are capable of forgetting information.
- Before the start of the next sprint, you and your team should be prepared. One of the best ways to conduct an end-of-sprint meeting is to come prepared with all the talking points. However big or small the talking points are, make sure that you include them in the meeting. It is better to discuss points, rather

than ignore them for being small and discovering later that those same small points are rather large issues.

Scrum Values

Having a certain set of values helps set up a collaborative and cross-functional approach for your Scrum. When people follow common values, you get them all to work together and focus on the same goals. When everyone's mind frame is synced, you effectively reduce the chances of conflict and improve cohesiveness in the team.

But the question arises, what values are you supposed to encourage your team to follow?

Here are some Scrum values that are important for every project.

Commitment and Focus

Commitment refers to the willingness of all the individuals involved in the project to dedicate themselves to the tasks and goals set forth. Focus refers to the concentration one applies to the task and hand, while simultaneously being answerable to their actions.

Commitment is important because it allows the team to agree on goals. The team as a whole becomes accountable for the accomplishment of the agreed-upon goals. This accountability works wonders for two vital reasons:

- If something goes wrong, then the entire team works together to correct the mistakes.
- If something goes right, then the whole team celebrates.

Both ways, you instill a sense of camaraderie among the team members. Without even trying to motivate them directly, you have brought them together using a simple technique.

At the same time, you do not have to worry about the focus on the team members. As a team, they are going to draw upon the focus of each other. How does this happen? Through a simple phenomenon called "pack mentality." Usually, this phenomenon has a negative connotation attached to it because of the way it has been depicted in movies and TV shows. However, in this case, it is going to work to your advantage. When the team is focused on their work, any remaining member who finds himself or herself losing focus will look at the others and motivate themselves to do more. This allows the entire team to become an independent machine, where each part works effectively to run the entire machine smoothly.

Openness

Being open with others is a sign of emotional maturity. It shows confidence and grace on the part of the individual who chooses to be transparent rather than bottle everything up inside. In order to develop high-performance teams, it is essential that people are open about the working conditions, projects, and anything else that affects their performance, productivity, or mindset. It is also easier to manage teams who are open and communicative than those teams that have members who aren't too forthcoming in their communications.

In some cases, the team members are strangers to each other or there might be one or a few new members who might feel like strangers. This is where you come in. You need to encourage everyone to speak during the morning meetings and ensure that the whole team is focused on one goal. You need to show that just because you know some members, it does not mean that you are only going to take their sides.

Respect

It does not matter if your team consists of people who have different opinions on things. What matters is that they learn to respect each other. Whatever their personal discussions are, they should be conducted outside work. While they are engaged in the completion of their work, they should remain professional and respectful of each other. It is also important for you to encourage the team to speak up. The others should, in return, respect feedback and opinions from other members. If everyone on the team simply said 'yes' to everything, then you are not going to have a high-performance team. When trying to find solutions, team members should feel free to contradict something, without having any nefarious intentions. If one member disagrees with another, then there should be mutual respect between them so that each person's viewpoints are heard without contempt. When you build such respect between team members, you are encouraging them to work together more efficiently. If two or more members are engaged in a conflict, then it is best to bring them together to sort out the issue or maybe find common ground.

Courage

Scrum can be challenging. This is why it takes a certain amount of courage to stick to the technique despite all the difficulties. Think about the above values for a moment. It takes courage to let go of your personal inhibitions and truly respect someone. It takes courage to be open and communicative. It takes courage to have a committed mind and take responsibility for your actions.

The way to bring out this courage in others is by displaying it within yourself. The phrase "practice what you preach" is quite appropriate here. When you show your team that you uphold the very values that you talk about, then you are indirectly influencing them to adopt them as well. In fact, if members ever felt that they could not follow Scrum values, then they might very well change their minds after seeing you.

Courage is vital for numerous other reasons as well, such as the ones shown below:

People who have courage are able to communicate bad news, even when it might be poorly received. It is important to be aware of bad news since the earlier you are aware of it, the faster you can try to fix it or prepare remedial measures.

Courage helps team members say 'no' when they want to. When someone feels like something is wrong or that they are unable to do something, they can confidently say no to the request, ideas, feedback, or plan.

Courage allows people to expect failure. You might think that having expectations of failure is a pessimistic way of looking at things. But in reality, it is important to prepare yourself for anything. Great entrepreneurs, business people, and leaders hone their minds to think about all the situations that could result in failures. It allows them to clearly picture what they should do in such scenarios. Expecting failure gives people the opportunity to prepare alternate plans and solutions for damage control.

AFTERWORD

At one point, agile was just a curiosity. It's like the idea of solar panels; sure they do not put a strain on the Earth's resources, but they are still something that is straight out of science-fiction. To most people, they are a passing interest. These days, with climate change a major topic around the world and the fact that we are rapidly depleting our fuel sources, which take millions (and sometimes hundreds of millions) of years to form, solar panels have become a bit more of a hot topic.

A similar scenario applies to agile. When organizations started noticing that they were unable to meet the requirements for technological innovations and customer demands with efficiency, speed, and quality, they began to look inwards. They realized that they were lacking in progress not because their competitors were going faster, but because they were going slower.

They needed to find a solution.

They needed agile.

It is important to note that agile is not just a process, it is also a mindset. It is about having a unique and organized approach to dealing with problems and challenges. Processing can be severely limiting. Agile aims to free individuals from such constraints because it gives so much freedom for people to think creatively, inventively, and even quickly. This is why agile focuses more on the aspects of adapting and learning, rather than creating a set of rules. It tries to incorporate principles rather than regulations. This aspect of having principles and teaching people is what allows users of agile to adapt so quickly and is what makes agile so innovative.

Agile might have started with the software industry, but its uniqueness was soon discovered by other industries. These industries realized just how adaptive agile can really be. And that's the best part about agile. It is truly flexible to fit into practically any situation. Remember how we mentioned that even though project-based businesses might not be able to completely use agile, they can still use some parts of it? It is this flexibility that allows for people to bring more of agile into their organizations.

Try to have an open mind about how you would like to achieve your goals. Gone are the days when people only relied on rigid systems to get the job done. These days, technology and innovations are moving at such a fast pace that organizations and businesses need to be flexible to changes. They need to adapt to the circumstances. In order to be adaptive, they need to have a framework that is flexible and adaptive as well.

Thankfully, there already exists such a framework.

It's called agile.

REFERENCES

Harvard Division of Continuing Education. Project Management Certificate. Retrieved 19 October 2019, from https://www.extension.harvard.edu/academics/professional-graduate-certificates/project-management-certificate

Napier, N. (2014). The Myth of Multitasking. Retrieved 22 October 2019, from https://www.psychologytoday.com/us/blog/creativity-without-borders/201405/the-myth-multitasking

State of Agile. (2019). 14th Annual State of Agile Survey. Retrieved 19 October 2019, from https://www.stateofagile.com/#ufh-i-521251909-13th-annual-state-of-agile-report/473508

CPSIA information can be obtained
at www.ICGtesting.com
Printed in the USA
LVHW030626240520
656398LV00002B/89